T5-BQA-975

RUSSIA:
A RETURN TO
IMPERIALISM?

Other Works by Uri Ra'anan and Kate Martin

Russian Pluralism—Now Irreversible?, edited by Uri Ra'anan, Keith Armes and Kate Martin, with an introduction by Elena Bonner (1992)

State and Nation in Multi-Ethnic Societies, edited by Uri Ra'anan, Maria Mesner, Keith Armes and Kate Martin (1992)

Staat und Nation in multi-ethnischen Gesellschaften, edited by Erich Fröschl, Uri Ra'anan, and Maria Mesner (1991)

Inside the Apparat*: Perspectives on the Soviet Union from Former Functionaries,* by Uri Ra'anan and Igor Lukes (1990)

The Soviet Empire and the Challenge of National and Democratic Movements, edited by Uri Ra'anan (1990)

Gorbachev's USSR: A System in Crisis, edited by Uri Ra'anan and Igor Lukes (1990)

RUSSIA:
A RETURN TO
IMPERIALISM?

URI RA'ANAN AND
KATE MARTIN,
EDITORS

ST. MARTIN'S PRESS
NEW YORK

RUSSIA: A RETURN TO IMPERIALISM?
Copyright © 1995 by Institute for the Study of Conflict, Ideology & Policy at Boston University

ISBN 0-312-12927-0

Library of Congress Cataloging-in-Publication Data

Russia: a return to imperialism? / Uri Ra'anan and Kate Martin,
    editors. — 1st ed.
        p.   cm.
    Includes index.
    ISBN 0-312-12927-0 (cloth)
    1. Russia (Federation)—Foreign relations. 2. Imperialism.
I. Ra'anan, Uri, 1926-   . II. Martin, Kate.
DK510.764.R85 1996
325'.32'094709049—dc20   95-481140
                                                                     CIP

First Edition: March 1996
10 9 8 7 6 5 4 3 2 1

Contents

Introduction

Considering Russia's and Eastern Europe's dizzying changes—first institutional and personal, subsequently systemic—the Institute for the Study of Conflict, Ideology and Policy (ISCIP) in 1988 decided that its first priority was the establishment of a database to facilitate research which would bring analytical clarity to an increasingly chaotic picture of the region. For this purpose, the Institute assembled an unusual team of gifted young analysts to constitute the database infrastructure, so to speak, and to enhance the Institute's research as well as its educational mission. A publication series was launched, including the journal *Perspective,* which draws heavily upon contributions by eminent Russians, from both official circles and the democratic sector.

In the initial stages, the Institute's emphasis was almost entirely on the Soviet and, subsequently, the Russian domestic scene, the assumption being that international policy would be dormant until and unless it was decided whether a potentially pluralistic (conceivably democratic) society, as opposed to authoritarianism at either end of the political spectrum, could be achieved. In other words, while the Institute was not inclined to accept *The End of History* as a fact, or even as a prognosis, it was prepared to consider it a legitimate question, at least during the euphoric weeks that followed the aborted coup of August 1991.

It became evident very quickly, however, that Russia's domestic developments and its attitude toward the other newly independent republics were simply two sides of the same coin. Despite Yel'tsin's, and, in his wake, the international community's, initial recognition of the independence and sovereignty of all the post-Soviet states, the "patriotic camp" in Moscow was not alone in its refusal to accept the shrinkage of empire as a fait accompli. Moreover, by the fall of 1993, there were indications that Russia had not come to terms with the full sovereignty of the East European ex-Warsaw Pact members, for example, their right to choose affiliation with another alliance. With the general direction of Russian policy thus indicated, Chechnya, in a sense, was the last straw, since it revealed the means that Russia's leadership was prepared to employ in the implementation of its aims.

At the same time, while some degree of pluralism had evolved in Russia, democracy and a law-based state seemed farther away than at any time since early 1992. Moscow's performance in the international arena vibrated in unison with regression at home. Yet the rest of the world, and particularly the West, seemed curiously unaware of or indifferent to these ominous developments. Analysts, decision makers, and the media alike had become habituated to chanting mantras, usually beginning with the words "since the end of the Cold War. . . ." From this premise, all kinds of assumptions followed, the most important being that only one superpower was left on the globe and, although many serious problems remained, the issue of Russia's attitude toward the rest of the world was no longer one of them.

Almost everyone seemed to forget how many times the "end of the Cold War" and the arrival of the "era of détente" had been proclaimed since Khrushchev met with Western leaders in 1955, during the "Geneva Spring of Nations." While 1991 marked a momentous, systemic, and qualitative change, it is questionable whether ideology really was the major issue at any time since the death of Stalin. Certainly, during the Brezhnev era the Soviet leadership's blatant cynicism concerning communist—not to speak of revolutionary—ideals was matched only by the Soviet population's utter indifference to and disbelief of ideological indoctrination. Some might say that the contentious schoolteacher Nina Andreyeva was the last true believer, at least within the boundaries of the former USSR.

Consequently, the real contest may not have been between the concepts of communism and capitalism; it may have stemmed rather from the fact that the USSR and, eventually, its Russian successor continued to act as the last truly imperial power at the very time when all the traditional empires had faded away, having experienced the penalties of imperialism in terms of blood, resources, and spillover onto the domestic scene.

The reason so many Russians, alas including would-be democrats, still are so responsive to imperial slogans and desires, the Afghan experience notwithstanding, may have to do with the difference between transcontinental and overseas empires. The latter experience far less of a wrench in separating from their possessions, with the ocean constituting, as it were, a clear "natural" demarcation between the metropolitan area and the colonies. An overland empire, Soviet or Russian, confronts no such geographic or demographic bounds, so that expansion of the dominant ethnic group and of the political entity can proceed unimpeded.

Be that as it may, in its research efforts the Institute confronted undeniable evidence of Russian doctrines and operations that could only be termed "imperial," or perhaps "neo-imperial." The signs of this development proliferated particularly in 1993 and 1994. The Institute's leadership decided that its immediate task was to establish whether its findings enjoyed peer support. In this endeavor, prominent scholars and other experts were approached. These included leading analysts of Russian affairs in three major research institutions, a former member of the CPSU Central Committee International Department, a distinguished former Moscow correspondent, an eminent expert on international law aspects of Russian operations, and the president of an institute surveying the progress of democratic policies and organizations, in addition, of course, to the appropriate academicians. All contributed to this volume.

Despite differences of emphasis and nuance, all of the authors evince deep concern that a distinctly imperial trend in Russian acts and statements is now unmistakable and that it holds ominous implications for the future of the Russian people itself, for non-Russians within the Russian Federation, for the 14 other former Soviet republics, for the independence and sovereignty of the other former Warsaw Pact members, and thus, ultimately, for the West as well. All are troubled by the failure of Western leaders to acknowledge these disturbing trends and to adjust their policies accordingly.

These analyses are presented here for readers to draw their own conclusions. The contributions are grouped in three sections: (1) The Neo-Imperial Theme: History and Motivations; Doctrines and Operations; Claims and International Law; (2) The Targets: The "Nearest Abroad"; the "Near Abroad"; the "Far Abroad"; (3) The Western Response: NATO; the United States (Descriptive); the United States (Prescriptive).

I wish to express my deep appreciation to all who made this work possible: Above all my colleague and co-editor, Kate Martin, whose unrelenting drive, dedication, and meticulous accuracy brought this enterprise to fruition; the distinguished contributors for their unique insights; the leadership of Boston University for its unfailing understanding and support; the Sarah Scaife Foundation for its generous and ongoing assistance and encouragement; the Earhart Foundation for its kind help to our graduate researchers; the ISCIP Database Research Team itself, and especially Peter Lorenz and Susan Cavan for their contributions to this work; the Institute's program manager, Tatiana Maneva; and the Institute's staff, Wendi Kern, David Percey, Kaara Peterson, and Karen Sim, for their unstinting labors in preparing the manuscript.

Uri Ra'anan
Boston, MA
1995

I

THE
NEO-IMPERIAL
THEME:

HISTORY AND MOTIVATIONS;
DOCTRINES AND OPERATIONS;
CLAIMS AND INTERNATIONAL LAW

1

Neo-Imperialism:
The Underlying Factors

Sergei Grigoriev

In the wake of the events of August and December of 1991, hardly anyone would have expected that the theme of the former Soviet Union's reintegration would be heard as loudly as it is in Russia today. The question of the reintegration of the former Union republics is becoming a focal issue for most of the political parties and movements; "What was the USSR?" and "Who lost the USSR?" may become the key questions during the 1996 presidential elections—if held.

Nostalgia for the USSR exists and—barring any positive changes in Russian political and economic life—its effects will be felt both in the post-Soviet space and all over the world. Today in Russia almost everyone is talking about reintegration. Some persons, like Vladimir Zhirinovsky, are speaking about the need for military preparation to conquer the territory of the former Russian Empire with sword and fire. The communists, who in principle are not against Zhirinovsky's methods, continue to talk about the possibility of reintegrating the former Soviet Union on the basis of popular referenda. Former Vice President Aleksandr Rutskoi announced the creation of the new political movement, *Derzhava* (Great Power), designed to rebuild the former USSR.

The "new centrists," like Presidential Council member Andranik Migranyan, are working urgently on a new "Russian Monroe Doctrine" designed to "reflect the place and the role of Russia in the post-Soviet space in the thinking of all the leading Russian politicians, beginning with the President and ending with the Foreign Minister Kozyrev. The key issue here is that all the geopolitical space of the former USSR constitutes the sphere of vital interests of Russia."[1]

Earlier, another politician from the same camp, Viktor Gushchin, had started the debate with his article "Russia Will Be An Imperial State!" in which he claimed that "life itself will soon give us a signal: it is time to act and in the direction that in reality leads towards the rebirth of Russia as a strong imperial power."[2] In a follow-up article summarizing the debates around the issue, Gushchin claimed that "those who advocated the disintegration of the Soviet Union . . . will have to recognize pretty soon that after the disintegration of the USSR, Russia, instead of being their older brother, will become now their imperial suzerain with all the corresponding implications for them."[3]

At the same time, others like Grigori Yavlinsky speak in favor of accelerating economic integration,[4] while groups of liberal orientation, like Yegor Gaidar's Russia's Democratic Choice, hold their conventions under huge portraits of Peter the Great.

What's Wrong with This?

While such debates were taking place in Russia and internationally, thousands of people were being killed in Tajikistan. Under the guns of the police of the self-proclaimed "Dniestr Soviet Socialist Republic," Moldovan women protested because their children were not allowed to study their native language. Refugees from Abkhazia who were forced into the Georgian mountains during the cold winter of 1993–94 still cannot return home. For a long time, in places like Armenia and Azerbaijan, children became too old too soon, simply trying to survive. The wars in these areas have something in common—Russian involvement—and in many ways these conflicts can be explained by Russian politics.

The war in Tajikistan reached such a large scale because Russia decided to support the most reactionary communist-Islamic fundamentalist regime there, obstructing the growth of democracy in that country. Russia and the Russian military, particularly the Fourteenth Army, continue to support the Dniestr Republic, which uses the old Soviet Union coat of arms and the red flag. This republic controls the local population, 67 percent of whom are ethnic Moldovans.

In Georgia the truce between the Abkhaz and Georgians was violated on the eve of Boris Yel'tsin's proclamation of Decree 1400 of September 21, 1993, dissolving the Russian legislature. What a coincidence! When the attention of the rest of the world was focused on Moscow, Georgian troops had to defend the city of Sukhumi against what were purported to be Abkhazian tanks and an Abkhazian air force (a concept as absurd as the notion of a Mongolian navy). Eduard Shevardnadze was trying to protect Sukhumi and claimed that he would die defending the city; instead he was forced to beg Russia to bring in its troops. He had to apply to the Russian government to allow Georgia to become a member of the Commonwealth of Independent States (CIS).

In the midst of these developments, Russian Foreign Minister Andrei Kozyrev traveled to New York and on national television claimed that Zviad Gamsakhurdia, not Shevardnadze, was the popularly elected president of Georgia.[5] Kozyrev's deputy, Boris Pastukhov, openly told the Georgian side at that time: "We will not let you win the war with Abkhazia!"[6] However, Russia then dealt with Shevardnadze once he prepared the agreement that grants Russia the right to keep five military bases on Georgian territory. Before Shevardnadze signed this appeal, he had to accept a situation that in the Caucasus is viewed as destroying any man who is a warrior or a politician. Tanks (this time described as the tanks of the Gamsakhurdia supporters) seized Shevardnadze's hometown for two days—long enough to make any politician lose face. No wonder that, according to INTERFAX wire service reports, Shevardnadze has now appealed to other CIS countries to stop playing games with independence and to admit that all such attempts are in vain. His ambassador in Moscow, Valerian Advadze, issued a statement on his behalf saying that "Georgia's independence depended to a great extent on the position of Russia" and that "Georgia would be independent only if Russia wanted it."[7]

Russian interference in the continuing conflict between Armenia and Azerbaijan cannot be ignored. Both sides are using Russian weapons in this conflict, and each side seeks Russia's aid every time the balance tips to the opposition. "The conflict between Armenia and Azerbaijan has many internal reasons," writes well-known Russian historian Yuri Afanasyev, "but it is also clear that Russia is not interested in making peace between them. The war between these states allows Russia to manipulate their interests, to keep both states in the sphere of its influence, and together with them—the whole of the Transcaucasus."[8]

Examples of Russian involvement in the affairs of other countries are too numerous to detail.[9] Amazingly, the major player in these intrigues is a country run by a reportedly democratic government, and the problem does not rest solely with the army, or with the power ministries. The decision that the Fourteenth Army should open fire on Moldovans was signed by the acting Prime Minister, Yegor Gaidar, in July 1992. It was the strong involvement of Russia's foreign minister, Andrei Kozyrev, that led to Russian armed interference in Tajikistan. In addition, under the instructions of Russia's defense minister, Pavel Grachev, Russian troops were "suddenly" withdrawn from the corridor separating the Georgian and the Abkhaz positions in Abkhazia on the night of September 15, 1993, allowing for a successful Abkhazian counteroffensive.

With the involvement of the Russian intelligence service (Sluzhba Vneshney Russkoy Razvedki, or SVRR), the armed forces helped to bring Geidar Aliev to power by supporting the coup that deposed Azerbaijan's popularly elected president, Abulfaz Elchibey. Russian taxpayers' money then was used to support the anti-Aliev forces once Aliev signed a contract with Western oil companies. It is clear today that Russia is preparing to put in power the puppet regime of Ayaz Mutalibov, who is now living outside Moscow in a safe house under FSK (Federal'naya Sluzhba Kontrarazvedki, or counterintelligence agency) protection.

Other Russian actions could be described as worrisome. When the parliament building in Moscow was still on fire in October 1993, two important decisions were adopted by the Russian government. One of them involved the extradition from Moscow of many persons from the Caucasus. Traders, businessmen, and many others were arrested in the streets, put into railroad cars, and sent home. Among those arrested and beaten up by the Russian police was the ambassador of sovereign Armenia.

Also in October 1993, under Yel'tsin's chairmanship, a meeting of the collegium of the Ministry of Defense and National Security Council members adopted the "Main Guidelines of the Military Doctrine of the Russian Federation" allowing for the utilization of Russian armed forces on the territory of the so-called Near Abroad, the newly freed non-Russian states, and also threatening all the other republics with a nuclear strike. The new military doctrine expanded Russia's security interests throughout the territory of the former USSR and rescinded the "no-first-use" nuclear weapons pledge of the Gorbachev era.[10]

In November 1993 the Russian government pushed Central Asia away from the so-called "ruble space," an action that placed the reformist regimes in Kyrgyzstan and Kazakhstan on the verge of bankruptcy. Kazakh Vice President Daulet Sembayev claimed openly that his country was "pushed out of the ruble zone" because of its attempts to seek economic cooperation with neighboring Turkey, Pakistan, Iran and other countries.[11] Facing the protests of the Kyrgyz and Kazakh governments, Russian Foreign Minister Kozyrev declared that "Russia is prepared to defend its citizens living in Kazakhstan . . . and in this purpose will use all its power, including economic sanctions and credit and financial policy."[12]

Following sporadic international criticism of its interference in the affairs of other republics, Russia has softened the sharpness of some of its verbal attacks; however, its meddlesome patterns remain the same. Is this an expression of postimperialism? France suffered from the postimperial syndrome when it had to leave Algeria, Vietnam, and Guinea. Yet, immediately thereafter, France was eager to be involved in international conferences to discuss the future of those newly independent states. Moreover, those conferences included representatives not only of other countries, but also of different political camps. Russia claims that the former Soviet Union constitutes its own sphere of influence, and external input is not welcomed. One senior US official told *The Washington Post* that "Russia is undermining internationally sponsored negotiating efforts by launching its own initiatives."[13]

Another popular opinion in Russia today is that reintegration is necessary because, within its present borders, Russia lacks sufficient resources to become economically independent and prosperous. This theory does not withstand any kind of scrutiny. Hitler had argued that Germany needed new resources and access to new territories; however, after his defeat West Germany became a prosperous economic state with about one-half the amount of territory Hitler had deemed insufficient.

One explanation for this negative outlook is that the country is undergoing a very difficult period of transition. While it is clear whence Russia is coming, its ultimate destination is unknown. Attempts to build a different country, for example, a democratic state, are accompanied by uncertainty, which worries many Russians. All the problems of the transition period, including obvious mistakes by the governments that have come to power since 1991, cause much of the population to feel nostalgia for the "good old days." Following the disintegration of the USSR in which Russians still played a leading role and where the ideology of Great Russian chauvinism had been maintained, the overwhelming majority of the population suddenly reached the painful realization that they were citizens of a Third World country. The lack of any alternate ideology in what had been a highly ideological state inevitably allowed for a sentiment such as nationalism to grow and consolidate.

Still, other factors connect Russia with the former republics, the economies of which continue to depend heavily upon Russia. There are (or were) 25 million ethnic Russians living in the former Soviet republics, and Russia continues to view the military installations there as its own. There are still very few border and customs posts and, in many cases, no demarcation lines between the newly independent countries. There are no professional Russian diplomats trained to operate in the former Soviet republics, and those who have been sent to these countries consider themselves exiled by the Ministry of Foreign Affairs.

Interrepublican ties and contacts between the representatives of the old Soviet nomenklatura and elites remain very strong. As a result, there have

been successful attempts by nomenklatura representatives in the former republics to return to power, often with Russian assistance; Russia considers
them more reliable and more predictable than their independence- and de-
mocracy-minded compatriots.

WHO RUNS RUSSIA TODAY?

Light may be shed upon these Russian actions by examining who precisely
came to power in Russia in 1991, namely, a broad anticommunist and anti-
Gorbachev coalition representing many different groups and movements,
from anarchists to monarchists. In addition to separate democratic groups,
the second and third echelons of the nomenklatura also played a prominent
role in that coalition. No wonder the breakdown of the old regime in Russia
is often described as the "revolution of the second secretaries."

Leading the first government were those young nomenklatura representatives who had been promoted during the Gorbachev years, such as
Pravda editorial board member Yegor Gaidar, senior executive of the Economic Department of the Central Committee Boris Fyodorov, and many
others. By the summer of 1992, Russia was ruled by a coalition government.

The old nomenklatura brought into this government its own members, the
so-called industrialists, such as Georgi Khizha, Viktor Chernomyrdin, and Vladimir
Shumeiko, while real democrats, representatives of the Interregional Group of
Deputies and of such movements as Democratic Russia, were forced to resign.
Following the departure of Gennadi Burbulis, the Yel'tsin administration was
abandoned by Arkadi Murashev, and Yegor Yakovlev; finally, the last persons
representing the democratic movements to be fired were Galina Starovoitova, in
November 1992, and Yuri Boldyrev, in February 1993. In December 1992, Yegor
Gaidar had been forced to leave the government; although he was brought back
to power in 1993, this move was intended to convince democratic forces in
Russia and the West that Yel'tsin's attempts to dissolve parliament were legitimate. Once this goal had been achieved, Gaidar's power evaporated.

Many government measures against the former Soviet republics were undertaken while Gaidar, for all his democratic posturing, was still in power. At the
time, however, it was believed that the government was not responsible for these
actions, which were blamed instead on the power ministries and the army in
regions where it was trying to establish its own control.[14] This assumption did
not turn out to be completely accurate. During the summer of 1992, Sergei
Stankevich, a prime representative of the democratic camp in Russia, did not
miss a single photo opportunity with Vice President Aleksandr Rutskoi posing
together in front of cannons in Sevastopol and in the Dniestr Republic.

Once Chernomyrdin came to power, the process of reform was stalled, allegedly due to the need for stabilization. As a result, the structure of the economy largely remains unchanged and the military-industrial complex retains a key position in that economy.

Since October 1993 Yel'tsin has become a hostage of the army. During the events of "Black October" both realized that Yel'tsin could depend only upon the army for support. Moreover, both for the nomenklatura and for Yel'tsin himself, the disintegration of the USSR was a necessary element in the struggle to remove Gorbachev and to legitimize their rise to power. These goals were of higher priority than the aspirations of the former Soviet republics to freedom and independence and the recognition of legitimate anti-Russian sentiments in those republics. At the same time, those politicians were sincere about their desire to have good relations with the West, primarily because they hoped to use Western assistance to modernize the country and to strengthen their power.

In many ways, the representatives of the old nomenklatura still view the former USSR as their own country. They have disposed of the communist ideology and the limitations the old rigid system had imposed upon the growth of their personal wealth. The new leaders came to power with the skills and experiences they had gained in their previous positions. Without a deep understanding of Russian history, they felt very comfortable when Russia was proclaimed the legal successor of the USSR. The well-known Russian historian Dmitri Furman explains:

> Today's elite is the old elite wearing new costumes. Former regional party secretaries may cause admiration among the US Senators proclaiming the end of the world communism. And they are sincere about it, they really think so, since in the back of their minds they always have been hating this communism, and they are happy that it is over, and that today they are given a chance to speak in front of the US Senators. But in the depth of their hearts they still remain regional party secretaries with all the correspondent habits and the way of thinking. They are happy today since they are being invited "to decent homes," and when they go out they put on their tuxedos. . . . But in the former USSR they still feel like they are at home. Here they put on their "field dress." Here they display their old instincts—chauvinistic, class, and so on.[15]

The Russian sociologist and writer Yuri Burtin describes this new Russian political elite as "nomenklatura democracy," where "democracy exists only for the members of the nomenklatura," and believes that Russia's new political and economic system should be described as "nomenklatura capitalism."[16]

RUSSIA AND THE REPUBLICS: A NEW STAGE

If, in 1992, Russia's interference in the affairs of other republics could have been explained as the instincts of the old imperial state, by the end of 1993 new reasons were evident. One concerned the development of what can be described as bureaucratic capitalism, namely, the system that transforms former ministries and departments into entities such as "holding companies" and industrial consortia that still depend upon the government. In 1991–92 they needed the help of the West, just to stand on their feet. By 1993, they were more stable but did not want to lose markets, especially in the former republics. One factor that has helped to maintain dependence on the state has been the use of the ruble at the time when other republics are using hard currency and preferring to purchase higher quality Western goods. Today Russia is looking for ways to avoid this development and to dump Russian goods in the other republics.

The growing appetites of Russian industrialists contributed substantially to a new orientation of Russian policy in the Near Abroad, with special attention to providing Russia access to natural resources in the former Soviet republics. As a result, Russian policy toward the CIS countries—and by January 1994 all the former republics, excluding the Baltic States, were persuaded by Russia in one way or another to join the CIS—has entered a new stage. Four months after the publication of his "Monroe Doctrine" for Russia, Migranyan was no longer concerned about the popularity of his concept among leading Russian politicians. He believed, correctly, that a consensus had already been reached. The key focus for him remained whether the "Russian political elite [would] build a consensus regarding such problems as the pace of integration and its principles." He even allowed that "for the sake of unification *(radi ob'yedineniya)* we might have to sacrifice our reform."[17]

The emergence of this "consensus" regarding the issue of "reintegration" was accompanied by negative predictions about the future of Russian democracy by a number of leading experts. Peter Reddaway, a well-known American expert on Russian affairs, warned in February 1994 that "behind the assurances about continuing the reforms, which the US has trustingly accepted at face value, a new course towards authoritarianism is being quietly prepared."[18] The Russian professor Yuri Davydov of the Institute for the Study of the USA and Canada warned that this "new authoritarianism would inevitably gain imperial features."[19]

Russian policy toward the CIS countries indeed has acquired some new features. Today it is being guided by certain pragmatic considerations. On the one hand, Russia does not want to accept any responsibility for what is happening in these republics. By applying all sorts of pressure, it gains access to their natural resources, attempts to control their economies, and tries to ensure that "friendly political forces" come to power there. On the other hand, Moscow is trying to minimize the expense and is unwilling to sustain losses, as in Belarus' when, despite earlier promises, Russia reneged on its pledge to merge the financial systems of both countries. Moscow decided that it was not in its interest to bail out the flagging Belarusian economy, and that an economically dependent Belarus' would be easier to pressure into accepting Russian demands. As Yuri Afanasyev pointed out, "this new tendency means politico-military and economic control of Moscow over the former republics of the Soviet Union, but not its responsibility for maintenance of parity with Russia in terms of living conditions and no responsibility for, let's say, living conditions in Uzbekistan, infant mortality in Azerbaijan, living standards in Tajikistan."[20] This has been accompanied by endless declarations that Russia is a great power and is entitled to have special rights regarding its neighbors.

To be able to utilize the post-Soviet space for its own interests, Russia has been trying to revive the institutions that had been established before, for example the CIS and its economic mechanism. Clearly, no one has asked the general public in the CIS countries, where there are strong anti-Russian feelings, whether a Russian-led CIS is acceptable. For elites trying to improve the economic situation in their republics and thereby legitimize their stay in power, however, the acceptance of the CIS structures might be a case of compromise to retain Moscow's support. Russia's efforts to turn the CIS into a Russian-led organization, instead of an association of equal partners, found its reflection during the seventeenth summit of the CIS leaders. In keeping with an earlier agreement, Azerbaijan's President Geidar Aliev was supposed to replace Yel'tsin as chairman of the Council of the Commonwealth's Heads of States, but during the summit it was decided to extend Yel'tsin's mandate.[21]

At the same time, Russian taxpayers have not been polled about their willingness and ability to carry the burden of Russian expansionism, despite an abundance of propaganda on the need for such structures and policies. Some analysts, however, have expressed their concern about the cost of revising imperial policies. "[N]either the president and government, nor the parliamentary opposition dare to announce honestly the cost of this new status: Russia will have to pay for it with oil and gas, with inflation, with deterioration of living standards, and maybe even with lives of Russian soldiers," writes Andrei Grachev, although, he adds "perhaps the Russian society is prepared to pay this price for the restoration of broken internal ties and the global role of their state."[22]

Yet it is clear that the matter of special concern for Russia in 1993–94 was guaranteed access to raw materials—the natural resources of the former republics. Russian industrialists believe that the costs of political, military, and economic involvement in the former republics will be offset by the costs of remonopolization of Moscow's control over the natural wealth in those republics. In Georgia, it is manganese and copper; in Armenia, molybdenum; in Kazakhstan, manganese, molybdenum, iron ore, copper, lead, and zinc; in Kyrgyzstan, stibium; in Uzbekistan, cotton and gold. Of special interest for Russia are the rich energy resources in Azerbaijan, Kazakhstan, and Turkmenistan: oil and natural gas.

Attempts by various Western companies, as well as by the governments of Turkey and Iran, to get access to those resources in the process of bilateral and multilateral cooperation have been assailed by Russia as efforts to build influence in the countries within its sphere of vital interests. The oil contracts between Azerbaijan and a number of major Western companies have been a major reason for tension in the relations between Russia and that country. The same could be said about Russia's relations with Kazakhstan. Many analysts argue that oil played the key role in the decision of the Russian government to start its brutal war in Chechnya. "Russian claims to Caspian oil make sense only when Moscow is in a position to control the oil pipelines," write Stephan Kiselev and Azer Mursaliyev.[23] Moscow has been insisting on transit of oil via Chechnya to the terminals in the port of Novorossiisk, but, as a result, it had to prove to its potential partners and opponents that "its territory and the route for the pipeline, part of which goes via Chechnya, is really safe and completely under control."[24]

At the same time, continuation of the conflict between Armenia and Azerbaijan allows Russia to block all attempts to design and build a pipeline from Azerbaijan to the Turkish port of Dzheikhan on the Mediterranean, since "one of the key sections of the projected pipeline—30 kilometers of the so-called 'Megrin corridor,' a small piece of land controlled by Armenia between Nakhichevan, which has the status of Azerbaijan's autonomous republic, and the rest of the territory of Azerbaijan—is within the zone of intense fighting."[25]

A number of different interest groups exist among Russian industrialists. Some are oriented to exports, such as the gas industry, which had been gradually privatized while preserving its organizational integrity and monopolistic position in the former USSR. This group does not mind borders between republics, since its members have learned how to make more money every time they have to pay custom fees and each time their products cross any border. However, the huge Russian manufacturing industries, which are first and foremost connected with the military–industrial complex, are suffering from the existence of borders. For example, in his October 1994 speech at Harvard University, Marshal Yevgeni Shaposhnikov, the former commander-in-chief of the Joint Armed Forces of the CIS, explained that to make a modern Sukhoi plane one has to utilize 45 enterprises; 39 of them are in Russia, the rest are dispersed over the territory of the former Soviet Union. Many enterprises would prefer to avoid paying custom fees and to cut off ties with their former branch enterprises, since in their attempts to survive those branch enterprises are beginning to look for new partners and new markets. The oil industry of the former USSR was not preserved as a monopolistic structure and, as a result, has fallen into a number of privatized and government-controlled companies competing for markets and profits. In addition, oil remains one of the main sources of hard currency revenues for the federal and local budgets.

A businessman from Yekaterinburg who travels to Boston quite often explained his point of view: "You know how long it takes for Russian goods to be shipped out of the port in St. Petersburg? At least ten months. The merchant marine facilities in St. Petersburg are overloaded; everything is stuck, and we have to look for something else. If the army will not help us bring back the ports in Odessa and Tallinn, we will do it ourselves. Don't ask me how, but we will have them at our disposal."

Aside from such attitudes in industry, there are throwbacks in the "tested and tempered fighters of the Cold War," that is, the power ministries. This is demonstrated by two reports from the Russian Foreign Intelligence Service headed by Yevgeni Primakov—one from November 1993,[26] and the other from September 1994. The first deals with Russia's reaction to the proposed inclusion of the former Soviet republics in the NATO Partnership for Peace (PfP) program, while the second focuses on Western attitudes toward the prospect of reintegration. Both are unprecedented cases of interference by the intelligence services in the affairs of the government. It is known that the Yel'tsin administration received the September 1994 report only two days before Primakov discussed it at a press conference and had it disseminated to the media. In a recent interview, Deputy Director of the Russian Foreign Intelligence Service Grigori Rapota stressed that his organization intends to prepare and publicize similar reports in the future.[27] Chauvinism also continues to be very strong in the Russian army.

The brutal character of the Russian military action in Chechnya and the fact that the decision to start this war reflected the attempts of the Yel'tsin administration to change the social base of its support in favor of a closer alliance with chauvinistic and nationalistic forces may serve as an illustration that the "party of war" in the Kremlin is gaining strength. This, in turn, may lead to the conviction that the interests of reform will be sacrificed in favor of "unification." So far, only the desire to obtain Western aid, in my view, is preventing Russia from taking stronger steps in this direction. As a result, because of possible reactions from the West, the so-called initiative about reintegration most likely will be funneled via republics other than Russia.

Due in no small part to Russian pressure, a number of the former Soviet republics will probably suggest reintegration, while Russia, as Stalin had done before, simply will sit back and "accept" those republics into the fold.

Quite symptomatic in this respect was a program broadcast on Russia's Ostankino Television early in 1995. Two days before the program aired, the anchorwoman, Marina Nekrasova, had been appointed head of the presidential administration's information department. During the program, the president of the Russian Sociological Academy, Dr. Gennadi Osipov, was introduced as a person with no less solid democratic credentials than Sergei Kovalev, the famous dissident and human rights activist. Dr. Osipov proclaimed that "although for a while it was good to let the republics have some degree of independence, so that they could feel themselves in isolation and their 'pro-independence elites' could lose their popularity . . . today it is time to correct the mistakes of the past and to begin the process of full reintegration."[28] In an obvious attempt to shift the blame for the disintegration of the USSR onto Russia's democratic forces, Dr. Osipov said, "Boris Nikolayevich Yel'tsin fully supports the decision. . . . All those guilty . . . will have to be punished."[29] Obviously, no one in the Russian political elite bothered to ask the opinion of the population in the former Soviet republics. Perhaps it is assumed that the population will support this move, or will have to support it as a result of a perceived lack of preferable alternatives, just as had been assumed in the case of Chechnya.

WHAT'S WRONG WITH THAT?

Historically, Russia's tremendous territorial space seemed to demand an authoritarian form of government. In Russia, the development of a modern culture, including political culture, traditionally took place only in the center, and then was dispersed to the periphery as part of powerful external expansion. The colonization and co-optation by Russia of other nations at different stages of economic, cultural, and political development played a very significant role in obstructing the process of democratization and the path of economic development.

Yel'tsin claims that Peter the Great is his favorite historical hero. Peter the Great is viewed often as a Westernizer, which is regarded as synonymous with being a reformer or modernizer. However, most of Peter's reforms were, in fact, dedicated to the modernization of the Russian army and the creation of the Russian military-industrial complex. The remainder represented a rather mechanical attempt to imitate Western institutions, although those imitations continued to play their traditional Russian roles under different names and remained important tools in the hands of a despotic ruler.

The nature of the Russian Empire set out by Peter, the built-in features of which were the hypertrophy of the power structures and messianic claims about the special role of Russia, became part of the genetic code of the Soviet communist state, which continued to colonize other nations under different banners, but with the same methods of exploitation. In that sense, the events of August and December of 1991 represented not only the crash of the Soviet communist model, but also "the crash of a certain model of Russian civilizational development set up by Peter."[30] Peter's model for Russia had allowed the country to compete with other more developed nations at the expense of any advance toward Western democratic values based on respect for freedom, individual rights, law, and order.

Under Peter, cruel treatment was the fate not only of the peasants, but also of the nobility, the educated class, and the entrepreneurs. The state, under a despotic ruler, imposed production quotas and also established the priority of the bureaucracy. This kept the population in constant tension, eased from time to time by the state renovating itself through perestroikas from above, such as the reforms of 1861, or those initiated more recently by Gorbachev. Still, under the rule of the most liberal tsar, Aleksandr II, the budget for defense and the military-industrial complex comprised 35 percent of state expenses while education accounted for only 1 percent.[31] In that sense, the experience of the Soviet state was a complete repetition of life as it existed under the tsars.

What Russia needs today is not the recreation of the same old empire under a new banner, but rather a development of the cultural and historical paradigm away from the imperial model. As the Russian scholar Yakov Shemyakin has stressed:

> in the minds of many, the collapse of this paradigm equals the collapse of Russia, its statehood and civilization. However, the necessary precondition for the preservation of any civilization is the law of integrity. While statehood plays a role, equally important factors include the system of values (i.e., its spiritual or moral culture) and economic activities (namely production and distribution). The best results are achieved only when all these factors work together.... A number of researchers studying various Latin American countries ... reached the conclusion that the hypertrophy of one factor tends to undermine the role of others....[32]

Similarly, earlier attempts at Russian modernization failed not due to a lack of consensus between the educated class and the people, but because of the hypertrophy of imperial thinking. The introduction of the principle of freedom of choice contributed in the most significant way to the collapse of the Soviet Empire. All attempts to return to the old paradigm of the imperial state will inevitably lead toward the deterioration of freedom of choice, human rights, and democratic values, even by the new regime and its supporters.

What kind of Russia can one expect in the near future—a gradually reviving empire slowly collecting its lost territory or a new peaceful Russian state involved in construction? Current attempts to substitute imperialism for national consensus will not allow Russia to become a democratic and market-oriented country and will only facilitate the resurgence of the military-industrial complex looking for a strong leader to practice its hegemonic aspirations. So far, it seems that some of the gloomy predictions may come true.

RUSSIA, NEWLY INDEPENDENT STATES AND THE WEST

A number of external reasons appear to be encouraging the return to imperial thinking in Russia. First of all, Russia understands that the West is very much concerned with the problem of nuclear weapons proliferation. In that sense, Russia will always be the focus of the West's attention. In addition, as the largest of the former Soviet republics, Russia will always receive most of the aid meant for the region. The disproportionate distribution of such aid supports Russia's belief in the inevitability of its special role in the region.

Other Western concerns, of a geopolitical character, such as the possible spread of Islam and the competition for the post-Soviet space of the USSR's various successors, could be viewed by Russia as justification for this special status. Such concerns might cause some in the West to believe that if any country were to move into that space, Russia would be preferable to a more volatile country. The lack of solid protected borders also evokes concerns of weapons and drug trafficking. These problems exist, and many Westerners sincerely believe that Russia will be able to stop such mischief by bringing in its own troops.

Danger lies in the possibility that the world will forget that other countries still exist in the post-Soviet space. With their own views, their own ideas, their own attitudes, and their own aspirations, they cannot be ignored.

NOTES

1. Andranik Migranyan, "Rossiya i Blizhnee Zarvbezh'e," *Nezavisimaya gazeta* (Moscow), 12 January 1994, p. 1. Unless noted otherwise, all translations are by the author.

2. Viktor Gushchin, "'Byt' Rossii Imperskoi!," *Nezavisimaya gazeta* (Moscow), 23 July 1993, p. 5.

3. Victor Gushkin, "I vsyo-taki Rossii byt' Imperskoi!," *Nezavisimaya gazeta* (Moscow), 17 September 1993, p. 5.

4. Grigori Yavlinsky, "What Does Russia Want?" *The New York Times,* 9 October 1994, op-ed page.

5. Andrei Kozyrev, interview by Larry King, *Larry King Live,* CNN Network, 27 September 1993.

6. Interview with Boris Pastukhov, *Moskovskiye novosti* (Moscow), no. 36, 5 September 1993.

7. INTERFAX *Daily News Bulletin,* no. 34, 28 September 1994, p. 8.

8. Yuri Afanasyev, "Agressiya—Kategoriya Ekonomicheskayan," *Moskovskiye novosti* (Moscow), no. 66, 25 December 1994, p. 4.

9. See Fiona Hill and Pamela Jewett, *Back in the USSR* (Cambridge, MA: Harvard University Press, 1994).

10. Yuri Afanasyev, "Russian Reform is Dead," *Foreign Affairs* 73:2, March/April 1994, p. 23.

11. Sembayev, quoted in "Moskva Postavila Alma-Ate Nepriemlivye Finansoviye Usloviya," *Nezavisimaya gazeta* (Moscow), 3 November 1993, p. 3.

12. Boris Vinogradov, "S Vvedeniem Natsional'nykh Valyut v Aziatskikh Stranakh SNG u Rossii Voznikli Novye Problemy," *Izvestiya* (Moscow), 20 November 1993, p. 3.

13. Daniel Williams, "Moscow's Troubling Intervention," *The Washington Post,* 21 June 1994, p. A11.

14. Thomas Goltz, "Letter from Eurasia: The Hidden Russian Hand," *Foreign Policy* no. 92, Fall 1993, p. 92.

15. Dmitri Furman, "Frak i Gimnasterka," *Moskovskiye novosti* (Moscow), no. 37, 12 September 1993, p. B8.

16. Yuri Burtin, "Emanispatsiya Apparata," *Moskovskiye novosti* (Moscow), no. 18, 1 May 1994, p. A6.

17. Andranik Migranyan, "Kto Osedlayet Integratsiyu," *Moskovskiye novosti* (Moscow), no. 30, 24 July 1994, p. 5.

18. Reddaway, quoted in John Lloyd, "A Familiar Spectre Haunts Europe Again," *Financial Times* (London), 15 February 1994, p. 3.

19. Yuri Davydov, "Zapad i Rossiya: Stavka na Zhestkuyu Ruku," *Moskovskiye novosti* (Moscow), no. 41, 10 October 1993, p. A13.

20. Yuri Afanasyev, "Agressiya-Kategoriya Ekonomicheskaya," *Moskovskiye novosti* (Moscow), no. 66, 25 December 1994.

21. INTERFAX *Daily News Bulletin,* no. 1, 10 February 1995.

22. Andrei Grachev, "Yesli Vypalo Imperiyei Rodit'sya . . ." *Moskovskiye novosti* (Moscow), no. 18, 1 May 1994, p. A11.

23. Stephan Kiselev and Azer Mursaliyev, "Chastniye Interesy Obscchei Voiny," *Moskovskiye novosti* (Moscow), no. 64, 18 December 1994, p. 8.

24. Ibid.

25. Umirserik Kasenov, "Chego Khochet Rossiya v Zakavkaz'ye i Tsentral'noi Azii," *Nezavisimaya gazeta* (Moscow), 24 January 1995, p. 3.

26. "Sblizhenie Politiki Rossii i Soedinennych Shtatov v Obkasti Oborony," *Nezavisimaya gazeta* (Moscow), no. 23, November 1993, p. 1.

27. Andrei Poleshchuk interview with Grigori Rapota, "Rossiiskiye Razvedchiki-Odny is Luchshikh v Mire," *Nezavisimaya gazeta* (Moscow), 28 January 1995, pp. 1–2.

28. Marina Nekrasova, "Moskva, Kreml' iz Pervykh Ust," ITA-Tsentr, Ostankino Television First Channel Network (Moscow), 26 January 1995.

29. Ibid.

30. Yakov Shemyakin, "Mimesis, Evokatsiaya Prizrakov Proshlogo i Problemy Izmeneniya Kulturnoistoricheskoi Paradigmy Rossiiskoi Istorii," *Svobodnaya mysl'* (Moscow), no. 17, November 1992, p. 65.

31. Vladimir Khoros, "Russkaya Ideya na Istoricheskom Perekrestke," *Svobodnaya mysl'* (Moscow), no. 6, March 1992, p. 38.

32. Yakov Shemyakin, op. cit., p. 66.

2

Imperial Elements in Russia's Doctrines and Operations

Uri Ra'anan[1]

Post-Soviet imperialism is manifested (1) by an assertion of domination over countries that the successor to the former imperial power and the international community have recognized as independent and sovereign; and (2) by the imposition of that domination by force or threat of force—the very attributes of aggression outlawed by Article 2, Paragraph 4 of the UN Charter. The unimpeded pursuit of an aggressive path, particularly by a major power, is, of course, entirely incompatible with the "New World Order" proclaimed triumphantly by President Bush and viewed in the West as the reason for downsizing defense. Euphoria swept the West with the defeat in Moscow of the aborted August 1991 coup; its aftermath—the dissolution of the USSR and the recognition by Russia's leader Boris Yel'tsin of the independence and sovereignty of the other former Soviet republics—seemed appropriate as a portent of the posture and policies of a new democratic Russian state. At the time, I was not immune to such euphoria.

Predictably, Western decision makers and their bureaucracies swiftly embraced the comforting assumptions of a supposed "new order," and became reluctant to consider data and analyses that questioned their suppositions. The interpreters of such data were written off as "the bearers of bad news," with all the usual consequences.

Even those who admitted that an ominous trend could be discerned in both Russian statements and actions assumed erroneously that this development was a *recent* result of the October 1993 bloody clash between President Yel'tsin and the "Red-Brown" opposition, or of the December 1993 elections, which boosted Vladimir Zhirinovsky's ultrachauvinistic forces and the revived communist party—both equally nostalgic for the "good old days," when the USSR dominated the space between the Pacific and the Elbe.

In fact, the doctrines and operations subsumed under the "neo-imperial" heading date back to May 1992 and March 1993. They emanated not from the "Brown" or "Red" opposition, but from the central apparatus of government itself, including President Yel'tsin's staff, his Security Council, the foreign ministry, part of the armed forces, and Yevgeni Primakov's Foreign Intelligence Service.

The doctrines in question passed through several stages that will be discussed in roughly chronological order, although, in fact, there may have been considerable overlap in time between them. The initial emphasis regarding the extension of Russian power into other former Soviet republics was markedly *ethnic.* Immediately after his victory over the aborted August 1991 coup, President Yel'tsin, even as he recognized the independence of the 14 other republics, indicated that at least some (presumably Ukraine and Kazakhstan) might have to purchase their freedom by agreeing to "revise borders," in other words, to allow Russian annexation of portions of their sovereign territory inhabited by sizable ethnic Russian populations.[2] However, since this assertion was received with evident concern by the international community, whose support Yel'tsin needed particularly at the time, he reversed his position within hours and specifically recognized all the former Soviet republics within their existing constitutional boundaries.

Early in 1992, Russian official circles began referring increasingly to the 25 million ethnic Russians now living in the Near Abroad. In May of that year the draft was published of a new Russian military doctrine (which was incorporated with some changes in the final version of the doctrine promulgated in the fall of 1993).

Under the subheading of "Possible Causes of *War* and Its Sources" [emphasis added], it listed the "violation of the rights of . . . persons who identify themselves ethnically and culturally with [Russia]." Under the subheading of "The Mission . . . of the Russian Armed Forces," the doctrine spoke of "the defense of the rights and interests of . . . persons abroad linked to Russia ethnically and culturally."[3]

By June 1992, Yevgeni Ambartsumov (then a Supreme Soviet critic of a supposedly "too liberal" Russian foreign ministry, subsequently an ambassador representing that same ministry—now much more to his taste) demanded that, in all treaties with former Soviet republics, Russia make "special provisions" for its "right to defend the lives and dignity of Russians" in the Near Abroad.[4] This message was spelled out even more clearly in the Russian foreign policy doctrine promulgated in the spring of 1993. It stated that the "rights of minorities"—described elsewhere in the document expansively as "persons of Russian origin" and "Russians and the Russian-speaking population"—in the Near Abroad would have to be secured "through persuasion, and in extreme cases also through the *use of force.*"[5] As pointed out earlier, not only the use but even the threat of force is outlawed under the UN Charter.

The assertion of a right to intervene militarily on behalf of ethnically related populations is uncannily reminiscent of the practice of the late 1930s—the Sudeten Germans come to mind. Since World War II, such claims have become generally inadmissible. Even military intervention on behalf of fellow *citizens* abroad has been viewed as acceptable only in the abeyance of law, order, and a functioning government in their country of residence, and then only if there is a palpable threat to their very lives. (The 1965 US intervention in the Dominican Republic may be a case in point.)

The Russian doctrines in question, however, did not speak of threats to life and limb but merely of a purported "violation of the rights" of the Russian diaspora, which some Western diplomats have confused with human rights. Actually the most that could be claimed in some instances was a dispute over *political status,* for example, the conditions and the period of time required for a Russian to become a citizen of a particular Baltic republic, and the kind of political participation and social services for which Russian residents would be eligible in the meantime. These are matters predominantly within the purview of the country of residence, and the claim that a neighboring state could use military force to impose its own views over such issues would turn international order into a Hobbesian jungle.

The theme of military pressure on behalf of the Russian diaspora was used extensively as an excuse for refusing to withdraw Russian forces from the Baltic States by the dates negotiated between the parties. Yel'tsin relented on this point in August 1994, only after President Clinton's Riga speech indicated American concern over this issue. However, at the same time, the Russian government issued an edict that comprised extensive demands regarding the privileges to be granted by the host countries to the ethnic Russian diaspora. The document spelled out Russia's economic sanctions if these requirements were not met, stressing, ominously, that these were "immediate measures" as far as the Baltic States were concerned.[6]

With Moscow's eventual realization that the "purely ethnic" argument evoked disagreeable associations, a new wrinkle was added, namely that ethnic Russians, having been Soviet citizens, should now be given Russian citizenship while simultaneously obtaining citizenship of the newly independent country in which they happened to be living. Thus, the doctrine of military intervention on behalf of Russian minorities was to be made more palatable. Consequently, the November 1993 version of Russia's military doctrine described "suppression of rights, freedoms, or the legitimate interests of Russian *citizens*" as one of the "main . . . sources of external military danger to [Russia]."[7]

Shortly thereafter, Foreign Minister Andrei Kozyrev claimed that, since Russia's constitution allowed dual citizenship, he could now demand the same of other republics in the Near Abroad: "If a Russian, an ethnic Russian, or a Russian-speaker, someone who feels close to Russia—there are Uzbeks and Kazakhs and Kyrgyz who consider themselves in essence Russian-speakers . . .—if all of these people, or some of them, wish to have Russian citizenship as well as Kyrgyz, Kazakh, or Uzbek citizenship, of course they will be under the protection of the Russian state. . . ."[8] Subsequently, he added that the question of dual citizenship had now become a key element in relations with the Near Abroad, and that "We should not leave regions that for centuries have been spheres of Russian interest."[9]

Of course, Mr. Kozyrev omitted mentioning that Russia's new approach meant compelling other countries to accept dual citizenship, which—as a matter under domestic jurisdiction—no state has the right to impose upon another. (In the second half of 1994, Russia attempted to compel Ukraine to accept dual citizenship as part of a bilateral treaty.[10] Earlier in 1994 Turkmenistan was compelled to accept such a clause.[11]) Most countries, in fact, do *not* accept dual citizenship; until recently, Americans could lose US citizenship for performing an act that implied citizenship of another country, such as voting in that country's elections or serving in its armed forces.

The issue of the Russian ethnic diaspora eventually yielded first place to two other demands on Moscow's agenda for the Near Abroad. One had to do with the location of the Russian Border Troops (a separate arm of Russia's military forces) and the other asserted Russia's monopoly over what were called euphemistically "peacekeeping activities."

Starting in 1993, Yel'tsin's apparatus and sections of the armed forces asserted that it was both too expensive and impractical to relocate the Border Troops along Russia's new frontiers with the post-Soviet republics and that they should simply be left in the existing (old Soviet) border installations.[12] By the fall of that year, Defense Minister Pavel Grachev reportedly informed an internal briefing that "a decision [had] been made not to pull back to Russia's borders but to maintain old Soviet borders, especially in Central Asia and the . . . Caucasus."[13] As a consequence, the three Transcaucasian republics and the five Central Asian republics could now be severed from the outside world by Russian troops along their southern frontiers, being enveloped at the same time by Russian military elements to their north, in the Russian Federation.

Colonel General Andrei Nikolayev, commander of the Border Troops, stated candidly, "the defense of the external borders of the [former Soviet republics] is being carried out, first and foremost, for us Russians, in the interest of Russia itself. Second, this involve[s] the guarantee of [our] national interests in the most important geo-political regions, where Russia's strategic interests exist, existed, and, hopefully, will continue to exist."[14]

Additionally, in the spring of 1993, President Yel'tsin requested that the United Nations "grant Russia special powers as guarantor of peace and stability in this region," but backpedalled in the face of unfavorable reactions.[15] Since then the demand for a Russian "peacekeeping" monopoly in the Near Abroad has been reasserted, not without some success. The concept is particularly bizarre because, in at least two instances, the actions of the Russian military and security sectors themselves have been responsible for the escalation of conflicts that, as a result, require "peacekeeping." One case concerned some 90,000 Muslim Abkhaz mountaineers living in a corner of the Georgian republic that happens to dominate a lengthy stretch of Black Sea coastline desired by the Russian navy.

As former Soviet KGB chief and Minister of Internal Affairs, Vadim Bakatin, has revealed, even before the dissolution of the USSR the KGB created "'fronts' in [those] Union Republics which showed obstinacy in their relations with the Center, [telling these Republics] if you don't want to obey then you may have [to deal with] . . . a 'front' which . . . will raise the question of the borders of the Republic and the legitimacy of the organs of power elected there. . . ." Consequently, another report disclosed, "the South Ossetian . . . and the Abkhazian [organizations] were formed . . . to counteract the . . . movements of the Georgian people aimed at liberation from communist dictatorship and the secession of Georgia from the USSR." The KGB's aim was "consolidation of the [mountain] people of the Caucasus . . . against Georgia." The eventual outcome was that an Abkhazian leader, Vladislav Ardzinba, declared secession from Georgia, supported by a "bloc of the revenge-seekers of pro-communist, pro-imperial, and national socialist orientation."[16]

As a result, in August 1992 armed conflict with Georgia erupted. By February and March of 1993, in the greatest miracle since the loaves and the fishes, backward Abkhaz mountaineers suddenly acquired a high-tech air force, including Russian (current generation) Sukhoi-25 and -27 planes, that bombed Sukhumi, a major city, and defeated the poorly armed Georgian forces. In the aftermath, most ethnic Georgians were expelled from Abkhazia. The Russian army then interposed itself between Abkhazia and the rest of Georgia, effectively preventing the return of the Georgian refugees. Moreover, the Russian navy blockaded Georgia's remaining port and Moscow demanded that Georgia accept Russian *garrisons*. Frantic pleas, by Georgia's leader Eduard Shevardnadze, for international help were ignored, despite this former Soviet foreign minister's once warm relationship with Western leaders. Abandoned, he was forced to surrender, whereupon, with his "consent," Georgia's major cities acquired Russian garrisons, and Georgia was sundered from the outside world to the south by Russian Border Troops. Apparently, that is Russia's now-classic definition of "peacekeeping."[17]

In Moldova, the Russian Fourteenth Army effectively bisected the republic by establishing itself along the Dniestr River, enabling ethnic Russians to the east of that waterway to proclaim a secessionist "Dniestr Republic." Now the excuse for keeping this army on Moldovan soil for at least another three years is that it constitutes the only available "peacekeeping" force.

Moscow utilized the dispute between Armenia and Azerbaijan over the Nagorno-Karabakh enclave to offer military support, first to one side then to the other, in the end demanding "compensation" in the form of Russian military bases in these republics, a request to which at least Armenia has acceded. A somewhat more complicated, but essentially also self-serving "mission" has established substantial Russian military forces in Tajikistan.

The topic of "peacekeeping" has become inextricably linked to the establishment of Russian "bases" and "garrisons" in former Soviet republics. Indeed, already in the fall of 1993 Foreign Minister Kozyrev stated openly that it would be unacceptable for Russia "to pull out completely from the zones of traditional influence which . . . were won over centuries."[18]

Eventually, a more sophisticated wrinkle was added to this endeavor, using the Russian-dominated Commonwealth of Independent States (CIS) as a "front." Russian military elements were to operate under the thin disguise of "CIS peacekeeping forces," although non-Russian contingents were practically nonexistent, and a UN mandate was to be sought ex post facto to legitimize these activities.

In response, the United States stipulated that (1) such activities required the freely given "agreement" of the countries on whose soil they were to take place; (2) the "peacekeepers" had to be "impartial" and "respect [the] territorial integrity" of the country in which they operated; and (3) they had to comport themselves "in accordance with the UN Charter and the principles of the Conference on Security and Cooperation in Europe (CSCE)." Moreover, a UN Security Council resolution permitting the operation was required *prior* to the introduction of such forces, if a genuine international mandate was to legitimate their actions. Additionally, the UN Secretary General stipulated that Russian troops could "account for no more than 20–30 percent" of a "peacekeeping" contingent on the territory of a former Soviet republic.[19]

In fact, none of these conditions has been met. We have seen how Georgia's "agreement" was obtained, how "impartial" the Russians have been between Georgia and Abkhazia and what this has meant for Georgia's "territorial integrity." Moreover, UN acquiescence was sought after the operation was completed, and Russians constitute the overwhelming majority—in Georgia's case the only contingent—of the force in question.

Nevertheless, the Russian army was prepared to offer the international community and/or the occupied republics one "privilege," namely to pay for the cost of these "peacekeeping" operations (a demand voiced by Defense Minister Grachev as long ago as the fall of 1993).[20] Russia has demanded that the CIS be viewed as a "regional agency" under Chapter VIII of the UN Charter, although that chapter emphasizes "pacific settlement of local disputes," an aim incompatible with Russian operations in Georgia.

Another bizarre aspect consists of Russia's demand that members of any CIS "peacekeeping" force be made to swear allegiance to their own republic and to *Russia.*[21] If enforced, Kazakh members of such a unit would swear allegiance not to Kazakhstan and the CIS, but to Kazakhstan and Russia, a foreign country.

Recently, yet another item has floated to the top of the Russian agenda, namely the "integration" of the CIS, originally defined in primarily economic and functional terms, but subsequently extended to comprise complete military integration, treating the CIS as a single military space, comprised of four "regional subsystems."[22] The term "integration" clearly is intended to evoke the image of associations of freely consenting states of roughly equal power, such as the European Union. However, some republics, at least, were coerced into CIS membership and that "commonwealth" is completely dominated by one overwhelmingly powerful state that does not hesitate to use force against fellow members.

President Yel'tsin's speech to the General Assembly in September 1994 included many of Russia's neo-imperial concepts in one package and, of late, the Russian media have taken to describing it as the "Yel'tsin Doctrine." He stated, "Russia's . . . priority is . . . the countries of the former union. Russia's link with them is . . . blood kinship" (what, between Russians and Tajiks?). He claimed that there was "a growing desire for . . . real . . . integration" in CIS countries. He warned that "attempts to play on the contradictions between countries of the Commonwealth [were] shortsighted" and that "the burden of peacemaking on the space of the former union [lay] . . . on the shoulders of . . . [Russia]." He then claimed that the Russian-imposed "Treaty on Collective Security . . . of the former union" constituted a "regional security system."[23]

The same concept of "integration," but with a notably more threatening tone, has been published in what must be a unique instance in intelligence history. In September 1994, while President Yel'tsin was in the United States, the head of Russia's Foreign Intelligence Service, Yevgeni Primakov, gave the press what was purported to be his agency's intelligence estimate. Presented as "intelligence options," the paper left little doubt as to Primakov's real message. It castigated "criticism of Russia's 'special role' in peacekeeping actions on the territory of the Commonwealth" and stressed that "it [was] necessary for Russia to stabilize the situation in the Near Abroad . . . and to restore order on the Commonwealth's external borders"—meaning the old Soviet frontiers—emphasizing that "with 'transparent' internal borders there is no doubt about the need to protect external borders." Primakov's paper called for "integration in the military sphere and a defense area with a unified command and unified subunits designed to protect external borders [and] undertake peacekeeping missions." It concluded by stressing "the objective nature of the reintegration processes on CIS territory," as opposed to a much more limited role for Russia, and stated flatly that "the second approach is unacceptable to Russia and . . . it will reject it."[24]

When President Yel'tsin was asked whether he had read the contents of this document, he gave an evasive answer to the effect that, just prior to his departure for the United States, he had been "advised" by Primakov of the planned presentation and was in general agreement. The whole episode raised the question of who precisely was making policy in Moscow.[25]

As indicated, Yel'tsin himself, at one time or another, has shown distinct traces of Great Russian national instincts but has displayed a slightly less bullying attitude than many other members of the old-new nomenklatura. This applies to the "Far Abroad"—the former Warsaw Pact members—even more than to the Near Abroad. Thus, in August 1993, Yel'tsin visited Prague, Bratislava, and Warsaw. In the Polish capital, he signed a joint declaration with his hosts that stated, "The presidents touched on the matter of Poland's intention to join NATO. President Wałęsa set forth Poland's well-known position on this issue, which met with understanding from President B. N. Yel'tsin. In the long term, such a design taken by a sovereign Poland in the interests of overall European integration does not go against the interests of other states, including the interests of Russia."[26]

At the same time, moreover, Yel'tsin was reported to have assured the Slovak president, Vladimir Mečiar, that "it [was] up to Slovakia to decide whether to join NATO or not."[27] In response to a question on the same issue in Prague, Yel'tsin gave an implicitly positive, but convoluted, answer, saying, "It is a question of integration between states and certain European organizations. We are not able to enumerate them. Each country selects its own."[28] Shortly thereafter, the head of Yel'tsin's press service stated that "the sovereignty of the NATO members and the former Warsaw Pact members has now become complete. Russia can no longer react the same way as the totalitarian Soviet Union might have reacted to the approach to, or cooperation with, NATO by certain countries."[29]

However, two weeks after Yel'tsin's visit, Russia's ambassador to Poland, Yuri Kashlev, claimed that the president's statements in Warsaw had been "oversimplified and misunderstood,"[30] while Foreign Minister Kozyrev was at great pains to stress that the issue was *not* to increase the number of NATO members but to change NATO itself.[31] Within another two weeks, Yel'tsin himself was to dispatch a letter to NATO members in which he warned "against expanding NATO by accepting the former socialist countries of East Europe into that organization."[32] Which was the real Yel'tsin?

Perhaps Yel'tsin personally, despite his own proclivities, might have proven amenable to Western leverage and curbed the excesses of Russia's current neo-imperial phase. However, given almost complete international silence concerning the resuscitation of Russian domination over most former "Soviet space," and of veto power over ex-Warsaw Pact members, Yel'tsin has no incentive to assert himself against those in his own entourage, not to speak of the "patriotic opposition," who insist on pushing Russian power rapidly outward. In this context, the economic exigencies under which Russian armed forces labor offer little solace. The military infrastructure of the non-Russian republics is so weak that the Russian operations listed—in the Transcaucasus, Central Asia, and Moldova—have required altogether considerably fewer than 100,000 soldiers.

The performance of Russian forces in Chechnya, it may be argued, weakens the contention that relatively small Russian military contingents suffice to overcome the weak opposition which can be mounted by the victims of Moscow's neo-imperialism. The fact is, however, that the Russian units initially poured into Chechnya were composed mainly of raw recruits or inferior echelons, untrained for the complexities of fighting under the conditions and on the terrain of the Caucasus.[33] Moreover, the mishaps of that clumsy operation should not mislead analysts into drawing far-reaching conclusions with regard to the capabilities of Russia's elite units and *strategic* forces. Observers should recall that fewer than 20 months intervened between the Red Army's abysmal performance in the Finnish Winter War and its successful repulsion of Germany's hitherto invincible armor at the outskirts of Moscow.

Disheartening as was Western—especially American—silence during weeks in which Chechens (and ethnic Russians) in and around Grozny were slaughtered indiscriminately, it is just as incomprehensible that Western spokespersons did not question the legitimation of this massacre as "Russia's domestic affairs." That claim might have been consistent at least had the West denounced Russia's military intervention in Georgia, a supposedly sovereign country recognized by Yel'tsin himself—an act of aggression that could not be characterized, by any stretch of the imagination, as "Russia's internal concerns." What is more, in that instance Russia acted in support of an avowedly secessionist element, the Abkhaz ethnic minority in Georgia's Abkhazian province.

Thus, implicit Western justification of the Chechen venture as a mere crackdown on secessionist "rebels" (a term repeated ad nauseam in our media) is a grim joke, considering that Russian planes had aided precisely such secessionist rebels in Abkhazia. Chechnya demonstrates that, after largely successful efforts to extend Russia's de facto borders by reabsorbing sovereign countries that were former Soviet republics, Moscow apparently recognizes no limits on the *means* that may be used to consolidate its empire, whether within the Russian Federation or beyond.

The trends described here are noted with sadness and regret. The historic opportunity offered by August 1991 is being frittered away at the expense not only of the briefly independent non-Russian republics and of international peace and order, but, ultimately, of the lawful socioeconomic hopes and aspirations of the Russian people. Chechnya has already led to truly chilling efforts by the Russian security services to intimidate the media and individual Russians who may have contact with the rest of the world, in however innocent a fashion.

On January 10, 1995, a "document" was leaked to the media by the Federal Counterintelligence Service. It referred to 500 Western academic and philanthropic institutions (including, surprisingly, some with a consistently pro-Russian past) as actual or potential "participants in subversive operations." Clearly, this slur was intended to make Russians shy away from any form of association with foreign organizations of whatever political hue. "Analysis of the Russian media" was mentioned specifically as one of Western intelligence's "ways of obtaining information."[34] In effect, this meant that anything printed in Russian publications might be analyzed by the Western institutions listed and, thus, ipso facto, could be viewed as a source for foreign intelligence. It is a document that could have been published at the very nadir of the grim mid-1930s. Similarly reminiscent of the "bad old days" are the transparent lies about the war in Chechnya that Russian leaders have told with a straight face (despite visual evidence to the contrary available to most Russians).

In this context, one has to view with particular concern the deafening silence of most of Russia's democratic movement in the face of the neo-imperial process, at least prior to Chechnya. The courageous voices that have refused to be silenced—particularly that of Sakharov's heir, Sergei Kovalev—provide heartening evidence that the Russian intelligentsia, as under the bolsheviks and tsars, still produces some truly brave individuals. Much less encouraging is the fact that those who have joined in protest have been pitifully few in number, and demonstrations against Yel'tsin's actions have been very sparsely attended. While the Russian imperialist chorus grows ever louder and is joined increasingly by former and even current "democrats," the paralysis of the democratic movement undermines any hope for genuine democratization.

NOTES

1. The author notes with deep appreciation the meticulous work on sources in this chapter contributed by Peter Lorenz, Research Fellow of the Institute for the Study of Conflict, Ideology & Policy.

2. TASS International Service in Russian, 1532 GMT, 26 August 1991, cited in FBIS-SOV-91-166, 27 August 1991, p. 71.

3. *Voennaya mysl'* (Military Thought) (Moscow), Special Issue, Ministry of Defense of the Russian Federation, May 1992, pp. 3–9.

4. *Izvestiya* (Moscow), 7 August 1992, p. 6, cited in Teresa Rakowska-Harmstone "Russia's Monroe Doctrine," in M. A. Mollot and H. v. Riekhoff, eds., *A Part of the Peace* (Ottawa: Carleton University Press, 1994), pp. 231–65.

5. *Foreign Policy Concept of the Russian Federation,* cited in FBIS-USR-93-037, 25 March 1993, pp. 1–20 (especially pp. 2 and 5) (emphasis added).

6. "On Measures to Support Compatriots Abroad," Russian Federation Edict dated 31 August 1994, cited in *Rossiyskaya gazeta* (Moscow), 22 September 1994, cited in FBIS-SOV-94-187, 27 September 1994, p. 1.

7. *Voennaya mysl'* (Military Thought) (Moscow), Special Issue, Ministry of Defense of the Russian Federation, November 1993, p. 5 (emphasis added).

8. Ostankino Television First Channel Network (Moscow), 1848 GMT, 15 December 1993, cited in FBIS-SOV-93-240, 16 December 1993, p. 9.

9. "CIS and Baltic Countries Are Focus of Russia's Immediate Vital Interest," *Krasnaya zvezda* (Moscow), 19 January 1994, p. 1, cited in FBIS-SOV-94-012, 19 January 1994, p. 8.

10. INTERFAX in English, 1048 GMT, 23 September 1994, cited in FBIS-SOV-94-186, 26 September 1994, p. 40.

11. "Russians in Turkmenia: They Are the First in the Near Abroad to Obtain Russia's Legal Protection," *Rossiyskiye vesti* (Moscow), 16 March 1994, p. 3, cited in FBIS-USR-94-033, 4 April 1994, p. 3.

12. *Segodnya* (Moscow), no. 53, 16 September 1993 (signed to press 15 Sep-

tember 1993), cited in FBIS-SOV-93-179, 17 September 1993, p. 4.

13. Steven Erlanger, "Troops in Ex-Soviet Lands," *The New York Times,* 30 November 1993, pp. A1 and A12, cited in Teresa Rakowska-Harmstone, op. cit.

14. Mayak Radio Network, 1930 GMT, 17 January 1994, cited in FBIS-SOV-94-011, 18 January 1994, p. 1.

15. ITAR–TASS, 1 March 1993, cited in Suzanne Crow, "Russia Asserts Its Strategic Agenda," *Radio Free Europe/Radio Liberty (RFE/RL) Research Report* 2:50, 17 December 1993, p. 2.

16. Svetlana Chervonnaya, "The Technology of the Abkhazian War," *Moscow News,* no. 42, 15 October 1993, pp. 1, 4.

17. For an excellent analysis see Fiona Hill and Pamela Jewett, *Back in the USSR* (Cambridge, MA: Harvard University, John F. Kennedy School of Government, Strengthening Democratic Institutions Project, January 1994), pp. 45–60.

18. *Nezavisimaya gazeta* (Moscow), 24 November 1993, pp. 1, 3, cited in Maxim Shashenkov, "Russian Peacekeeping in the 'Near Abroad,'" in *Survival* 36:3 (Autumn 1994), note 11 (p. 66).

19. Madeleine K. Albright, "Realism and Idealism in American Foreign Policy," *Department of State Dispatch* 5:26, US Department of State, 27 June 1994. Also Moscow NTV, 1700 GMT, 3 April 1994, cited in FBIS-SOV-94-064, 4 April 1994, p. 6.

20. See note 11.

21. *Izvestiya* (Moscow), 7 April 1994, p. 2, cited in FBIS-SOV-94-068, 8 April 1994, p. 3.

22. Lt. Gen. Leonid Ivashov, "Perspectives for the Integration of CIS Armed Forces," *Nezavisimaya gazeta* (Moscow), 18 October 1994, p. 5.

23. Russian Television Network, 1927 GMT, 26 September 1994, cited in FBIS-SOV-94-187, 27 September 1994, pp. 7, 8.

24. *Rossiyskaya gazeta* (Moscow), 22 September 1994, pp. 1, 6, cited in FBIS-SOV-94-185, 23 September 1994, pp. 1–9 (especially pp. 1, 5–7).

25. Ostankino Television First Channel Network, 1518 GMT, 4 October 1994, cited in FBIS-SOV-94-193, 5 October 1994, p. 11.

26. ITAR-TASS, 25 August 1993, cited in Suzanne Crow, "Russian Views on an Eastward Expansion of NATO," *RFE/RL Research Report* 2:41, 15 October 1993, p. 21.

27. Aleksandr Kuranov, "Looking at the Rear," *Nezavisimaya gazeta* (Moscow), 25 August 1993, p. 1.

28. Radiozurnal Prague Radio Network in Czech, 1102 GMT, 26 August 1993, cited in FBIS-EEU-93-165, 27 August 1993, p. 8.

29. Gabor Horvath interview with Anatoly Krasikov (undated), *Nepszabadsag* (Budapest), 16 September 1993, p. 3, cited in FBIS-SOV-93-179, 17 September 1993, p. 8.

30. PAP (Polish Press Agency) Newswire, "Russian Stand on Poland's NATO Membership Biased by Media," 15 September 1993.

31. *Moskovskiye novosti* (Moscow), no. 39, 26 September 1993, p. A7, cited in Suzanne Crow, op. cit.

32. Vladimir Lapsky, "Russian President Urges West Not to Expand NATO by Incorporating East Europe," *Izvestiya* (Moscow), 2 October 1993 (1st edition), p. 4, cited in FBIS-SOV-93-190.

33. Benjamin S. Lambeth, "An Ailing Army Needs Our Help," *The New York Times,* 28 February 1995, p. A23.

34. "The Federal Counter-Intelligence Service Is Disturbed by the Activities of American Researchers in Russia," *Nezavisimaya gazeta* (Moscow), 10 January 1995, p. 3.

3

Peacekeeping:
Russia's Emerging Practice

Harry H. Almond, Jr.

Peacekeeping is an instrument of policy that can be wielded by states or by the United Nations. It affords the means to invoke coercive as well as persuasive strategies.[1] Under current practice, states may attempt to engage in peacekeeping missions and activities to achieve exclusive interests of their own: One of the primary themes of this inquiry is an assessment of Russian practices and the extent to which national interests are the primary concern of that state when it turns to peacekeeping efforts outside its borders.

The current framework of peacekeeping regulation mainly addresses states and their uses of force.[2] It separates the *jus ad bellum*—or action in defense against aggression—from action by way of attaining United Nations objectives under the UN Charter.[3] The *jus in bello,* regulating the conduct of hostilities among states, is only now commencing to expand as a regulatory framework for other uses of force.[4]

Under current practice, states have claimed the legitimacy of their peacekeeping efforts, but such legitimacy can be sustained only by showing that the states in question are acting to attain the objectives of the UN Charter. They must operate pursuant to that charter and to customary international law and, where possible, under mandates established or monitored by the Security Council of the United Nations.[5]

The fundamental issue faced by the United States and other Western governments is the global regulation of peacekeeping. The difficulty of this task is exacerbated by the underlying need to couple the legitimation of peace-keeping activities with the rules of engagement that the peacekeeping mission may require.[6] Peacekeeping activities afford a convenient means for resorting to force under the mask of legitimacy, and to establish legitimacy under the claim of promoting "stability."[7]

Any legal appraisal of Russian practices must be interdisciplinary. Law is policy-oriented toward future behavior, and therefore embraces numerous themes—strategy, defense, security, global-order goals, and policy in general.[8] The assessment comes at a time when the practices still may be changed; although malleable, the guidelines and criteria of the UN Charter afford a sufficient and firm framework of future conduct. The key element is the will of the West, and especially the United States, to maintain, through leadership and forcible example, the promotion of the Charter. The core principles of United States policy must be formulated to oppose Russian policies wherever the concept of peacekeeping is invoked to achieve Russian national goals. Failure to do so would undermine the mission of the United Nations and international law. Of particular concern is Russia's apparent commitment to expansionism, to hegemony over the former Soviet republics, and to a general policy of "gradual reintegration."

Default in leadership to ensure that peacekeeping furthers the objectives of the Charter has serious repercussions: It promises a gradual weakening of the United Nations structure, primarily because peacekeeping is an institution that is authorized to use (and is the source of authority for using) coercion or force to achieve peacekeeping goals. A breakdown in this institution is tantamount to a weakening of our grasp upon the regulation of the use of force. This in turn may compel the United States to refrain from leadership roles because of a lack of resources to confront unregulated proliferating conflict.[9] Thus the United States would lose the initiative in shaping the future of global order.

This inquiry includes an assessment of relevant United States peacekeeping perspectives that can be considered in juxtaposition with those of Russia. The perspectives here share one common theme: They focus on policies and decisions that can impose control over conflicts, disputes, or the impermissible outbursts of force that have aroused the concern of the global community. There are three relevant categories:

1. Those perspectives associated with United States' claims to be recognized as a major power, but presupposing an arena in which it finds itself competing for power with other states, such as a newly empowered Russia. In these perspectives the competitive arena and competitive process continue to prevail in state relations.

2. The differing perspectives from which the United States is perceived as a peacekeeping leader, both in the political and military sense, and hence as an actor in peacekeeping missions operating in its own right as a member of the loosely organized global community. The need to maintain dominance in power and influence prevails, but it demands the continuous and scrupulous exercise of will on a timely basis when peacekeeping is required.[10]

3. The perspectives of the United States that encourage the strengthening and shifting of peacekeeping powers, authority, or competence to global order entities, or, in the more immediate sense, to direct United Nations control. In this context the purpose is to build upon global order and to strengthen the presently loosely organized institutions and organs of the global community to operate in the power process.

The Clinton administration policy stresses the determination of national interest in deciding when to participate in peacekeeping operations. It also emphasizes the need to achieve leadership in peacekeeping activities, the avoidance of military hostilities, and outcomes that are consistent with the objectives of the UN Charter. According to the first operational policy element expressed in the Presidential Memorandum titled, "The Role of Peace Operations in US Foreign Policy":

When our interests dictate, the US must be willing and able to fight and win wars, unilaterally whenever necessary. . . . UN peace operations cannot substitute for this requirement. . . . Since it is in our interest at times to support UN peace operations, it is also in our interest to seek to strengthen UN peacekeeping capabilities and to make operations less expensive and peacekeeping management more accountable. . . . UN and other multilateral peace operations will at times offer the best way to prevent, contain or resolve conflicts that could otherwise be more costly and deadly. In such cases, the US benefits from having to bear only a share of the burden. We also benefit by being able to invoke the voice of the community of nations on behalf of a cause we support. Thus, establishment of a capability to conduct multilateral peace operations is part of our National Security Strategy and National Military Strategy. . . . The US does not support a standing UN army, nor will we earmark specific US military units for participation in UN operations. . . . It is not US policy to seek to expand either the number of UN peace operations or US involvement in such operations. Instead, this policy . . . aims to ensure that our use of peacekeeping is selective and more effective. . . .[11]

The term and the concept of peacekeeping are ambiguous; they entail differing, opposing, and combative policies. This ambiguity permits creative actions that can be self-serving for the states involved. It also can create confusion about if and when action is required, and how much.[12] Peacekeeping is largely appraised in terms of the changing functions associated not only with its traditional meaning, but also with notions of peace-keeping pursued through "peace support."[13] Much of this is abstract, but peacekeeping is significant in one sense that we share; it is a problem relating to the public order, both as it applies within states and among them.

The starting points can be stated by reference to the UN Charter. The objectives in a global order, or in processes aimed at the distant attainment of global order, are to maintain international peace and security, and to promote human rights and human dignity.[14] These are broadly stated, but they have one element that gives them precision: The reasonably precise operative provisions of the Charter add up to a global claim to achieve these objectives.[15]

According to the conclusions of the *Basic Report*:

> Peacekeeping was originally intended to be a service to the international community as a means of maintaining peace. Since the end of the Cold War, peacekeeping has increasingly become applied to the traditional military and political policies of nation states. Peacekeeping itself is becoming as much a source of instability as it is an attractive new label of old-style intervention. Even more paradoxically, the new peacekeeping order seems to be leading to a growing unwillingness to intervene effectively, in instances where an impartial military presence could make a difference to the fate of countless innocent civilians.[16]

Yale University Professor W. Michael Reisman suggests that the problem today may consist of trying to rally states around common interests, espe-cially among the Permanent Five UN members that control the veto in the Security Council. While Reisman calls attention to the uncertainties of UN control, and to the necessity of common interests, it is evident that the appli-cable law relating to peacekeeping is to be found in UN practices and in customary international law. He states the need to establish common inter-ests as a problem that requires overcoming the competitive attitudes among states:

> There is as yet no broad and enduring identity of interests between the Permanent Five. If the Permanent Five can establish a specific common interest with regard to a particular candidate for peacemaking, they can now use the United Nations and possibly use it effectively, as they did in Namibia. In the absence of that specific common interest, either the organization cannot be used for peacemaking at all or peacemaking will be ineffective or cosmetic.[17]

RUSSIAN CLAIMS CONCERNING IDEOLOGICAL AND DIPLOMATIC SUPPORT FOR RUSSIAN PEACEKEEPING INITIATIVES AND ACTIONS

Russia cannot claim that it is authorized under the Charter or international law to invoke peacekeeping efforts for members of the Commonwealth of Independent States (CIS) (on the grounds, for example, that it has a responsibility to stabilize order in the area) if that claim is inconsistent with the Charter or law. Such a claim would replace the assertion and recognition of sovereignty of these states. Russia cannot legitimately claim to be a special power, and thereby authorized to regain great power status.

Valuable insights into what Russia is claiming and demanding from the West can be gathered from recent articles by Russian Foreign Minister Andrei Kozyrev. These insights are of great importance in appraising attitudes of the Russian elite concerning the future shape of international law and of the global legal order. They echo some of the notions heard earlier from communists in the Soviet Union relating to peaceful coexistence and to the special law for the "socialist commonwealth of states."[18]

Kozyrev has suggested that the re-establishment of a greater Russia is essential for security and global public order. He offers for these purposes a pragmatic perspective:

> At first, after the disintegration of the Soviet Union, the West openly recognized the role of Russia as the stabilizing factor and engine of economic reform in the former Soviet Union. We never refused that role, even though it costs us billions of dollars. *What is wrong with Russia announcing as its goal the gradual reintegration—primarily economic reintegration—of the post–Soviet space on a voluntary and equal basis?* The situation is similar to that of the European Union, where the economic leadership of the larger states like France and Germany is recognized.[19]

A policy of this nature is far-reaching in projecting freedom of action and policy for Russia, outside the current framework that depends upon the UN Charter. The CIS states have little choice: Kozyrev asks, "Is there an alternative?" He wonders whether the West is prepared to pay the billions of dollars owed by Ukraine, Georgia, and the other CIS states for oil and gas delivered by the former Soviet Union, repayment of which is demanded now by Russia.[20]

He likens the objectives of the Russian program that he is describing to the voluntary efforts of the European states in forming the European Union. This approach bypasses the problem raised under the notion of "voluntary" because, he quickly adds, the former Soviet republics have no alternative.[21] Kozyrev does not propose, for example, that these states will be assisted through peacekeeping in strengthening their territorial integrity or political independence, factors familiar from the UN Charter.[22]

In claiming objectives that call for a departure from the precepts of the UN Charter, Russia apparently is seeking a new foundation of authority to govern its actions. From the juridical point of view these objectives indicate that the legal authority for Russian activities in this sphere, and the legal order supportive of those activities, will be "special." Having made the remarks just cited, Kozyrev declares, "That is why Russia's *special role and responsibility within the former Soviet Union* must be borne in mind by its Western partners and given support."[23] To cement this legal foundation,

Kozyrev proposes a partnership linking countries that "now share common democratic values." A premise of this Russian-formulated notion of partnership is evidenced in the perspectives about human rights. Russians, according to Kozyrev, now have an increased and awakened "respect [for] human rights." However, the concept of human rights has switched from the communist doctrine that linked human rights to economic progress—under communism and "socialism"—to the notion that human rights in general are meaningless without recognition of the rights of individual Russians, to wit, "relatives and friends who are suffering from one form or another of discrimination or who have become refugees."[24] This, in turn, has led to the pronouncements that Russia would resort to force if necessary to protect those individual "human" rights.

These matters are given wide publicity, but the inherent nature of such publicity leads to the tolerances associated with both the making and the enforcement of law—domestic and international. Law, whether customary international law or the law that develops from treaties and international agreements, evolves from a pattern of shared expectations.[25] Kozyrev's perspectives are deliberately designed to manipulate thinking in neighboring countries and in the West. They focus on matters that can be promoted readily under the blanket of a strengthened CSCE,[26] and are designed to encourage among other states and their citizens tolerance regarding Russian behavior in enforcing such claims.

The "human rights" problems are, of course, what Kozyrev would resolve by gaining special recognition of the Russians in the Near Abroad—the CIS states and the Baltic States—with demands for such countries to adopt domestic policies giving Russians special status. Some sources even indicate that Moscow's policies would extend to Russian-*speaking* peoples, or to those with cultural ties and other affiliations to the Russian Federation. Russian doctrines stress that such rights must be backed by military force if necessary. The legal framework that emerges from these proposals affords a basis for restoring Russia to the position of a great power and, concurrently, establishes its authority, self-interpreted, to take the necessary actions (including force or threat of force) to achieve this goal. Democratic Russians would be faced with a major task to change this shift once it had become firmly entrenched. Such actions are not merely contrary to the Charter, but could lead only to weakening the Charter and international law.

Accordingly, to achieve his goals, Kozyrev proposes a partnership, still "lagging" at the time of publication of his article in 1994, that would co-opt all states as active, supportive members in the restoration of Russian economic and political strength—and in the restoration of Russia with its reintegrated CIS states as a great power among states in the global order.

The reach of his strategy, in paraphrase, would be "pragmatic"—a "full-scale scheme."

Kozyrev proposes that his strategy of control for the global order is best achieved through a partnership which would include "mutual recognition" of states committed to "democracy, human rights and responsible international behavior." It would close the "institutional gaps between Russia and the West," by transforming the G-7 states to a G-8, restructuring NATO to fit the post–Cold War world, but by implication looking to NATO's dismantling.

This strategy affords an opening for a "unified non-bloc Europe" that best can be pursued by restructuring and giving greater authority to the CSCE.[27] For decision-making purposes the partnership would not operate under rules, but instead rest upon "mutual trust." The last factor would lead ultimately to a decision process in which Russia would participate as a strong and active partner.[28]

This would presumably overcome the potential of the UN Security Council to falter as the intended guardian of global security and shield against threats of aggression. There are romantic elements in the Kozyrev vision. It presupposes that states will shift from the competition that now shapes their behavior to cooperative and joint enterprise; it presupposes that trust among nations is compatible with their competition for resources, wealth, and power; and it presumes that the cultural differences, especially varying and deep-rooted perspectives about social order and how it is governed, will be overcome.[29]

Kozyrev's strategy must also be read against the realities of current Russian behavior. Most importantly, it must be measured under the reciprocal principle that is key to the evolution of both international relations and international law. Thus, the United States action in Haiti is perceived by Russia to be a factor supporting Russian intervention in the states of the Near Abroad. Such interventions are contrary to the rights of states to self-determination, and, to the extent that Russian interventions are intended as permanent, they are contrary to the rights of independent states under the Charter.

Boris Yel'tsin, for example, reportedly proclaimed a policy in which Russia would have "the prime responsibility for ensuring peace and stability among those neighboring states." Thus, based upon the intervention by the United States in Haiti, Yel'tsin is arguing in substance that Russia "has a similar right to intervene in the smaller and weaker countries of its neighborhood." However, there is a major distinction. The United States seeks peacekeeping in which it restores or initiates democratic processes and then leaves as quickly as possible. Russian elites intend to move in and, through "gradual reintegration," stay there. Asserting a position some consider to be a renewal of the "spheres-of-influence" concept, Yel'tsin declared that his country's "economic and foreign policy priorities lie in the countries of the Common-wealth of Independent States. . . . Russia's ties with them are closer than tradi-tional neighborhood relations; rather, this is a blood relationship."[30]

The same report indicates the full scale of the Russian position, reach-ing beyond the usual foundations of spheres of influence to claims linked to "blood." Yel'tsin insisted that the desire for economic integration of the former Soviet republics is shared by those states and has "a foundation of goodwill and mutual benefit." Russia's historic claim to police activities, imposed through peacekeeping, is supported. The report observes that Yel'tsin "left no doubt that Russia considers conflicts in the region 'a threat to the security of our state. . . . The main peacekeeping burden in the territory of the former Soviet Union lies upon the Russian Federation.'"[31] Hence the gradual tight-ening of the Russian claims, and the accumulation of authority and control through incremental but almost irreversible stages, can be launched under the cloak of legitimacy. Yel'tsin has insisted that these efforts have led to peace: "A solid truce has been established in Moldova. The peace process in Georgia is developing; the hope of stopping bloodshed in Nagorno-Karabakh is emerging; the first agreements on Tajikistan have been reached."[32] The action taken to "protect" Russian or Russia-affiliated minorities from the CIS countries and the Baltic States has been established as part of the need to promote human rights; the security of the area has been proclaimed as a matter of the foremost priority.[33]

Yet this vision too is important in assessing Russian perspectives—at least at the highest level in Moscow. A legal order derived from Kozyrev's proposed partnership would be based, in fact, on states whose weight in decisions is ultimately linked to the power they possess and have the will to invoke. The partnership does not replace the existing arenas in which states carry out their affairs. It simply imposes a vision to reduce some of what Kozyrev views as undesirable conduct of relations among states. It does not reflect the emerging social and legal order among states.[34]

The laws relating to what peacekeeping activities are permissible, what objectives are legitimate under community perspectives, what special privi-leges are permitted and under what conditions they are permitted are still evolving. However, they are laws that depend upon the coalescence of per-spectives of states in the global community, not the laws claimed or de-manded from the community.

Russia cannot demand special privileges for its own interpretation of the applicable law. It cannot claim the right to replace the sovereignty of the newly created independent states on the basis of establishing itself as a great power, or upon ambiguous notions about stability in the region. It cannot demand that a part of the resources or wealth of the Near Abroad rightfully belongs to Russia so as to achieve its goals, and to do so by establishing a stronger economy.

To consider the permissibility of Russian claims for its peacekeeping practices, and the legitimacy of its missions and objectives, one must put these claims into focus. For this purpose, it is appropriate to look at states that make demands upon each other and, when the demands reflect opposing policies and points of view, claim legitimacy for the demands they are making. As this process progresses, the resulting pattern of expectations is tolerated among states. They are engaged in making laws to regulate their future activities.

Claims are made as to meeting the standards of Chapters VI and VII of the UN Charter. Claims are also made as to the permissibility of using force based upon a theory of consent: Force is presumptively required where the peacekeeping mission is legitimate, sanctioned under the United Nations, and faced by mutually hostile states that refuse to provide their consent.[35] Charles Dobbie, author of the British manual on peacekeeping, observes that consent in this context entails the impact of a number of elements: to wit, impartiality is strengthened, legitimacy is more readily established, mutual respect is supported, minimum force is applied, credibility of the action and its effectiveness is promoted, and transparency in the sense of publicizing the missions and their objectives is maintained.[36] He cites an example of when force would lead only to greater involvement by the peacemakers, jeopardizing the humanitarian and peace-oriented goals, or perhaps even opening opportunities to shape the outcomes of the crisis:

> There is unanimity at *battalion* level that without a substantial level of local support, UN efforts to restore security will be fruitless and more seriously, the day-to-day security of military bases and humanitarian relief personnel could not be guaranteed. For example, as long as the Pakistan Brigade in South Mogadishu concentrated its urban security operations against individuals, criminals, and small gangs of bandits it enjoyed the support of the local people. However, when UN policy, and consequently battalion operations, began to act against the interests of the local warlord, he mobilized his resources against them and the Pakistanis' security of movement and the *modus vivendi* of the district were seriously jeopardized.[37]

Put into the situation that Russia faces, it is evident that consent elicited by force or the threat of force will shift the peacekeeping mission from a humanitarian and peace-directed effort to a differing goal: The only likely aim will be that which serves Russian interests. These have been outlined by the leading public officials and are inconsistent both with the UN Charter and with the UN practices that are traditionally expected to mature into customary international law.

The claims described below deal primarily with issues concerning a peacekeeping mission's legitimacy following its authorization by a globally recognized authority (such as by law or by the decision of the United Nations), issues concerning the permissibility of the activities involved (especially the resort to force), and questions relating to facts.

Russia's Claim Relating to Peacekeeping Missions

Claim that a particular peacekeeping mission, including its objectives, is a legitimate activity aimed at legitimate goals and objectives under community standards and international law.

Many of the violations of international law and the UN Charter arising from Russian actions involve missions or activities that are impermissible. The test is whether the Russian practices violate the self-determination of the people in the republic to which the mission is sent, and whether the disputes they have raised justify the actual or threatened deployment of military forces.

If the CIS states were presupposed to waive their claims to independence and sovereignty by adhering to the treaty documents, this would be inconsistent with international law. The documents would imply duress, or threats of coercion, contrary to the Vienna Convention on the Law of Treaties and the assumption of membership in the United Nations.

Specific activities violate international law, such as establishing claims based upon "dual nationality," and Russia's alleged right to protect individuals who, it decides, are Russian—regardless of their official citizenship status. These claims have extended to persons with Russian bloodlines or ethnic backgrounds and to a variety of protectorate arrangements with regard to citizenry.[38] Other claims violating the sovereignty of such states or imposed through duress relate to the deployment of Russian military forces in the territories of the CIS states, compelling such countries to provide funding for the deployed forces, and pressuring them to become members of the CIS, as well as applying other pressures associated with the "gradual reintegration"—into the economy, and ultimately military and political union—of the CIS states with Russia itself.

Actions such as these are expressed under the guise of peacekeeping.[39] The tendency is to invoke ambiguities, or to impose arbitrary elements of legitimacy on those who claim authority under the notion of "peace," bypassing the primary objectives and practices of the United Nations and its peacekeeping efforts. If Russian peacekeeping activities are not among those authorized by the Security Council, then such missions and activities cannot claim legitimacy under the authority of the United Nations.

Claims of peacekeeping are interwoven with specific demands for the transfer of sovereign powers or competence, with calls on third-party states to recognize the legitimacy of these claims, and with assertions of special circumstances to avoid the allegation that Russian "peacekeeping activities" are in effect circumventions of the Charter aimed at Russian objectives of hegemony and great power status. Such claims extend far beyond those authorized by the Charter, and most importantly, extend beyond the requirement of consent, freely given and freely protected, of the CIS states involved.

Russian Claims Regarding the Resort to the Use of Force

Claims that, in a given incident or by way of the general competence of the peacekeeping mission, the resort to the use of force is permissible under international law and the applicable provisions of the UN Charter.

Claims Relating to Military Capabilities. Secondary claim that the deployment and mobilization of military capabilities are permissible as long as they do not constitute threats of aggression against third parties.

Claims that the use of force or threats to use force are permissible must offset the provisions in the UN Charter, especially those which relate to refraining from aggression. The former Soviet republics are subordinate in power and dominance to Russia, so their claims would be judged by the global community, rather than exclusively by the proclamations of their officials who have no choice but to defer to Russian demands.

The UN Charter regulates this matter as a treaty operating on long-standing developments in customary international law. Roberts indicates that major uses of force have led to situations in which the actions of the peacekeepers may be faulted, or impermissible and illegal. He mentions the use of excessive force or threats in Namibia in April 1989, in Bosnia-Herzegovina, and Somalia, introduced for the purposes of legitimacy as part of preventive diplomacy. In terms of Russian actions in the Near Abroad, the intimacy of the states has become an excuse to strengthen that intimacy through the overall policy of "gradual reintegration."[40]

Russian Claims Relating to the Scope of Authorized Activities to Be Associated with Peacekeeping

Claims that for given states or given situations the peacekeeping institution and its activities when "necessary and proper" are legally permissible in view of special conditions relating to that institution or mission.

Claims Invoking Necessity. Secondary claim that states can act on their own discretion when compelled by vital interests or self-preservation.

The claim to a special and protected right to provide peacekeeping for the former republics of the Soviet Union made by Yel'tsin in February 1993 exceeds the expectations of the evolving practice of the global community. However, Yel'tsin's demand has apparently been unopposed by the Western community. He stated, "I believe the time has come for distinguished international organizations, including the UN, *to grant Russia special powers as a guarantor of peace and stability in the former regions of the USSR.*"[41]

This stability, according to Russian elites, includes ensuring the attainment of Russian military and political policy objectives. Peacekeeping is then an instrument to achieve these goals. To do so, however, the Russians must skirt the need for consensus and cooperation envisaged in the peacekeeping operations. The failure of Western countries to oppose this implies a tolerance of such action, which would allow demands in the future to be considered "legal."

The danger here is to the overall legal framework. Even if Russia gained this authority by agreement among states, in authorizing Russia to act as guarantor they would, in effect, be creating a sphere of influence and acting inconsistently with the fundamental goals and objectives of the Charter. The demand for special treatment is tantamount to ignoring the UN Charter and the customary international law that provides the constitutive framework of global order. It allows a given state to defend conduct that is not permissible in the global community by a claim of "necessity."

Russia claims special responsibility and authority to provide military force in order to control former Soviet republics and to serve as a peacekeeper deployed for long periods of time in those states—as well as to intervene in "all armed conflicts" and to work toward the full integration of those states into a Russian-dominated "federal" system. All these are objectives inconsistent with the sovereignty, independence, and equality under law and under the Charter asserted by the former republics and recognized by Russia itself in 1991. Numerous Russian statements put forward naked claims to special Russian rights and responsibilities, without citing the authority for those claims.[42]

Claim Relating to the Use of Force

Counterclaim by the global community that peacekeeping invoked as a reason for imposing force or coercion is regulated under the UN Charter and customary international law and is not entitled to exceptional treatment for the special circumstances of states that have asserted that they are peacekeepers.

This claim by the global community opposes practices by Russian leaders in which their peacekeeping missions are established and guided by their own mandates. The Charter provides a framework in which the permissible use of force is limited primarily to self-defense and to more circumscribed applications associated with humanitarian or other forms of intervention. Mandates formulated by Russia without the participation and approval of the UN Security Council establish authority which conflicts with and overrides that of the United Nations. Much of the debate about peacekeeping activities relates to whether the mission for peacekeeping is entitled to use force, whether the use of force must be authorized by the United Nations (especially the Security Council), or whether the use of force, though not fully expressed, is "necessary and proper" to achieve what is conceded to be a legitimate mission.

We must look to the Security Council's mandate[43] to determine whether a "peaceful measure" peacekeeping action or an enforcement action affording the use of force to achieve given objectives has been authorized (Chapter VI).[44] This would require a survey of Russian actions in the CIS to determine whether they comport with the understanding of the members of the CIS or are inconsistent with the fundamental claims and rights of the newly independent states under the Charter and under international law.

Citing the case of the *Certain Expenses of the United Nations,* Professor Eugene Rostow declares that these were matters to be appraised under the UN Charter and international law, and not under objectives selected by states for their own purposes:

> The Charter makes no express provision for UN peacekeeping activities [of the kind that are implicitly endowed with the authority to use force]. But the International Court of Justice has decided that the General Assembly or the Security Council have broad implied authority to organize and use such forces as they may deem "necessary and proper" in order to carry out diplomatic efforts to promote the peaceful settlement of disputes.[45]

Content of Peacekeeping and Peacemaking

Claims that peacekeeping constitutes the intervention of military forces or political entities intended to achieve one or more of the following: preventive diplomacy (bilateral or multilateral, or by way of coalitions), preconflict peacemaking (where distinguished from preventive diplomacy), peacekeeping, peacemaking, peace enforcement, and postconflict peacemaking.

In practice, the operational roles of peacekeeping have not been frozen. They may extend to sanctioning goals long associated with deterrence, prevention, restoration, rehabilitation, and reconstruction discussed in great depth by McDougal and his associates.[46] The peacekeeping entities may be those authorized by the United Nations, or more ambiguous entities—a reference to the peacekeeping function that resides in the regional organizations and arrangements. Nonetheless, the secretary general of the United Nations would seek to promote the Charter objectives by ensuring that these regional entities aim at, and are monitored to achieve, the objectives listed above. The normative standards for states involved through regional groupings in peacekeeping must be established—largely through customary international law—with authority based upon an amendment or supplement to the UN Charter.

At present, customary international law would link a state's authority to the practices and current authority of the United Nations. Here consultation, deliberations, and the formulation of peacekeeping entities before they are introduced—to ensure that they have met Charter standards—would be needed. As in other situations, these call for particular emphasis upon the sovereignty and equality of the states involved. The failure to comply with these principles constitutes Russia's major violation of the newly created independent states— the incremental takeover of their sovereignty. As stated in *An Agenda for Peace:*

> In the past regional arrangements often were created because of the absence of a universal system for collective security; thus their activities could on occasion work at cross-purposes with the sense of solidarity required for the effectiveness of the world Organization. But in this new era of opportunity, regional arrangements or agencies can render great service if their activities are undertaken in a manner consistent with the Purposes and Principles of the Charter, and if their relationship with the United Nations, and particularly the Security Council is governed by Chapter VIII.[47]

Military Doctrine and Rules of Engagement

Russia's claim that its own policy instruments such as military doctrine, rules of engagement, etc., relating to the (international) legal and political authority of peacekeeping validate these Russian policy instruments under international law.

The question of military doctrine leads to controversial claims. According to Professor Uri Ra'anan, the Russian view of military doctrine is both military and political in nature: The doctrine spells out what is asserted as permissible and legitimate in Russian interests, and establishes itself as a source for that legitimacy as interpreted by high domestic Russian authority. Ra'anan cites the doctrine as one which declares that Russia's interests include "violations of the rights of Russian citizens and persons who identify themselves ethnically and culturally with [Russia] in the former republics of the USSR," and has additional provisions declaring that "a particular task of the armed forces, may consist of . . . the defense of the rights and interests of Russian citizens and of persons abroad linked to Russia ethnically and culturally."[48]

Such actions may, in fact, cross the line from a legitimate claim of self-defense under the Charter and customary international law to one that amounts to aggression, especially when the state involved in peacemaking has assumed the exclusive competence to judge its military doctrine and then to project that doctrine to cover its use of military forces for political or other goals.[49]

Ambiguities expressed in a military doctrine are far-reaching in themselves, but are given greater range when coupled with political doctrine. The communist parties of Europe and the Soviet Union offer ample illustration of this. Ambiguities as to what constitutes legitimate policy goals can be exploited in such matters as these because Russia can claim that it is, after all, pursuing peace or stability in relations with its neighbors, or is attempting to quiet the outbursts of conflict that will draw in the larger community of states, as well as Russia.

This approach, however, would run counter to the carefully designed procedures for decision making and policy making expressed and implied in the UN Charter. Hence even the formulation of policies that contradict or operate inconsistently with the Charter must be assessed for their legitimacy.[50]

Ambiguities in doctrine and practice have led the Russians to give precision to their own procedures and practice without consulting others in the United Nations, and without close adherence to the UN Charter. The overall policy is reintegration, and tactical measures must be avoided that would interfere with achieving that policy.[51] Peacekeeping is then channeled through political objectives and tactics that operate hand in glove with the military instrument—at least ever since Clausewitz—as the public use of force to act as a political instrument of the state.[52]

The problem may not necessarily concern the legitimacy of the mission as such but rather the establishment of the authority to pursue the mission, and the expectation that the authority will limit the role of the peacekeeper to what is reasonable in the context of the global community as envisioned under the Charter. To act otherwise entails the risk that a country will act as a rogue state, unilaterally exempting itself from the authority of the Charter.[53] Hence one element of the problem is the expectation that states will act in good faith to strengthen the shared and common public order, and that the principles for doing this consist of deliberation, consultation, and consensus—proposed by Foreign Minister Kozyrev in another context, when Russia sought support from the West.

CONCLUSION

The general conclusion of this inquiry is that Russia has adopted a peacekeeping practice that operates as a strategic and policy instrument to promote or to probe the promotion of national interests—particularly the restoration of former Soviet borders and full power, jurisdiction, and control over the territories thus embraced—as well as to promote expansion beyond the purpose of protecting Russian national interests. An analysis of claims and counterclaims regarding the permissibility of these activities and goals indicates an array of Russian practices inconsistent with the UN Charter and customary international law. Briefly stated, the problems and the violations that emanate from such practices are

- the breakdown of principles favoring the self-determination of peoples in a given newly independent state;
- the weakening of the claims of independent states to their sover-

eignty and equal treatment under international law, and denial of the
expectations of former Soviet republics that those joining the Commonwealth of Independent States would be establishing a confederation of equal, sovereign, and independent states;

- Russian tendencies in deploying and resorting to force that involve
aggression under the Charter and under customary international law;
- Russia's drive toward hegemony, inconsistent with self-determination,
through the exertion of practices premised upon the false claims of
"spheres of influence";
- the adoption of self-serving military doctrine formulated unilaterally
by Russia as its authority for future action;
- the formulation and adoption of peacekeeping mandates designed to
legitimate Russian peacekeeping actions used to achieve national interests; and
- the claims generally of the overriding impact of Russia's national
interests including its claim to be restored as (and to be given the
respect owed to) a "great power."

Some of these practices, to be sure, are not violations of international law or impermissible as such under international law. Taken as a
whole, however, they amount to a demand that the framework of the UN
Charter and international law be reshaped to enable Russia "peaceably"
to achieve goals inconsistent with the understandings, expectations,
and commitments that states have adopted by ratifying the Charter.
Such actions as imposing and establishing the notion of dual nationality to expand Russian interests outside its territory and deploying
military forces in the newly independent states form examples of impermissible behavior.

The *Basic Report*'s conclusions may be summarized as follows:

- Russian thinking about peace operations increasingly reflects Russian national interest.
- Russian peace operations obviously seek international mandates, but
with limited international influence on the conduct of operations.
- Russian peace-operations thinking includes limited contributions to
US or CSCE operations (for example, in former Yugoslavia), but
favors CIS collective defense arrangements within the former USSR
or in ad hoc coalitions where vital interests are at stake. *Unilateral
action, if necessary without a mandate, is seen as a Russian policy
option.*
- Wherever Russia considers multilateral action, command-and-control
is seen as crucial, as is legitimation via international mandate and
sharing of the financial burden.

• Russia's geographical area of vital interests is currently more limited than the US/NATO area (within a manageable compass for immediate territorial or hegemony goals).
• Russia's peace operations are likely to be conducted by dominating (that is, unreasonable) force if combat operations are probable.

Hence, according to the Basic Report, there is an apparent conflict between Russia perceiving itself as a great power, or within reach of achieving such status, and the West perceiving Russia's actions as expansionism needing to be checked. The West, according to the Basic Report, assumes it will succeed in checking Russia on the basis of its "superior political, economic and military power."[54] But the more appropriate basis for judging the evolution of peacekeeping as an instrument of peace is in terms of control. Our concern is with actions that are within the control of the community at large and that are under the control of its rule of law, operating under the authority provided by the community and under the "consent" of the community. Control that operates outside this framework is almost inevitably aimed at the exclusive policies of a particular state, and this is what now appears to be Russia's policy. We are engaged in a struggle for a world legal order as well as for a global strategy and public order. In such a struggle we must ensure controls over violence in general and over uncontrolled violence in particular.

NOTES

1. See *NATO, Peacekeeping and the United Nations, Report 94.1* (London and Washington: British American Security Information Council, prepared with the cooperation of the Berlin Information Centre for Transatlantic Security, September 1994), hereinafter *Basic Report.* In its findings, the *Report* declares: "The peacekeeping debate is no longer about how the major military powers can best serve international peace. Now the debate is about competing national interests and how these are played out in inter-institutional insights over legitimation and resource allocation" (p.ii). Other findings refer to the "militarization of peacekeeping policies," to pressure for restructuring the collective defense organizations, especially NATO (North Atlantic Treaty Organization), WEU (Western European Union) and the CSCE (Conference on Security and Cooperation in Europe), to the possibilities of a takeover of the CSCE by NATO, and to related developments. A recent survey also appears in Robert D. Blackwill and Sergei A. Karaganov, eds., *Damage Limitation or Crisis: Russia and the Outside World,* CSIA Studies in International Security No. 5, Center for Science and International Affairs, John F. Kennedy School of Government, Harvard University (London: Brassey's, 1994). The editors conclude: "So with 'partnership' an empty slogan, Russia and the West should instead energetically pursue policies of damage limitation designed for narrow cooperation when possible, and seek to

forestall crisis in Russia's relations with the outside world. This will not be easy. Ukraine is the key. The outlook is bleak" (p. 17).

2. See, generally, W. Michael Reisman, "Peacemaking," *Yale Journal of International Law* 18:1, Winter 1993, pp. 415-23. Clearly, as Reisman points out, a major goal is to restore order, overcome instability, terminate conflicts, and impose the rule of law. "Peacemaking is quintessentially a political operation," aimed at achieving order, drawing upon military means if necessary. The realities are therefore political, and if these oppose the imposition of a normative framework such as law, then there is little to be said about the application of that law. The realities draw us to the elites who make the effective and enforceable decisions—in the context of the United Nations, this involves the playing out of differences at least among the Permanent Five members (United States, Russia, China, France, and the United Kingdom—each with the veto). Reisman argues that to establish effective peacemaking it is necessary to recognize and clarify the realities of the political contest, and then exercise leadership domestically as well as globally toward the goals associated with those in the UN Charter. This of course may come to a head in those situations where the destabilized community is large, and where large military forces and substantial resources are required.

The legal regulation of the use of force appears as a normative standard, and as a commitment, among members of the United Nations. Article 2(4) of the UN Charter is the key operative article establishing the normative standard for "defining" aggression. The obligation to refrain from using force as declared in Article 2(4) is not absolute, but balanced by its complementary opposite, to wit, the rights and authority of states singly or collectively to respond in self-defense. Hence Articles 2(4) and 51 regulate the use of force under the perspectives of aggression, but such regulation operates through states acting individually as well as collectively, through their own practices as well as the practices under the United Nations. Article 2(4) declares: "All Members shall refrain in their international relations from the threat or use of force against the territorial integrity or political independence *of any State,* or in any other manner inconsistent with the Purposes of the United Nations" (emphasis added).

The commitment to refrain from using force does not apply exclusively to members of the United Nations, but to all states: the legal responsibility for non-members is established under customary international law. Article 2(4) is supplemented in scope and weight by Article 2(3), to wit: "All Members shall settle their international disputes by peaceful means in such a manner that international peace and security, and justice, are not endangered." For a discussion of the implications of regulating peacekeeping as an instrument or vehicle for projecting force (usually military force when wielded by states), see Eugene Rostow, "Is UN Peacekeeping a Growth Industry?" *Joint Force Quarterly,* Spring 1994, pp. 101–105, hereinafter referred to as "Rostow."

3. Secretary General Boutros Boutros-Ghali has put forth his views on peacekeeping under the United Nations in *An Agenda for Peace (Preventive Diplomacy, Peacemaking and Peacekeeping)* (New York: United Nations; UN SCOR,

47th Sess., UN Doc 5/24111, 1992). Although this document is not the definitive statement of the legal authority under the United Nations or the UN Charter regarding peacekeeping, it comes from a high authority and constitutes a guideline to future policy. Accordingly, it sets the stage for further refinements, traditionally coming from the claims and counterclaims of states. The recommendations in this document are of interest for the same reasons. For example, the secretary general suggests the creation of a UN Peace Endowment Fund with an initial goal of one billion dollars. He wants autonomy for this entity, that is, control over the decisions regarding the use of the funds. In the general sense, the proceeds "would be used to finance the initial costs of authorized peacekeeping operations, other conflict resolution measures and related activities." He also seeks access to additional funds from the members of the United Nations to be applicable to peacekeeping support and recommends that these funds once provided be placed under the control of the United Nations. See pp. 41–44.

4. The conceptual and legal framework for peacekeeping is not explored in detail here. The present inquiry, however, indicates the complexity and difficulty in formulating such notions as "force," "peace," and so on. For an approach to a comprehensive map of regulation, see, generally, Scott Thompson et al., eds., *Approaches to Peace* (Washington, D.C.: United States Institute of Peace, 1993), especially "Law and Peace," by Myres McDougal. For the major work on this subject, see Myres S. McDougal and Florentino Feliciano, *International Law of War (Transnational Coercion and World Public Order),* formerly referred to as *Law and Minimum World Public Order* (Dordrecht, the Netherlands and Boston: New Haven Press, 1994).

5. An interesting analysis of the peacekeeping institution under the United Nations appears in Antonio Cassese, *United Nations Peacekeeping* (The Hague: Sijthoff, 1978). See especially the articles by von Gruenigen, "Neutrality and Peacekeeping"; Rosalyn Higgins, "A General Assessment of United Nations Peacekeeping"; and Dan Ciobanu, "The Power of the Security Council to Organize Peacekeeping Operations." An introduction to the related problem of self-determination appears in K. Shehadi, "Self Determination," *Adelphi Paper* 283 (London: Brassey's, 1993). This study provides the historical background commencing with the 1648 Peace and Treaty of Westphalia, observing that the first cases of self-determination arose with the United Provinces, Saxony (Poland), North America, and Spain between 1581 and 1814. It continues with state practice under the Concert of Europe following the Congress of Vienna of 1815, the practice of the League of Nations, and finally of the United Nations.

6. Because peacekeeping involves coercion or the use of force, and because so much of such actions are left to the interpretations of the individual states (or to collective entities such as the coalitions established for the Desert War), and as to when they are to be initiated, how much force is to be used, and so on, it is evident that a full treatment of this subject calls for a comprehensive inquiry into the global order security process expected from the United Nations. According to a recent commentary published by the US Army War College, the collective notion of

going to war can be traced from early history of human tribes, that is, from the beginnings of the urbanization of peoples, and their shift from the nomadic existence that depended upon hunting to an agricultural society. This in turn has led gradually—over millennia in fact—to growing demands of the peoples to participate in major decisions regarding the making of war. See, generally, Richard A. Gabriel and Karen S. Metz, *A Short History of War* (Carlisle, PA: Strategic Studies Institute, US Army War College, 1992). The pressure to participate in both declaring and making war commenced with the notions of the "just war"—appearing as early as St. Ambrose and St. Augustine—refined over the subsequent centuries, and finally reaching the criteria proposed by former Secretary of Defense Caspar Weinberger in 1983. For an in-depth study of this trend, see Alan Ned Sabrosky and Robert L. Sloane, *The Recourse to War: An Appraisal of the "Weinberger Doctrine"* (Carlisle, PA: Strategic Studies Institute, US Army War College, 1988). Weinberger, notably, calls for commitment of United States forces abroad only if "vital interests" are identified justifying armed combat and further calls for support of the American people and their representatives in the Congress. Former Secretary of State George Shultz concurrently called for the use of force by the president acting on his own judgment in major crises and proposed a doctrine that did not depend upon public support for specific situations. See, ibid., pp. 19-26. Shultz argued: "American must never be timid. . . . We will use our power and our diplomacy in the service of peace and our ideals."

7. W. M. Reisman, in "Criteria for the Lawful use of Force in International Law," *Yale Journal of International Law* 10:2, Spring 1985, p. 279, observes: "Law includes a system of authorized coercion in which force is used to maintain and enhance public order objectives and in which unauthorized coercions are prohibited. . . . Law is made when there is disagreement; the more effective members of the group concerned impose their vision of common interest through the instrument of law with its program of sanctions. Law acknowledges the utility and the inescapability of the use of coercion in social processes, but seeks to organize, monopolize, and economize it."

8. See Robert J. Art, *Strategy and Management in the Post-Cold Pentagon* (Carlisle, PA: Strategic Studies Institute, US Army War College, 1992), indicating the major change that is separately occurring in inducing the military services to adopt the strategy of joint military operations. This shift to jointness has been referred to as a "major cultural change." But strategy is a complex matter according to David Jablonsky, *Why Is Strategy Difficult?* (Carlisle, PA: Strategic Studies Institute, US Army War College, 1992), p. 65. He points out: "In the future, as US military means decline, the interaction of national military strategy will grow more complex. In particular the reduction of military forces will mean less margin for error in the application of military power along with other national means." See also Edward Mead Earle, ed., *Makers of Modern Strategy: Military Thought from Machiavelli to Hitler* (Princeton, NJ: Princeton University Press, 1945) and the revised edition, Peter Paret, ed. See also the analysis in the framework of decision analysis, in Admiral J. C. Wylie, *Military Strategy: A General Theory of Power Control* (Westport, CT: Greenwood Press, 1980). The difficulty, according to these

authors, arises in strategy operating as an art rather than as a science, averting the attempts to create order and discipline, or an organization approach. The problem of strategy must await a follow-on paper. Perceiving strategy as an art, it is apparent that the attempts to establish peacekeeping and peacemaking in a scientific framework is at best a means to establish a given perspective, not an operational perspective. John Mackinlay in "Improving Multifunctional Forces," *Survival* 36:3, Autumn 1994, indicates the attempts made to reduce peacekeeping to a list of required standards. He cites Goulding to the effect that the related peace-support activities should "be organized and authorized by the UN; be deployed with the consent of the parties involved; act impartially; be provided with sufficient military assets and finances by member states; only use force in self-defense" (p. 150). These are neither strategic nor legal criteria. The Russian practice of peacekeeping, for example, must be judged upon how it is affected and whether it violates the UN Charter and international law. It can also be judged upon United Nations practice to determine how it affects the emerging trends among states in the peacekeeping activities. One approach is implied by Charles Dobbie, "A Concept for Post–Cold War Peacekeeping," ibid., pp. 124–48: The functions include conflict prevention, humanitarian relief, military assistance, demobilization operations, and duration and denial of movement.

9. See, generally, Donald M. Snow, *Peacekeeping, Peacemaking and Peace-Enforcement: The U.S. Role in the New International Order* (Carlisle, PA: Strategic Studies Institute, US Army War College, 1993). Snow cites former General Colin Powell on decisions, policies, and costs of engaging in military actions, in the form of the most pertinent questions and issues: "Is the political objective we seek to achieve important, clearly defined and understood? Have all other nonviolent policy means failed? Will military force achieve the objective? At what cost? Have the gains and risks been analyzed? How might the situation that we seek to alter, once it is altered by force, develop further, and what might be the consequences?" (p. 27). As Snow points out, the use of force has led to demands for greater participation in the decisions relating to declaring and making war often buried under the expression of engaging military force: "Vietnam spawned the Weinberger "doctrine" as a set of criteria that should guide American response to crises and the engagement of military force. The criteria were very conservative and cautionary, which was and is appropriate. At the very base of the criteria was the caution that American force requires the Clausewitzian trinity of unity among the people, the government and the military" (p. 36).

10. The challenge to the United States is to establish its leadership in peacekeeping and to do so in the larger political context and in terms of the preferred outcomes of the United States, especially with regard to the application of law and shaping the practice of states and the United Nations to ensure their consistency with the applicable law and the objectives of the Charter. The key elements of the Presidential Decision Directive, PDD 25, are presently contained in the White House Press Release, May 1994 draft, "The Clinton Administration's Policy on Reforming Multilateral Peace Operations." These call for the following US policy:

When our interests dictate, the US must be willing and able to fight and win wars, unilaterally whenever necessary. . . . UN peace operations cannot substitute for this requirement. . . . UN and other multilateral peace operations will at times offer the best way to prevent, contain or resolve conflicts that could otherwise be more costly and deadly. In such cases, the US benefits from having to bear only a share of the burden. . . . While the President never relinquishes command of the US forces, the participation of US military personnel in UN operations can, in particular circumstances, serve US interests. . . . The US does not support a standing UN army, nor will we earmark specific US military units for participation in UN operations. . . . It is not US policy to seek to expand either the number of UN peace operations or US involvement in such operations. Instead, this policy . . . aims to ensure that our use of peacekeeping is selective and more effective. . . ." (*Peacekeeping Monitor,* May/June 1994, p. 14).

The list of policy elements indicates that United States policy is expected to make "disciplined and coherent choices about which peace operations to support" (facing the problem of the national interests and the scarcity of available resources for these operations and missions); reduce the costs; define the command and control of the US military forces; reform and improve the United Nation's capability to manage peace operations; improve the way the US government manages and funds its peace operations; and create better forms of cooperation within the US government and including the American public regarding peace operations. (See also the summary in *Basic Report,* p. 34).

11. Presidential Decision Directive, PDD 25, from the White House release, May 5, 1994 entitled "The Clinton Administration's Policy on Reforming Multilateral Peace Operations." The US position on peacekeeping should be distinguished from that presently adopted by Russia. The preferred outcomes of the United States with regard to peacekeeping missions appear to be aimed at global objectives and at the application of community standards, especially those embodied in the UN Charter, whereas the Russian preferred objectives are those associated with its vital interests, to wit, those that will support Russian expansionism, hegemony, control over the former Soviet republics, and so on, coupled with a program for "gradual reintegration," and a demand of "hands-off" Russian policies in using peacekeeping for achieving these goals.

12. See the *Basic Report,* op. cit., p. 35, showing the ambiguity between the US Department of Army and NATO regarding the concept and meaning of the term "peace enforcement." NATO declares that "peace enforcement missions . . . generally employ conventional combat operations to achieve their objectives." The army uses the term "to describe the protection of humanitarian assistance, guarantee and denial of movement, enforcement of sanctions, establishment of, and supervision of protected zones and the forcible separation of belligerents as peace enforcement activities." According to the *Report*:

[Charles Dobbie, the author of the British manual on peacekeeping, states]: "We regard as intellectually flaccid the idea that peacekeeping and peace enforcement are differentiated only by the degree of force being used." He expresses a concern that considerations such as popular support, negotiations, mediation and conciliation will matter less and that traditional peacekeeping would fade in favor of "a doctrine more orientated towards warfighting." Turning to NATO's draft curriculum for peace support training, one is forced to agree.

13. The concept of "peace support" seems to have been adopted by the policy councils of NATO. According to the British American Security Information Council's, *NATO, Peacekeeping, and the United Nations,* 94.1, US policy is linked to invoking NATO and the military forces that it would provide. As expressed in PDD 25, May 1994: "The policy stresses that the US wants to maintain the leadership role in peace operations, no matter if it is involved solely with its own forces or not. For the US to have the most control over peacekeeping operations, the preferred multilateral institution to act in peace operations is NATO" (p. 33).

14. Reference is made to the preambles, and to Articles 1, 2 and others in the Charter. The objectives of the Charter form the context for Western and democratic thinking about the future of global order, and institutions such as peacekeeping are judged against their consistency with these objectives, especially where more precise rules are missing.

15. For a brief survey of the UN objectives, see N. D. White, *The United Nations and the Maintenance of International Peace and Security* (Manchester, UK: Manchester University Press, 1990). Other books and materials on this subject are very numerous. The compendium referred to as the *Peacekeeper's Handbook* (New York: International Peace Academy-Pergamon Press, 1984) is a helpful source. See also Henry Wiseman, ed., *Peacekeeping: Appraisals & Proposals* (New York: Pergamon Press, 1983), and for representative documentation about peacekeeping in the past, see Robert C. R. Siekmann, *Basic Documents on United Nations and Related Peacekeeping Forces* (second edition) (Dordrecht, the Netherlands: M. Nijhoff, 1989).

16. See *Basic Report,* op. cit., p. i. The report concludes that the competition is over which of the institutions is to be dominant, to maintain control over peacekeeping in a showdown situation, and so on. The report also declares that if the role of the UN and CSCE operating together is reduced, their acts will be exclusively to legitimatize peacekeeping—that is, presumably through the Security Council acting without imposing its veto. Competition arises for this reason: "There is no consensus between the major and powerful players in the West on the issues of peacekeeping. In fact, there are major contradictions, which reflect different military practices and culture, as well as deep divisions regarding the political expediency of peacekeeping" (p. ii). On this matter, see William J. Durch, *The United Nations and Collective Security in the 21st Century* (Carlisle, PA: Strategic Studies Institute, US Army War College, 1993). Durch points out:

Impatience with peacekeeping has led to calls for greater UN involvement in peace enforcement. UN blessing for a military operation does give it the greatest legitimacy international law can currently convey, and the backing of a General Assembly resolution gives it the broadest possible international political support. But all proposals that suggest that the UN should go further and either develop its own military forces or actively command forces seconded to it from member states will sooner or later run up against the basic resistance of national sovereignty, even eroded as it has been over past decades. (p. 33)

17. Reisman, op. cit., pp. 415, 418.

18. These notions appeared ultimately in the last constitution of the Soviet Union. They presupposed the devolution of foreign affairs power upon the Communist Party of the Soviet Union and led, ultimately, to a complete deferential or subordinate power position to be assumed by all of the Soviet satellites—that is, by the "socialist" or communist states to Soviet conceptions of international law and its application. Such law became under this practice an instrument for promoting or projecting the policy and the power of the Soviet Union. The Soviet Union and its ruling communist party knew or discovered that control of a society is achieved through control, and the legitimation afforded by control, of the law. The values of the society, the behavior expected and punished, and so on are all clearly within the reach of the controlling lawmaker.

19. Andrei Kozyrev, "The Lagging Partnership," *Foreign Affairs* 73, May/June 1994, pp. 59, 69 (emphasis added). See also A.V. Kozyrev, "Russia and NATO: A Partnership for a United and Peaceful Europe," *NATO Review* 42:4, August 1994, pp. 3–6. Speaking in general terms, Kozyrev welcomes cooperation, the processes of rapprochement, the clearing away of differences in the new relations between Russia and the West, and so on. The controlling and operable element is that of the "gradual integration" of the former Soviet republics and, unless checked, their territories, and ultimately, their jurisdiction and control. But he proposes that the partnership would be best served by

transforming the NACC (the North Atlantic Cooperation Council) into an independent body which would be closely linked to the CSCE and which would promote military-political cooperation in the Euro-Atlantic area. Generally speaking, the CSCE should aim at coordinating the activities of NATO, the European Union, the Council of Europe, the WEU and the CIS in the sphere of enhancing stability and security, promoting peacekeeping and protecting human and national minority rights. Of course, this does not mean establishing the CSCE as a hierarchical leader or "commander." (p. 4)

This geopolitical vision of course would indeed strengthen the CSCE and enable it to consolidate its strength, weaken the primacy of NATO as a regional and collective security organization, while taking on new functions under the CSCE aimed at using the peacekeeping institution as an instrument for asserting national policy and invoking Russian perspectives about human rights—that is, the forcible protection of Russian minorities including those who are Russian-speaking. He subsequently refers to peacekeeping in general terms, but observes that for Russian-controlled peacekeeping in the former Soviet republics, "Our Western partners could cover a part of expenses for logistical back-up and training of our peacekeeping units." These remarks might be compared with the objectives in PDD 25, cited previously.

20. Ibid.

21. A member of the Russian Duma, Grigori A. Yavlinsky, in "What Does Russia Want?" *The New York Times,* Sec. 4, p. 15, argues in favor of an economic union among CIS states, but only if Russia bases its policies

> on explicitly formulated, intelligible principles, that reflect moral absolutes. . . . If Russia truly wants to remain democratic, these should be the principles: the states that appeared after the collapse of the Soviet Union must remain politically independent; integration must be voluntary, without any pressure from Russia; economic union should be the basic form of integration—and in Ukraine, Belarus and Moldova the only form.

Yavlinsky would, symbolically at least, guarantee the states in the economic union their standing as states; there is, of course, the possibility that they may devolve their foreign affairs powers upon Russia. He continues:

> Is economic reintegration without political integration possible? Yes. But Russia must understand that it must refrain from any political union with Ukraine, Belarus and Moldova whatsoever—even if these states invite it—because there would be only two possible outcomes: failure or neo-imperialism.

22. The UN Charter refers, for example in Article 2(4), to a fundamental objective of states in general, to wit, promoting the territorial integrity and political independence against aggression. "Gradual reintegration" necessarily entails strong pressures, without alternatives, that would lead the CIS states toward accepting reintegration. This would lead to the assimilation of the CIS states by peaceful—that is nonmilitary—pressures, but with coercion implicit with regard to those that might reject the program. However, it is unlikely that this would stop at some form of economic union. The experience of European states in such matters as the attempt to create a customs union between Austria and Germany after World War I with the natural leaning toward political integration following economic integration is a familiar example. See Earle, op. cit., pp. 138-142. See also Sun Tzu, *Art of War* (New York: Oxford University Press, 1963): the matter of "supreme importance in war is to attack the enemy's strategy" (p. 77). The tendency of the European Union to move toward political integration is obvious. Notwithstanding Kozyrev's remarks in "The Lagging Partnership," the European actions in tightening their European Union are voluntary among equal states and states traditionally treated as equal, and the policy he proposes has no alternatives, hence the potential for coercion and duress, and for legitimatizing action involving coercion and duress as inevi-

table in the authority afforded Russia by the wide support it presumably seeks to achieve in making these claims. Even with the European Union, it is unlikely that the economic union and the economic gains expected by the European states is achievable without moving toward a political union, in large measure because control over the budget and funding is political in nature. This subject has been exhaustively reviewed in the literature about the European union and prospects for its success.

23. "The Lagging Partnership," op. cit., p. 69 (emphasis added).

24. Ibid., pp. 69–70. Kozyrev insists that Russians are not seeking for their citizens in other states the same privileges Hitler had sought for the Sudeten Germans. They want something different. The Russian minorities and Russia itself seek "not privileges, but normal citizenship and equality for Russians in those states." It is noteworthy that the facts relating to these matters need to be held in focus: In some Estonian cities, for example, what once was a dominant and majority Estonian population has been replaced by a near exclusion of all Estonians by the alien Russian population. This form of territorial conquest is clearly insidious in its implications: It would support by precedent takeovers along the Russian borders in general. Kozyrev also insists that this is a matter already under the authority and pronouncements of the High Commissioner for Ethnic Minorities, established in the CSCE through "a lot of effort" by Russia. But according to Kozyrev the commissioner's "recommendations to the Latvian and Estonia authorities are not being implemented, while the West stands idle. Here we also have the right to expect understanding and support" (p. 70).

25. For an in-depth inquiry into international law appraised in the terms used in the text, see Myres S. McDougal and Associates, *Studies in World Public Order* (New Haven: Yale University Press, 1960); see also Myres S. McDougal and Florentino P. Feliciano, *Law and Minimum World Public Order* (New Haven: Yale University Press, 1961).

26. In December 1994, the Conference on Security and Cooperation in Europe (CSCE) was renamed the Organization for Security and Cooperation in Europe (OSCE). For this book, the earlier name is used.

27. See M. Sapiro, "Dispute Resolution: General Methods and CSCE Mechanisms," *ASIL1 Insight* Sept.-Oct. 1994, p. 1. Ms. Sapiro points out that the CSCE expectations are broad-ranging, but they are binding politically and not legally. However, it is evident that the step, though gradual, toward a takeover of policy by the CSCE and the reduction of the United States leadership in Europe may be the beginning of this process. It presumably will be expedited by tendencies evolving around the use of the CSCE and its institutions such as the dispute resolution system mentioned here, and by the reach of the CSCE into numerous areas not covered by NATO. It is also encouraged by Russian participation, not occurring in NATO.

28. Ibid., pp. 65–66.

29. Journalist Roger Cohen reports upon the disagreements between NATO and the United Nations as to when force should be used (and presumably how much force, what kinds of force, and the duration of imposing force); this debate raises the unresolved problem of how to handle conflicts in authority, in this case, between the United Nations and a regional organization, each authorized to operate in the amorphous and overlapping realm of peacekeeping. See Roger Cohen, "At Odds Over Bosnia," *The New York Times,* October 2, 1994, p. 14. Should force be used in this specific matter for deterring the Serbs or to protect, by way of self-defense, the UN's peacekeeping force?

30. John M. Goshko, "Yeltsin Claims Russian Sphere of Influence," *Washington Post,* Sept. 27, 1994, p. 10. For the perspectives of a noted anthropologist on the insecurities arising with the destruction of large political or tribal entities, see Harold R. Isaacs, *Idols of the Tribe* (New York: Harper & Bros., 1975), pp. 1–25. For an extended assessment see the present author's "The Struggle for a World Legal Order: An Overview of an Adversary Process," *Marquette Law Review* 61, 1977, pp. 1–21.

31. Goshko, op. cit. As also noted, the claims even include the "linkage" of Russian-speaking peoples to Russia, operating upon the precedent found in the historic claims of the tsars to be the protectors of Slavic peoples but adding to the reach of those claims.

32. Ibid.

33. Russian director of the Secret Service, Yevgeni Primakov, is cited in the same report as stating that efforts by the West to stand in the way of reintegration of the former republics are "dangerous and should be reconsidered." Primakov does not bother to cite the linkages cited by other Russian spokespersons. Yel'tsin stated that interventions by others in this process of reintegration would be "extremely short-sighted." And his view about human rights was reported by Goshko as follows: "Russia's interest in its neighbors is not limited to trying to sort out the tensions between different ethnic factions that have plunged some of these states into bloody civil war. He also asserted a right to protect the interests of 'millions of Russians in the newly independent states who looked on these places as home and who now live there as guests—and not always welcome guests'" (Ibid., p. 10). Ideological language supported these assertions—a mixture of demands, threats, and claims. W. Michael Reisman of Yale University, in "Criteria for the Lawful Use of Force in International Law," *Yale Journal of International Law* 10, Spring 1985, points out:

> Coercion should not be glorified. The promulgation of a norm such as Article 2(4), for all of its ineffectiveness, is a major achievement. But it is naive and indeed subversive of public order to insist that coercion never be used, for coercion is a ubiquitous feature of all social life and a characteristic and indispensable component of law. In a contest with an adversary that does not accept the prohibition, to forswear force is to disarm unilaterally. . . .

The critical question, in a decentralized international security system such as ours, is not whether coercion has been applied but whether it has been applied in support of or against community order and basic policies, and whether it has been applied in ways whose net consequences include increased congruence with community goals and minimum order. (p. 284)

The issue here also involves the use of force in relations among states in a sanctioning system—that is, a system aimed at supporting global order and which operates consistent with the standards imposed by the global community, presently under the United Nations. See Reisman's papers, "Sanctions and Enforcement" and "Private Armies in a Global War System: Prologue to Decision," pp. 381 and 142 respectively, in Myres McDougal and W. Michael Reisman, eds., *International Law Essays* (Mineola, NY: Foundation Press, 1981).

34. Kozyrev gets down to details:

If a partnership is built on mutual trust, then it is natural to recognize other rules as well; the need not only to inform one another of decisions made, but also to agree on approaches beforehand. It would be hard to accept an interpretation of partnership in which one side demands that the other coordinate its every step with it while the former retains complete freedom for itself. Partners must have mutual respect for each other's interests and concerns. (Ibid., p. 66)

Clearly these remarks are designed to relax views on customary international law, at least those perceptions of law as a community's shared expectations about future behavior and as standards applicable to a community with exceptions applied in terms of law, not of power. The "Partnership for Peace" is a broad vision for moving toward global order, but under the control and policy enunciated by NATO. Much of the content of this partnership must be provided through future NATO practice. See for summary Box P of the *Basic Report,* p. 26. Most importantly, NATO assumes control of its own peacekeeping activities; it does not devolve that control upon the Security Council or the United Nations in general.

35. Adam Roberts, *Survival* 36: 3, Autumn 1994, p. 100, argues that Boutros-Ghali's statement in *An Agenda for Peace,* para. 20, p. 11, is controversial. He observed that peacekeeping "is the deployment of a United Nations presence in the field, *hitherto* with the consent of all the parties concerned. . . ." The concern related to the arbitrary shift of the accepted meaning of peacekeeping, suggesting that at least some elements of a common framework had been adopted. Also of concern was the possibility of expanding the claims and legitimacy of claims for interventionist peacekeeping. Roberts's discussion indicates that Russian claims on the above grounds would meet with determined opposition—that is, consent is the critical element, and the controversy that remains concerns only whether consent is needed for all activities in which force is or may be used. Roberts notes in particular:

The "hitherto" in this definition became the subject of much comment by individuals and states. There were two main grounds for concern. First, tried-and-tested principles of UN peacekeeping were being changed and, perhaps, fatally weak-ened without a full discussion of all the implications. Second, many individuals and states (mainly small states and/or developing) feared a new interventionist peacekeeping.

36. See Dobbie, op. cit., p. 132 et seq. Dobbie considers in detail how force should be used and regulated. Although his formulation has not been adopted here, it comprises a standard of reasonableness, especially with regard to the legitimate use of force and the permitted intensity and duration of force applied. Force, Dobbie points out, may work in situations of low-intensity violence, but major force may lead to the peacemakers becoming a participating belligerent. The impact of this upon accepted notions and policies of the neutrality of states, of the notions of co-belligerency, let alone the application of the laws of war, require far deeper treat-ment than has been attempted so far.

37. See Dobbie, op. cit., p. 128. Dobbie presses consent in this situation to relate to the interests of the parties, and consent given to support, rather than op-pose, those interests.

38. See, generally, the findings of Uri Ra'anan in his paper "The U.S., the New World Order, and NATO" (Cambridge, MA: Harvard University/CFIA, 1993). Ra'anan cites Yel'tsin as including under Russian protection "the rights of ethnic Russians and the Russian-speaking population," a claim that would include many who would have no desire to be involuntarily assimilated under Russian authority.

39. For background, see Ra'anan, ibid. The report cites the current reactions to Czechoslovakia's experience of Soviet (subsequently Russian) threats of domina-tion by incremental measures that impinge upon Czech claims and projection of sovereignty. See, for example, remarks of Václav Havel, president of the Czech Republic, cited in the *Basic Report,* p. 6.

40. See Roberts, op. cit., pp. 101-117. For a US view see Presidential Decision Directive 25 of May 5, 1994, cited and discussed by Roberts, pp. 108–109.

41. See Fiona Hill and Pamela Jewett, *Back in the USSR* (Cambridge, MA: John F. Kennedy School of Government, Harvard University, January 1994) (herein referred to as the *Harvard Report*) (emphasis added). Russia's current goals are largely the historic geostrategic objectives, according to the *Harvard Report*: maintaining access to ports in the Black and Baltic seas and a buffer zone between Russia and rivals around its borders; preserving Russian hegemony; retaining control over resources in the former republics; retaining control over the defense-industrial complex, including nuclear power plants and nuclear hard-ware; and guaranteeing markets for its products.

42. See, for citations, *Harvard Report,* pp. 4–6. The statements of Yel'tsin and Kozyrev, for example, are replete with mention of the "legitimate rights" of Russian-speaking minorities in former Soviet republics, with claims for volun-tary reintegration, and with the continuation of peacekeeping missions in vari-ous conflict zones on their territory.

43. Note in particular that the Security Council is the organ primarily authorized to determine the maintenance of peace, breaches of the peace, and threats to the peace. This wording of the Charter raises questions whether the Security Council is actually the organ *exclusively* in authority once seized with a given situation involving peace. See especially Chapter VII of the UN Charter.

44. These terms are ambiguous and even controversial. The United Nations presumably takes the view expressed in Boutros-Ghali's, *An Agenda for Peace* (New York: United Nations, 1992). See p. 11 for definitions of preventive diplomacy, peacemaking, and peacekeeping; p. 32 et seq. for postconflict peace building; pp. 26-27 for peace enforcement; and p. 35 et seq. for the amorphous problem of cooperation with regional arrangements and organizations.

45. See Rostow, op. cit., p. 104. See also the case in the International Court of Justice, *The Certain Expenses Case,* 1962 International Court of Justice (ICJ), p. 151 ff. But this case provides an advisory opinion, that is, a legal opinion rather than decision upon a legal question submitted pursuant to the UN Charter procedures (see pp. 165-166). The only cases in which force was authorized for actions by states were those relating to Korea in the Korean War and to Iraq in the Desert War. These were enforcement actions authorized under Chapter VII of the Charter. The problem must therefore be faced as an issue for amending the Charter to express authorization. For a general discussion, see Boutros-Ghali, op. cit.

46. See Myres McDougal, Harold Lasswell, and Lung-Chu Chen, *Human Rights and World Public Order: Basic Policies of an International Law of Human Dignity* (New Haven, CT: Yale University Press, 1980), ch. 5.

47. See Boutros-Ghali, op. cit., p. 36.

48. Ra'anan, op. cit. Ra'anan cites subsequently Russian observations that the neighboring states or those of the Near Abroad may lead to local conflicts and local wars, and because these "impinge upon the vitally important interests of the Russian Federation then Russia would be entitled to take defensive measures of . . . even military nature commensurate to the threat posed" (p. 2).

49. See the observations of Eugene Rostow, op. cit. See also John W. R. Lepingwell, "The Russian Military and Security Policy in the 'Near Abroad,'" *Survival* 36:3, Autumn 1994. Lepingwell concludes that the authority claimed by Russia under its own legal and political authority—expanded to conform with its military doctrine—amounts to authority formulated and interpreted entirely by Russia; the purpose is to enable Russia to extend or reach out its authority as needed, and to claim that in doing so it is acting consistent with law and the Charter. Hence, even if the terms of reference embraced in the self-serving instrument referred to as "military doctrine" are already operating on the margins of community standards, the actions taken under the terms tend to provide interpretations and actualization of policy that go even further. "The new doctrine [i.e., military doctrine] while important in presenting a framework for Russian military and security planning, is not by any means a comprehensive or rigid guide to Russian military interests or behavior. More revealing have been both the comments by key military actors and the actions of the troops on the ground" (p. 74). Lepingwell

and others refer additionally to the impact of the military doctrine upon political doctrine—hence upon perspectives about law or what, generally, is permissible in resorting to the use of force through peacekeeping or otherwise.

50. This problem may spill over into the formulation of rules of engagement. See, for example, J. A. Roach, "Rules of Engagement," *Naval War College Review* 36, January-February 1983, pp. 49-60; J. Devorkan, "Rules of Engagement, Somalia," *Military Review* 74, Sept. 1994, p. 26. The United States has had considerable experience in formulating its rules of engagement; however, such rules differ from "military doctrine" as apparently formulated by Russian authorities. The rules of engagement apply to the conduct of hostilities themselves. They superimpose the requirements of international law thereby linking the actions of the military commanders and armed forces with the overall perspective of international law and the law of war. In other words, they are designed to restrain as far as possible—consistent with the necessities and humanitarian principles—the use of force during combat that may lead to attacks on, or harm, or damage to, the noncombatants. Military doctrine with its justification of military force and military objectives reveals a political component in the Russian practice. If the rules of engagement are formulated to establish exclusive national objectives and are inconsistent therefore with the objectives of the Charter or of international law, they would be inconsistent with US practice and probably the practice of a majority of states in the global community. They would then shift away from their primary objective of linking military actions to humanitarian outcomes and toward ensuring that military practice does not become practice entirely justified by a given state's claim of necessity—a rewriting of the old German maxim of *Kriegsraison.* See Dobbie, op. cit., note 8, and his discussion about strategic direction and military doctrine, pp. 141-145. The Russian approach is likely to lead to belligerents or others using more than the minimum force expected in peacekeeping or peacemaking, ibid., p. 145. Dobbie specifically points out the need for the doctrine and related instruments and concepts to meet objective standards such as impartiality, minimum force, and credibility; failure to do so leads to the emergence of a destabilizing influence, and a mandate outside the expectations of the United Nations and its Charter, ibid., p. 145.

51. Maxim Shashenkov, "Russian Peacekeeping in the 'Near Abroad,'" *Survival* 36, Autumn 1994, pp. 46, 56, describes the current Russian standards, though subject to modification and withdrawal at the option of Russia as the formulator of these standards, as evincing a readiness to use peacekeeping while fighting occurs; involvement in the operations of their military contingents and those involved in the conflict; a determination to maintain Russian pre-eminence gaining control in the operations, yet drawing in other CIS members; determination to use high levels of force and the appropriate weaponry to conduct the operations; reliance on specially trained professional soldiers, presumably including the *spetsnaz* forces, or special military-political forces specifically trained for such missions and in particular for achieving the goals of such missions; close coordination between the peacekeepers and local authorities; and a desire to maintain an appearance of neutral third-party intervention. Formulations of this kind obviously are in the

control of the peacekeepers, their formulations and doctrine, and not subject or subjected to the authority and control of the overriding principles or provisions of the UN Charter.

52. Lepingwell, op. cit., pp. 70-92, observes that Russia is gradually achieving through the diplomatic channels associated with new agreements and accords, with bargaining and economic pressures, and so on, the "ability to influence strongly the outcome of such negotiations" as apply to military facilities. He suggests that, while doctrine is important to consider, "more revealing have been both the comments by key military actors and the actions of the troops on the ground." He provides examples also shown in the *Harvard Report,* op. cit., concerning the Caucasus, Central Asia, Ukraine and Moldova, and the Baltic States, and considers the retention of the Russian armed forces but restructuring and redeploying them to achieve goals commensurate with Russian policy. Part of the problem in assessing peacekeeping activities arises from the indeterminate nature of the institution. It is no longer clear, for example, that consent is required for nonforcible peacekeeping activities. The Russian practice is putting the element of the peacekeepers' neutrality from the conflict or crisis in doubt, and along with it, the elements of impartiality and consent. Russian practice tends, at least, toward exclusive controls and authority over its peacekeepers whenever they are operating within the territory formerly under the jurisdiction of the Soviet Union. Lepingwell observes:

> The narrowing of Russia's interests from those "ethnically and culturally identifying themselves with Russia" to Russian citizens did little to alleviate fears in the near abroad. Instead, by making citizenship the operative element of the clause, the doctrine has focused more attention on Russia's calls for dual citizenship agreements with its neighbors. Indeed, Russian has been increasing its diplomatic efforts to gain dual citizenship agreements since late 1993. A Russian proposal on minority rights, first presented at the Ashgabat CIS summit meeting in December 1993, met with a cool reception, however, and so far only Turkmenistan has signed a treaty on dual citizenship. . . . So far, only about 150,000 people residing outside Russia have taken up Russian citizenship, a minute fraction of those who might be eligible if dual citizenship were extended throughout the former republics. [citations not included] (p. 74)

53. See Roberts, op. cit., p. 97, indicating the new types of tasks for UN peacekeeping. Many of these are tasks requiring actions such as demilitarization of a specified area, or providing specific humanitarian relief, or reporting violations of the laws of armed conflict by belligerents. However, Roberts stresses the linkage to the United Nations in pursuing the peacekeeping missions. He believes that to shift from this is to shift peacekeeping to a quasi-sovereign activity, free of claims that it might be contrary to law.

54. Basic Report, op. cit., pp. 41, 60. Pursuit of these themes must be set aside for a subsequent paper. The possibilities are seen in Shashenkov, op. cit., p. 46, and in the separately authored chapters in Blackwell and Karaganov, ed.,

op. cit. The key element in Russian thinking is that of "gradual reintegration"—as long as this prevails and guides policy it will lead to the gradual return of Russia to the status of a great power that may not be committed to the democratic values we had sought. Assimilation of "reintegration" with the notions of "sovereignty" and "legitimization" is a likely prospect in view of past trends.

II

THE TARGETS:

THE "NEAREST ABROAD";
THE "NEAR ABROAD";
THE "FAR ABROAD"

4

The "Nearest Abroad":
Russia's Relations with Ukraine and Belarus'

Adrian Karatnycky

Relations with Ukraine and Belarus' stand at the center of the new Russian state's self-definition. It could not be otherwise since, for centuries, Russia, Ukraine and Belarus' existed as part of a seamless imperial unit. As a consequence of this long history of shared statehood, the relationship of Russians to their Ukrainian and Belarusian neighbors today reflects deep-seated ambiguities. While the political elite in Ukraine and (to a lesser extent) Belarus' emphasize their own distinct ethnic identities as the basis for post-Soviet sovereignty, Russia's political elite and most Russians, as well as many other citizens in the three now-independent states, are ambivalent about the several-years-old status quo of independence and statehood. This state of affairs influences policy and has created a perilously tentative set of relationships among the three Slavic states. It also means that relations between these states—especially between Russia and Ukraine—exist in a perpetual state of dangerous tension.

It is unquestionable that the three Slavic nations of the former USSR share traditions and cultural influences. The Kievan state that emerged on the territory of what is now independent Ukraine brought to the three peoples Christian faith and a Cyrillic alphabet. Still, linguistic differentiation into separate ethnic groups began as early as the eleventh century. By the fourteenth century there were clear reordered and idiomatic differences. And, certainly by the seventeenth century, Russians, Ukrainians, and Belarusians had evolved into distinct national groups.[1]

Yet despite such differentiation, the Russian imperial elite did not countenance the separate identities of their brethren. In 1864, the architect of Russian imperial education policy, Mikhail Katkov, wrote these patronizing words: "We love the Ukraine in all her peculiarities in which we see the token of future riches and variety in the common development of the life of our people." Katkov, whose ideas influenced tsarist efforts to ban literary Ukrainian, went further: "We love the Ukraine, we love her as part of our Fatherland, as a living beloved part of our people, as a part of ourselves, and this is why any effort to introduce a feeling of mine and thine into the relationship of the Ukraine towards Russia is so odious to us."[2]

Such ideas, redolent of the patronizing sentiments of imperialism, reflect the views of most of Russia's contemporary political and cultural elite to this day. Such proprietary attitudes also suggest that relations between Russia and her Ukrainian and Belarusian neighbors are likely to remain complex and dangerous for years to come.

As 1995 began, after three years of independence, Russia's identity crisis was growing more acute. Russia's leaders continued to seek ways to restore some form of unitary state or federal superstructure over the independent states that had emerged as a result of the collapse of the USSR. Many of Russia's political parties and their leaders reflected extremely aggressive views, ranging from the rantings of Vladimir Zhirinovsky's Liberal Democratic Party to the anti-Western conspiracy theories of Gennadi Zyuganov's Communist Party of the Russian Federation. Russia's foreign policy could be described as—at best—unpredictable and inconsistent and as—at worst—imperialist and aggressive. The Russian assault on Chechnya late in 1994, complete with its immense brutality and severe force, raised in stark relief worrying trends that had been developing in the country's external policies vis-à-vis its most proximate neighbors, and further afield, in places such as Iran, Iraq, and Cuba.[3]

Although there are ample reasons to be troubled by Russia's foreign policy and by its conduct in much of the Near Abroad, Russia's relationship with the "Nearest Abroad"—Ukraine and Belarus'—will determine whether Russia re-emerges as a global superpower or whether it evolves into a normal state and regional power. In the first three years of independence, Russia's policies vis-à-vis Belarus' and Ukraine were not characterized by the brazen military interference that was observed in its engagement in the Caucasus, in Moldova, and in Tajikistan. Such military interventions—some sanctioned by the Russian authorities, others rogue operations backed by segments of the military and security structures of the evolving Russian state—helped destabilize and even topple the official authorities of sovereign states in the former Soviet space.

In the case of Belarus', interference by Russian military or security was not an issue because of the absence of a will to statehood on the part of the vast majority of its citizens and on the part of its political elite, most particularly President Alyaksandr Lukashenka, who was elected on June 13, 1994. While President Lukashenka's election by a second-round margin of 80 to 19 percent signaled the victory of an avowedly pro-Russian leader, the first three years of the country's independence had also been characterized by a tacit acceptance of Russia's dominance. The inclination to bend to Russia's will was shared by the country's ruling nomenklatura, by the majority of its parliament, and by the government headed until mid-1994 by Prime Minister Vyacheslau Kebich. Indeed, this pro-Russian trend had been only partly resisted by the country's moderate parliamentary speaker Stanislau Shushkevich, who held his post from 1990 until his removal in January 1994. The only resolute opponent of close cooperation and outright merger with Russia was the Belarusian Popular Front, headed by Zyanon Paznyak.

While Belarus's relatively small population of 10 million made it difficult for the country to resist the pressure of its powerful neighbor, Ukraine's size and population of 52 million, coupled with its substantial military potential, made it risky for Russia to resort to aggressive efforts at reasserting dominance. As the Ukrainian experiment with independence proceeded amid mounting economic crisis, the country maintained a degree of political stability as a result of a growing consensus within the republic's ruling elite to preserve independence. This consensus made Ukraine a dangerous target for Russia's hegemonic inclinations.

While many of Russia's leaders believed Ukraine's status as a sovereign state was a reversible accident of history, they also understood that efforts to absorb or destabilize Ukraine could be dangerous for Russia's economic interests. Nevertheless, in the first years of Ukrainian independence, Russia pursued policies to maximize its influence in that country, and sought to keep open the prospect of an eventual economic, political, and military integration.

As 1994 drew to a close, it was clear that Russia's ambitions no longer matched its capabilities. Its "great power" ambitions and search for grandeur remained part of the country's rhetoric, but the longer the experiment with independence persisted in Ukraine, the more difficult it became for Russia to reintegrate its southern neighbor into a confederation or a military structure, much less a unitary state.

In a sense, the underlying theme of contemporary Ukraine's relations with Russia is "buying time." For Ukrainian foreign and domestic policy makers, the main issues are how to secure statehood and stability amid an acute economic crisis and how to create a set of circumstances that discourages aggressive Russian behavior.[4] This task is partly in the hands of the leaders of Ukraine and other newly independent non-Russian states, but it is also partly dependent on Western statecraft and United States leadership.

Ukraine and Belarus' are unquestionably Russia's Nearest Abroad—geopolitically, economically, and culturally. Geographically, Ukraine shares a border of over 650 miles with Russia and there are particularly close economic links between the Ukrainian east and Russia. Ukraine's trade with Russia during the Soviet period reflected the high levels of mutual interdependence that were part of a planned strategy of mutual dependence. The disruptions occasioned by the emergence of two distinct and separately evolving economies are regarded by the public as a major reason for economic decline in both countries. Belarus's largest border, too, is with Russia. And both countries are heavily dependent on Russia as the major provider of their energy needs.

Both countries also represent the Nearest Abroad from the geopolitical perspective. They are central to Russia's capacity to project its power in Central and Eastern Europe. Without them, Russia has only a small external border (Kaliningrad) with Poland. With Belarus' and Ukraine as part of a unified state or in a Russian-dominated federation, Russia would have access to a lengthy external border with Romania, Slovakia, Poland, and Hungary.

Equally important, from a strategic viewpoint, were Ukraine's and Russia's involvement in highly interrelated defense production as part of the Soviet military-industrial complex. Ukraine was the site of twenty-two Soviet central weapons manufacturing complexes. The Yuzhmash—the Southern Machine Building factory in Dnipropetrovsk, once headed by Ukraine's current President Leonid Kuchma—produced the intercontinental ballistic missiles of the Soviet nuclear arsenal and was one of four major missile plants on Ukrainian soil.

This region also represents the Nearest Abroad in the cultural sphere, containing populations that speak East Slavic languages with significant linguistic similarities. Many prominent exemplars of Russian cultures—writer Nikolai Gogol, poet Anna Akhmatova, novelist Mikhail Bulgakov, and filmmaker Oleksander Dovzhenko—were either ethnic Ukrainians or had roots in Ukraine. In addition, because Russia, Ukraine, and Belarus' trace their origins to a common Kievan-Rus state, and because their peoples spent centuries as integral parts of the tsarist empire and the USSR, Russians, many Belarusians, and a significant portion of Ukrainians regard the division of the three states as unnatural. Moreover, many

Ukrainians and Belarusians are deeply influenced by Russian culture, as demonstrated by the dominance of Russian books, television, the press, and films in Ukraine's and Belarus's markets.

Centuries of tsarist and Soviet policies aimed at the forced Russification of Ukrainians and Belarusians also have led to the dominance of the Russian language in both countries. In Ukraine, less than half the population uses Ukrainian as the language of daily discourse, and a significant segment of those who do speak Ukrainian daily live in rural areas, and are thus far removed from the urban centers in which political and cultural life is shaped. In Belarus', the percentage of ethnic Belarusians speaking their native language is even smaller. Moreover, only 70 percent of ethnic Belarusians regarded Belarusian as their native tongue.[5]

Among Russians, attitudes toward Belarus' and Ukraine coincide. A nationwide poll taken in September 1993, by the Moscow-based ROMIR research firm found that 72 percent of Russians either completely agreed (37 percent) or somewhat agreed (35 percent) that Ukraine must be reunited with Russia.[6] Only 4 percent of those polled completely disagreed with the statement. Only one-fifth of Russians agreed with the assertion that it is "natural for Ukraine to be independent." And only 1 percent of Russians agreed that Crimea, an internationally recognized part of Ukraine, should remain part of that country. Moreover, nearly three-quarters of those polled completely (47 percent) or somewhat (27 percent) agreed with the view that "it is a great misfortune that the Soviet Union no longer exists."[7] Ukrainians, particularly in the Russian-speaking eastern regions, also reveal sentiments in favor of close integration or reintegration of the two states. A poll conducted in Ukraine's southern and eastern regions found that 47 percent would vote against independence while only 24 percent would vote for it.[8]

Polls have shown similar attitudes in Belarus'. Such sentiments should hardly be surprising. After all, both Ukraine's and Belarus's independence did not occur as the result of protracted struggle, but because of the rapid collapse of the old Soviet state. In Ukraine, the entrenched Communist Party nomenklatura, under intense pressure from nationalist anti-communists organized around the *Rukh* popular front, quickly adopted the nation-building agenda of their political opponents in a successful bid to hold onto power after the collapse of the August 1991 putsch. Although these local Ukrainian communist leaders had not resisted the coup, they rapidly agreed to ban the Communist Party and proclaim independence, subject to a nationwide referendum, in the hours after the coup was defeated.

The declaration of independence was ratified in a December 1, 1991, referendum that was backed by over 90 percent of the population. In Belarus', independence was less a matter of volition or an attempt to avert a clash with a powerful nationalist opposition—as in Ukraine—than an inevitable consequence of decisions made by the Baltic States, Moldova, the states in the Caucasus and in Ukraine.

Because of this awkward genesis, several years after the agreements between the leaders of the three countries at the Belovezhskaya Pushcha to dissolve the USSR, Russia's citizens, including the majority of its political elite, are not reconciled to the permanent independence of Ukraine and Belarus'. They are likely to find encouragement in polling that shows growing discontent with the statehood experiment in Belarus' and Ukraine.

Today, Russian political life is filled with lively discussion about the restoration of a larger state through the ingathering of the now dispersed former Soviet republics. These views range from outright restoration of the Soviet Union to schemes aimed at creating a Eurasian commonwealth—an idea proposed by Kazakhstan's President Nursultan Nazarbayev.

Pan-Slavic ideas also have been advanced in Russia. The prominent Russian writer Aleksandr Solzhenitsyn has called for the reconfiguration of a new Slavic state consisting of Russia, most of Ukraine, Belarus', and northern (ethnically Russian) Kazakhstan. That Solzhenitsyn advanced these ideas in the official setting of an address to the Russian State Duma in December 1994 has been a source of some unease within the Ukrainian political and state establishment.

While many Russian leaders openly question the continued existence of Ukraine as a state, others question the current configuration of Ukraine's borders. For example, they wish to contain Crimea and parts of eastern Ukraine within Russia's borders. The Russian military leadership, in particular, is eager to restore a unified military made up of the armed forces of the countries of the CIS. As part of this effort, the chief of staff for CIS military coordination, General Viktor Samsonov, has devised a plan that calls for "the strategic nuclear forces of Russia to fulfill the function of restraint against all CIS participant states."[9] Minutes of an October 9, 1993, session of the Russian Security Council underscore the desire of Russia's leaders to reassert hegemony within the borders of the former USSR.

This pattern of acquisitive Russian attitudes has created unease among many Ukrainian political leaders. In this uncertain setting, it is important for the political elites of Russia to behave with restraint and to have an accurate understanding of internal political processes within the Ukrainian state. There also needs to be a realistic understanding of Russia's capability to restore Russian domination of Ukraine, which currently has a standing army of nearly half a million, and whose military forces possess no less than 40 percent of the tanks, artillery, and armored personnel carriers that Russia has on European territory, west of the Ural Mountains.

Absent the military assets of Ukraine, Russia lacks the hardware and manpower to re-emerge as a military superpower on European soil. The reintegration of Ukraine into Russia's military, political, and economic sphere, therefore, has become a pre-eminent objective of Russia's foreign policy. This has meant devising non-military means of exerting greater influence within Ukraine.

Part of this effort is an attempt to maintain a Russian military presence on Ukraine's soil through the Russian component of the Black Sea Fleet. The Russian foreign and defense establishments have sought also to keep unresolved a dangerous range of issues, including open acknowledgement of Ukraine's territorial integrity and its current borders.

Of the entire complex of post-Soviet issues, the question of Ukrainian-Russian relations is central to the nature of the post-Soviet order in Central and Eastern Europe. A glance at recent history shows that the relationship between the newly independent Ukrainian state and Russia has been filled with recrimination since its inception. Just days after the Ukrainian parliament voted to support Ukraine's statehood, Russian President Yel'tsin's press spokesman Pavel Voshchanov questioned the integrity of an independent Ukraine's borders.[10] Initially, as Ukraine's leaders pressed for independence, President Yel'tsin did not seek a similar status for Russia. Rather than aim for the dissolution of the USSR, the Russian president hoped to reorganize the USSR as a confederation. It was the December 1, 1991, independence referendum in Ukraine which forced President Yel'tsin to accept the inevitability of Ukraine's statehood and led him and his advisers to conclude that the USSR must be dissolved and not transformed. Such a course was of tactical advantage to Yel'tsin in his power struggle with Soviet President Mikhail Gorbachev.

Ukraine's uncompromising path toward statehood led Yel'tsin, Ukrainian President Leonid Kravchuk, and Belarus's parliamentary chairman Shushkevich to the Belarusian forest and to the Belovezhskaya Pushcha agreement to form the CIS and put an end to the USSR. While Yel'tsin accepted the arguments of some of his aides—most notably Yegor Gaidar and Gennadi Burbulis—that it would be impossible to achieve fundamental economic reforms on a USSR-wide scale, he had an ambivalent view of what should succeed the USSR. The CIS structure was a highly malleable idea that sought to satisfy the fundamentally different views of the leaders of Russia and Ukraine. In the Russian view, the CIS was intended to preserve a unified strategic and economic space. For Ukraine, the Commonwealth was seen as an instrument for a "civilized divorce."

Moreover, Russian relations with Ukraine were haunted by diametrically opposed concepts almost from the beginning. In the first days after the dissolution of the USSR, Russian officials, in particular the Russian defense ministry and its counterpart in the CIS command, were surprised by Ukraine's efforts to create its own military and to compel loyalty oaths from all troops serving on its soil. Within days of the December 1991 referendum that ratified Ukrainian independence, Ukraine proceeded to build its own armed forces through a process of new loyalty oaths.[11]

Ukraine's efforts provoked a Russian response. On January 9, 1992, President Yel'tsin declared that the Black Sea Fleet—which Ukraine asserted as its own—was, is, and always will be Russia's, and the Russian parliament began to examine Moscow's claim to ownership of Crimea and the port city of Sevastopol. Soon after, Vladimir Lukin, at the time chairman of the parliament's foreign affairs commission, circulated a memorandum that suggested Russia encourage separatist sentiments in the Crimea as part of a campaign aimed at making encroachments on Ukraine's sovereignty.[12] Lukin argued that Moscow should stir up challenges to Ukraine in an effort to strengthen its hand vis-à-vis Kiev.

Lukin's memo, however, did not win universal support. Sergei Filatov, then deputy chairman of the Russian Supreme Soviet and later President Yel'tsin's chief of staff, criticized the memo as inappropriate, bullying, and unacceptable. The foreign ministry, which was pursuing a conciliatory policy toward Ukraine at the time, also distanced itself from Lukin's tough line. At the same time, President Yel'tsin's apparat leaked word of a draft decree that would have placed all former Soviet troops under Russia's jurisdiction. Although the decree was never introduced in 1992, relations between the two states began to reveal other strains and points of disagreement including comments by Russian officials that Russia would respect Ukraine's current borders, but only within the context of Ukraine's membership in the CIS.

Such pronouncements strained relations and led to the dispatch of a high-level delegation to Kiev, headed by then Vice President Aleksandr Rutskoi. The mission appeared to allay Ukraine's fears of Russian intentions. Yet the absence of a firm policy and an emerging political struggle between President Yel'tsin and his opponents in the Russian parliament rapidly undermined these understandings.

A mid-1992 Russian draft of a friendship treaty between Ukraine and Russia revealed the gap between the two sides by completely contradicting Kiev's views. The treaty envisioned a unified defense policy, Russian military installations in Crimea and throughout Ukraine, as well as economic integration. The Russian Congress of Peoples Deputies further contributed to Ukraine's unease when in July 1992 it passed a resolution calling for the re-examination of the status of Sevastopol and an investigation into the legality of the 1954 transfer by Khrushchev of Crimea from the Russian Federation to Ukraine.[13]

Throughout 1993, with no bilateral treaty in sight, relations between

Russia and Ukraine continued on a downward spiral. This coincided with the development of a more tough-minded Russian external policy and the emergence of the concept of the Near Abroad. As part of this tougher Russian line, on February 28, 1993, at a congress of Arkady Volsky's Civic Union, President Yel'tsin called on the United Nations to grant special powers to Russia as a guarantor of peace and stability on the territory of the former Soviet Union.[14] In April 1993, Russian diplomats began a campaign to discourage Western countries from establishing large embassies in Kiev, because Ukraine's days were numbered. While some of these statements were disavowed by the Russian foreign ministry, they continued to emanate from Russian diplomats.

In June 1993, Russian foreign minister Andrei Kozyrev, while on a visit to Sevastopol, proclaimed support for Ukrainian-Russian reunification. In July 1993, Russia began to restrict gas and energy supplies to Ukraine and to charge near-world market prices. As a result, Ukraine began to accumulate debts it could not service, in part because of the weakness of Ukraine's own currency. For a one-month period Russia even shut off gas and oil deliveries to Ukraine for non-payment.

In September 1993, Russia followed with a diplomatic démarche, signing an agreement with Poland to construct a gas pipeline that would travel through Belarus' and Poland, bypassing Ukraine. Such a pipeline would reduce Ukraine's ability to exert pressure on Russia. It also reflected a measure of Russian distrust of Ukraine. As a result, President Leonid Kuchma, who was then prime minister, labeled the move an anti-Ukrainian action.

Ukrainian-Russian relations reached a nadir at the summit between President Kravchuk and President Yel'tsin in the Crimean resort of Massandra.[15] At issue in Massandra was the disposition of the Black Sea Fleet. The fleet had been a bone of contention since the emergence of the Ukrainian armed forces after independence. Ukraine had claimed the right to the entire fleet. In turn, Russia had argued initially that the fleet was part of the strategic forces of the former USSR, and later simply that these vessels were Russian property.

A few months before the Massandra summit, Ukraine and Russia had agreed to divide the fleet equally. At Massandra, the Russian position appeared to shift. It was there that President Yel'tsin took an aggressively hard line. Much to the surprise of Ukrainian officials, Russia demanded that Ukraine transfer its part of the fleet to Russia in partial settlement of Ukraine's accumulating energy debts. If it did not, President Yel'tsin threatened to cut off fuel supplies to Ukraine.

The Ukrainian side was taken aback by the Russian position, which had not been suggested in the preparatory meetings leading up to the summit. At a press conference at the end of the summit, President Yel'tsin explained that Ukraine had accepted the Russian proposal to sell the balance of the fleet to Russia and to allow its long-term stationing in Ukrainian waters. President Kravchuk said nothing to contradict President Yel'tsin's unexpected remarks.

In the days that followed, Ukraine's political life was thrown into tumult. Nationalist parliamentary deputies denounced Kravchuk's capitulation. The events at Massandra clearly rattled the Ukrainian foreign policy and defense establishments. Defense Minister Kostyantyn Morozov, an ethnic Russian who became an ardent Ukrainian patriot, voiced his opposition to the arrangement. The pressure from Ukraine's political leaders worked. President Kravchuk denied he had ever agreed to transfer the entire fleet to Russia.

Back in Russia President Yel'tsin and Defense Minister Pavel Grachev boasted of the summit's success—the recapture of the Ukrainian debt and the establishment of a permanent military beachhead in Ukraine. The entire episode created a great deal of animosity between the foreign ministries and defense establishments of the two countries. Ukraine's leaders became more protective of their country and more suspicious of Russia's conduct. Distrust of Russian intentions grew after Russia's December 1993 parliamentary elections, in which ultra-nationalists and neo-communists won the greatest electoral support. In a sense, this climate of suspicion contributed to the process of Ukrainian nation building.

In 1993, Russia had sought also to exploit international concern about Ukraine's tactical and strategic nuclear weapons by skillfully portraying the new Ukrainian state as an unreliable member of the international community, led by a president who was a neo-communist turned nationalist. While Ukraine sought security guarantees in return for surrendering the nuclear arsenal it was bequeathed after the collapse of the USSR, Russian officials sought to muster Western pressure against Kiev's allegedly dangerous nuclear policies. International pressure on Ukraine to accede to the Nuclear Non-proliferation Treaty (NPT) helped to isolate the new Ukrainian state by denying it desperately needed early economic assistance, and to weaken its hand vis-à-vis Moscow. Ironically, such Western pressure was exerted according to Russian—not Western—strategic priorities. For Ukraine was pressed first to rid itself of its tactical nuclear weapons—which could be deployed as a deterrent against Russia—and not the strategic nuclear arsenal, which was targeted originally at the United States.

On January 14, 1994, President Kravchuk agreed to abide by the NPT and to adhere to the START (Strategic Arms Reduction Talks) Agreement.[16] By the fall of 1994, the Ukrainian parliament ratified START and the NPT in return for vague security assurances from the nuclear powers.

In 1994, Ukraine was on the eve of a new political season with March elections for parliament and June-July elections for the presidency. Russia, which in 1993 had drastically reduced the supplies of energy to Ukraine, exerted no similar pressure on Ukraine when its delinquencies on payments climbed in the winter of 1993–94. This constructive Russian position was based on a calculation; any effort to heighten tension between the two states might strengthen the hand of anti-Russian forces and weaken the hand of the candidate Moscow felt was clearly preferable—the challenger Leonid Kuchma.

While Kuchma was a Ukrainian patriot, who as prime minister had done nothing to undermine Ukraine's sovereignty, he ran a campaign against Kravchuk that was clearly calculated to maximize Kuchma's support in Ukraine's pro-Russian east and south. Kuchma had denounced Kravchuk's stridency and accused him of undermining Ukraine's historically good relations with Russia. Emphasizing close relations with Russian industrialists, Kuchma, who served as head of the Ukrainian Association of Industrialists and Entrepreneurs, promised he would work to repair economic links between the two countries. He further spoke of a strategic partnership with Russia. The effect of the campaign was to create an image of Kuchma as the pro-Russian candidate. Kuchma's anticipated defeat of Kravchuk was an important reason behind Russia's restraint in handling a growing crisis in Crimea, where local officials sought to establish their sovereignty from Ukraine.

Although the defeat of President Kravchuk in July 1994 appeared to set the stage for a warming of relations between the two countries, matters quickly reverted to past patterns. It turned out that the new President Kuchma may well have been inclined to cooperate, but he was unwilling to bend to Russian pressure and proved an able defender of Ukraine's national interests against Russian encroachments. Russian officials believed that the election results signalled the growing desire of Ukraine's citizens to reunite with Russia, but such Russian expectations were predestined for disappointment. In discussion with this author Kuchma prided himself on being a tough-minded negotiator and promised to inject an element of pragmatism into inter-state relations.[17] He asserted that President Kravchuk had resorted to needless political posturing. Russia, by Kuchma's reckoning, was Ukraine's natural trading partner and the major market for Ukrainian goods. However, Kuchma indicated Ukraine should not be part of a political-military alliance with Russia, and said he opposed the establishment of a unified currency between the two states, because a currency was an essential attribute of sovereignty.

Indeed, while Kuchma's election opened a door for better Ukrainian-Russian relations, it also demonstrated that three years of independence had created a powerful Ukrainian elite which identified its interests with the perpetuation of statehood. Moreover, even the pragmatic positions taken by

President Kuchma were not enough to accommodate a more assertive and aggressive Russian foreign policy or to overcome tensions that issued from Ukraine's inability to pay Russia for oil and gas imports.

The interregnum in Ukrainian–Russian relations appeared to be over when President Kuchma visited Moscow on January 25, 1995. There he was publicly upbraided by President Yel'tsin for not accommodating Russia's wishes in negotiations concerning the issue of dual citizenship. In the days that followed Kuchma's visit to Moscow, Ukraine and Russia initialed the outlines of a major bilateral treaty in which Russia appeared to accept most of Ukraine's demands. The terms of the agreement appeared to be compatible with the Ukrainian position on citizenship, rejecting Russia's insistence that residents of Ukraine be permitted to take Russian citizenship. The agreement included language that unequivocally recognized Ukraine's territorial integrity. The draft agreement also provided for the final division of the Black Sea Fleet into a Russian and Ukrainian fleet, for basing of the Russian portion of the fleet in Sevastopol, and for the placement of the main Ukrainian naval contingent in Balaklava.[18]

Why did Russia appear to accede to Ukraine's positions? The most compelling answers were two: Chechnya and a looming CIS summit. The Russian adventure in Chechnya had isolated Russian diplomacy and frozen or put into question some Western aid programs. At the same time, CIS member states were alarmed by Russia's behavior in Chechnya. As tensions between Russia and the international community grew with the prospect of a much more hostile environment for Russia within the new, Republican-dominated US Congress, and with Central European states angry at Russia's efforts to block NATO expansion eastward, Russia was aware that it needed to shore up support and cooperation with its most proximate neighbors.

Thus, ironically, Russia is more—not less—likely to seek cooperation with Ukraine whenever it feels isolated or under pressure from the international community. At the same time, Russia saw the February 1995 CIS summit as an opportunity to advance the process of reintegration of the post-Soviet states. Russian officials believed that, for the first time, the sentiment for closer economic and strategic integration within the CIS was growing. Russia's calculation, however, was in error, for Ukraine—joined by Turkmenistan, Uzbekistan, Georgia, and Moldova—rejected Moscow's effort to take joint responsibility for policing CIS external borders and for moving toward the creation of a unified military-political space. This failure of Russian diplomacy underscored an important point in Russian-Ukrainian or Russian-Belarusian relations: Russia's behavior is not simply a matter of Russian intentions and declarations; its policy in the Nearest Abroad is also shaped by Ukraine's and Belarus's responses and by the overall international climate.

Moreover, official and semi-official Russian declarations and strata-gems are not unequivocal or immutable. As is the case with much of Russian thinking, the situation is in a constant state of flux. In fact, Russia does not speak in one coherent foreign policy voice. Not only are there natural differ-ences between the legislative and executive branches, or even differences between ministries and services or between the Russian government and the presidential administration, but frequently they are internal, within a ministry or in the president's inner circle. Clearly, there is no unity or uniformity in conception and execution of Russia's policies with regard to Ukraine and Belarus'. As is the case with much Russian policy in the Near Abroad, the Russian military and the Russian defense ministry appear to pursue one set of policies, the security services another, the finance ministry its own, and the prime minister his own.

The lack of clarity in Russia's relations with Ukraine and—secondarily—Belarus' is to some degree a hopeful sign. For it reminds us that an unequivocal and clear-cut Russian position has yet to be formed and, thus, can be influenced. Finality is unlikely, for Russia remains deeply uncertain of its place in the post-Soviet world. While such a situation offers reasons for hope that Russia will eventually accept Ukraine's independence, it suggests also that the Russian pub-lic and elite will support efforts aimed at eroding Ukraine's sovereignty.

For the moment, Moscow appears to be interested in pressing for the economic and political reintegration of its Slavic rim. Clearly, Russia is ac-tively seeking economic and political means to establish itself as a hegemon in the region; however, there is no clear signal that Russia is capable of reintegrating its Slavic neighbors into a single state. Still, Russia has signifi-cant resources to assert some degree of dominion over Ukraine and Belarus'.

SECURITY SERVICES

Yevhen Marchuk, who in March 1995 was named Ukraine's acting prime min-ister, had revealed in May 1992, when he headed Ukraine's National Security Service, that influential Russian industrial interests were actively transferring considerable funds to support separatist and pro-Russian movements in the Crimea and the Donbass. While Marchuk did not charge Russia's security services with similar activities, in private background discussions Ukrainian officials worried about the activities of Russia's security services on their terrain.

A high-ranking foreign ministry official put it this way: "We know they are doing this business; but skillfully, so that the official roots are hidden. . . . Offi-cially and in public we do not raise this issue."[1]

ETHNIC RUSSIAN MINORITIES

Russia's consistent assertion of its right to defend ethnic Russians and Rus-sian-speaking populations is problematic from the perspective of Belarus'

and Ukraine. In Belarus' the Russian-speaking population is about 80 percent and in Ukraine there are 11 million ethnic Russians and around 16 million Russian-speaking Ukrainians, representing together a majority of the
population. And while Ukraine has only one region with an ethnic Russian
majority—Crimea—Russia's ability to try to play the Russian ethnic card
represents a constant source of tension. An association of Russian commu-
nities has emerged as a powerful voice in Russia's internal political life. The
group has worked in alliance with ultranationalist Russian political groupings and has sought the support of Russia's communist and agrarian parties.
Its support of Russia's insistence on dual citizenship is part of this strategy
of organizing a base of support within—and legitimating Russia's direct engagement in the domestic politics of—Belarus' and Ukraine. As part of its
efforts to exert a greater influence on events in Ukraine, Russia is to open
new consulates in Lviv and Odessa.

RUSSIAN DIPLOMACY

Ukrainian foreign ministry officials confirm that Russian diplomacy continues to be the "legal successor to that of the USSR" in style, if not in
content. Russian diplomacy has inherited some of the traits of Soviet—
and, before it, tsarist—diplomacy. It is characterized by extreme toughness
in negotiations and by the capacity to mobilize global pressure in pursuit
of bilateral goals. This approach has characterized Russian efforts to press
Ukraine on denuclearization.

MEDIA

Russia dominates television in Ukraine and Belarus'. Some 70 percent of the
Ukrainian population watches Russia's Ostankino Television, which trans-
mits the strongest national signal inside Ukraine. Ostankino broadcasts allow Russia's government and political leaders to influence debate inside
Ukraine and Belarus'. Russian newspapers, including *Argumenty i Fakty,
Izvestiya,* and *Trud* are among the most popular periodicals in Ukraine. The
strength of Russia's currency also means that Russian media are able to purchase popular Western films, subscribe to Western wire services, and maintain bureaus around the world, unlike their Ukrainian and Belarusian
counterparts.

ECONOMIC PRESSURE

Russia is the major trading partner of Ukraine and Belarus'. Both countries
are highly dependent on Russia for oil and natural gas. Russia's current
technocratically oriented crop of economic pragmatists, including Deputy
Prime Minister Anatoli Chubais, is unlikely to support economically harmful
policies in pursuit of geopolitical advantage. However, the same cannot be

said with assurance about the Russian leaders who may emerge after the December 1995 parliamentary and June 1996 presidential elections.

Despite Russia's broad array of resources, Ukraine possesses enough important resources of its own to resist Russian encroachments. As the Ukrainian condition of statehood persists, it reinforces a bureaucracy that associates its power and influence with the preservation of national sovereignty. Even the Ukrainian Communist Party, many of whose leaders favor the restoration of the USSR, has seen the emergence of a powerful pro-statehood faction associated with the writer Boris Oliynik, the head of the Ukrainian parliament's foreign affairs committee.

Local Ukrainian business interests, too, are increasingly eager proponents of statehood. While they seek greater access to Russian markets and, so, support closer economic integration between Russia and Ukraine, they are also fearful of losing their share of the domestic Ukrainian market to more powerful Russian commercial interests. Ukraine's emerging generation of private entrepreneurs is fearful that Russian business, with its more powerful currency, might sweep in and buy up Ukrainian enterprises and property on the cheap.

Such Ukrainian resistance to Russian encroachments means that there is a reasonable prospect that Ukraine's sovereignty can contribute to transforming Russia into a normal state that respects the sovereignty of its neighbors. For if Russia is rid of its age-old imperial impulse, it can at last join the ranks of its European neighbors.

Russia's foreign policy for the years ahead will be settled in the 1995 and 1996 elections, if held. Whatever choices voters make, Russia's relations with Ukraine will continue to be the single most important objective of Russian foreign policy. Without Ukraine, Russians understand that they remain a regional power. However, Russia's behavior toward Ukraine is likely to be all the more aggressive if Ukraine appears a weak and inviting target, internally divided between its nationalist west and Russian-oriented east.

What role can Western and, particularly, US policy play in terms of Russia's relations with the Nearest Abroad? With regard to Belarus', Western policy should recognize that there is little possibility for mobilizing the Belarusian public to resist Russia's siren song of "reintegration." Belarus's public and its political elite favor close integration, and such a preference cannot be reversed from the outside. Nevertheless, Western policy should urge Belarus' to preserve its constitutionally defined status as a neutral state and should make it clear to Belarus's leaders that its long-term interests— including access to Western aid—rest in preserving sovereignty. The West also should be open to the possibility that Belarus's political elite and public may alter their views on reintegration with Russia, should ultra-nationalists or militarists gain the upper hand in Russian political life.

With regard to Ukraine, the West should strengthen and reinforce the country's already substantial sentiments of sovereignty. Western diplomacy should make it clear that the preservation of a sovereign Ukraine is crucial to a peaceful order in Eastern Europe. The best way to strengthen Ukraine's independence is through promotion of the country's economic stability. This means that the United States and other advanced industrial nations should make Ukraine's economic recovery a major focus of aid and technical assistance.

In the longer term, it is clearly in the West's interests to promote the diversification of Ukraine's trade. This means that Europe and the United States should be prepared to open their markets to Ukrainian business and products. Ukraine will also need assistance to purchase oil and natural gas and to increase the more efficient use of its energy resources.

At the same time, even as NATO plans to expand eastward, it must look to a formula that does not isolate Ukraine from the West. Part of this effort must include active Western diplomatic pressure on Russia to recognize unequivocally Ukraine's territorial integrity, to renounce claims on Crimea, and to move rapidly to implement agreements on the final division of the Black Sea Fleet.

Constructive pressure by the West will rein in the more confrontational and expansionist sentiments within parts of Russia's political elite and will enhance Ukraine's sense of security. Such pressure is, therefore, essential to preserving regional peace and stability. For, although several years have passed since the collapse of the USSR and the emergence of independent states, the Russian public—and, in even greater proportions, the Russian cultural and political elite—has not reconciled itself to the permanence of Ukraine's and Belarus's independence.

Such potentially dangerous sentiments need not be decisive in defining Ukraine's—and to a lesser extent, Belarus's—future. For while Ukraine is fated to remain within Russia's area of influence, it can resist efforts to make it part of Russia's sphere of dominance, and should be assisted in its resistance.

NOTES

1. Francis Dvornik, *The Slavs* (New Brunswick, NJ: Rutgers University Press, 1962), pp. 307-309, 348.

2. Mikhail Katkov, quoted in Ivan Dzyuba, *Internationalism or Russification* (London: Weidenfeld and Nicolson, 1968), p. 96.

3. See the author's, "Grrrr . . . Russia's New Hard Line," *National Review,* 6 February 1995, pp. 55-58.

4. In a September 4, 1994 background discussion, a high-ranking official of

the Ukrainian Foreign Ministry told the author that "well over . . . half of Ukraine's foreign policy efforts and personnel are focused on Russia. This is really a ministry of Russian and foreign relations."

5. Ann Sheehy, "Russian Share of Soviet Population Down to 50.8 Percent," *Radio Liberty Report on the USSR,* 20 October 1989, p. 3.

6. USIA Opinion Research Memorandum, 8 December 1993.

7. Ibid.

8. Report (in English) issued by Democratic Initiatives. Polling was conducted between 15 May and 2 June 1994 in the oblasts of Dnipropetrosk, Donetsk, Zaporizhge, Luhansk, Mykolaiv, Odessa, Kharkiv, and Kherson, and the Republic of Crimea.

9. See Adrian Karatnycky, "Resurrection of the East-West Divide," *Wall Street Journal Europe,* 18 August 1994, and "Russia's Nuclear Grasp," *The New York Times,* 30 August 1994, p. A21.

10. REUTERS report, 26 August 1991.

11. See Adrian Karatnycky, "The Ukrainian Factor," *Foreign Affairs* 71:3, Summer 1992, p. 93.

12. Chrystia Freeland, "Wild Card in Volatile Game of Nuclear Power Poker," *Financial Times,* 10 February 1992, p. 2.

13. Fiona Hill and Pamela Jewett, *Back in the USSR* (Cambridge, MA: Harvard University Press, 1994), p. 72.

14. ITAR-TASS Report, March 1993.

15. Bohdan Nahaylo, "The Massandra Summit and Ukraine," *RFE/RL Research Report,* 17 September 1993, pp. 1-6.

16. See John Lepingwell, "The Trilateral Agreement on Nuclear Weapons," *RFE/RL Research Report,* 28 January 1994, pp. 12-20.

17. Meeting at Freedom House in Washington, D.C., 21 April 1994.

18. See "Ukraine and Russia Initial Political Treaty," *The Ukrainian Weekly,* 12 February 1995.

19. September 4, 1994, background discussion with the author and a high-ranking Ukrainian foreign ministry official.

5

Revisiting Russia's Turbulent Rim:
Caucasus, Central Asia, and Moldova

Ariel Cohen

For a millennium the southern rim of Russia was highly unstable. After the Turkic invasions of the ninth to fifteenth centuries came Moscow's expansion into the steppes and mountains of southeastern Europe, the Caucasus and Central Asia, which lasted until late in the nineteenth century. After World War I, Bessarabia reverted to Romania, while its appendix east of the Dniestr was declared an autonomous republic in the Ukrainian SSR. The Transcaucasian republics experienced a brief period of independence (1918-20), but were reconquered by the Red Army with Western acquiescence. The bolsheviks subjugated Central Asia's lands with great brutality and crushed the remnants of independence enjoyed by the khanates of Khorezm and Bukhara.[1]

The USSR made major efforts to assimilate fully the non-Russian territories of the former Romanov empire, but despite heavy-handed interference in their affairs by Stalin and his heirs, the idea of national independence remained alive. Georgia, Armenia, and Azerbaijan received union republic status after the dissolution of the short-lived Transcaucasus SSR. Four of the five Central Asian republics (Kazakhstan, Kyrgyzstan, Turkmenistan, and Uzbekistan) were created by Stalin primarily to forestall the emergence of a unified Turkic nation in Central Asia. However, the education and cultural policies of the CPSU allowed for the growth of national awareness among the republican elites. With central controls growing feeble under Gorbachev, nationalist movements emerged that pushed for sovereignty, in other words, a greater degree of autonomy from Moscow.[2]

With the collapse of the Soviet Union following the August 1991 coup, the non-Russian republics (as well as Russia itself) declared independence. While this development served the interests of the local republican elites, the central bureaucracy in the imperial capital remained rigidly opposed. Bureaucrats and officers would be denied posts, promotions, and control over the vital resources of raw materials and manpower. At the same time, the union elites were paralyzed at critical moments by the power struggle between the Russian (RSFSR) faction led by Boris Yel'tsin, which was nominally opposed to continuation of the Soviet imperial arrangement, and the USSR/CPSU faction led by Mikhail Gorbachev, which advocated a rejuvenated federation.

The collapse of the August 1991 putsch and the dissolution of the Soviet Union in December 1991 left many in the political class—first and foremost in the military and the security services, as well as in the former Gosplan and branch ministries—extremely dissatisfied and still hoping for the restoration of past might. The struggle for the re-establishment of the empire started early in 1992, almost immediately after the declaration of Russian independence. Preceding a putative full-scale military involvement, this struggle has come to employ a broad spectrum of military, covert action, diplomatic, and economic measures. Geographically, all of the former Soviet periphery is involved. The whole southern tier of the former USSR is a zone of feverish Russian activity aimed at tightening Moscow's grip in the aftermath of the Soviet collapse. In addition, the Baltic States, Ukraine and Belarus' have come increasingly under Russian pressure.

SETTING THE STAGE

In order to analyze adequately attempts to re-establish the postimperial state, the interests and ideologies of the metropolitan (Moscow) and peripheral elites must be closely examined. Also to be considered are economic concerns, the position of the military hierarchy, and the location of large individual units and bases, as well as the attitudes of major powers and international organizations. Transnational factors such as religion and technology have to be scrutinized, as well. In addition, the model of a "turbulent frontier," a highly unstable and fluid environment in which local players and mid-level metropolitan bureaucrats drive the process of imperial acquisition, cannot be ignored. As the development and decline of other empires demonstrates, this is a complex scenario, with socioeconomic and politico-military components that must be addressed as a whole.[3]

Bemoaning the collapse of the Soviet Union, the USSR's last Chairman of the Council of Ministers, Nikolai Ryzhkov, called for the restoration of the federation with Russia in a "leading role."[4] From the other side of the spectrum, Aleksandr Solzhenitsyn has advocated the *Anschluß* of Ukraine, Belarus' and "South Siberia" (that is, Northern Kazakhstan).[5]

However, not only unrepentant communists and Russian nationalists use imperialist language. Dr. Sergei Blagovolin, Andrei Kozyrev's foreign policy adviser and a senior official of the Russia's Democratic Choice party (headed by former Acting Prime Minister Yegor Gaidar), told a gathering of American academicians that "Kazakhstan and Armenia are crawling on their hands and knees to be accepted into the federation with Russia."[6]

Kozyrev, once an ardent advocate of Russia's de-imperialization, has stated on many occasions the alleged right of Russia to defend its "sphere of historic interests." Moreover, on November 19, 1994, he called for a transformation of the CIS military-security system into "a politico-military union of republics united by common history and the common CIS border, for they simply do not need another border."[7] Kozyrev argued that a Russian-led CIS would end "existing conflicts" and "stabilize this entire space, contributing to European and world security." The Russian foreign minister dismissed Western concerns:

> Let the West react as it pleases, we will do our work as we need. We have nothing to explain to anyone, we won't have to justify ourselves. . . . There are of course, those who see any strengthening of Russia or the CIS as harmful because they prefer a weak partner to a strong one. Well, let them think that way while we strengthen both Russia and the CIS.[8]

Vladimir Shumeiko, Yel'tsin's ally and chairman of the Council of the Federation (the upper house of the Russian legislature), has called for an "increase of the role of the CIS," and the creation of a supranational legislative body to which deputies would be elected by direct vote.[9] Shumeiko complained that the West reserved for Russia merely the role of a regional power and a raw material supplier. He also claimed to possess a map of the USSR on which Western corporations had allegedly staked out and divided among themselves the resources of the ex-Soviet republics. To prevent this alleged scenario from developing, Shumeiko stated that Russia must keep its armed forces, intelligence and the military-industrial complex.[10] These pronouncements are similar to those statements constantly issued by his predecessor, Ruslan Khasbulatov, from whom he inherited the job of CIS Interparliamentary Commission chairman.

Upon dismembering the Soviet Union, President Yel'tsin called for a re-examination of Russia's borders to the detriment of her neighbors, especially Ukraine and Kazakhstan. After returning from a state visit to the United States in September 1994, he reiterated the right of Russia to conduct "peacemaking" in the Near Abroad, to protect Russian speakers, and to exercise freedom of action in its purported sphere of influence.[11]

ECONOMICS AND GEOPOLITICS

Perceived economic interests play a role in Russia's desire to re-establish the union, the empire, or the federation. However, this agenda is hardly rational. No one in Moscow knows the costs or the revenues that could be generated by such a reintegration, either on a case-by-case basis or in toto. Uzbek cotton and natural gas, Tajik uranium, Baku oil, Ukrainian sugar, and the ports of the Black and Baltic seas are all mentioned by Moscow decisionmakers as national patrimony that needs to be repossessed.[12]

The production of components for the military-industrial complex is often cited as another rationale for "reintegration," as if such components cannot be purchased through normal market channels. However, the high costs involved in reintegration hamper the official enthusiasm to assume the burdens of empire. The aborted economic merger with Belarus' in December 1993–January 1994 and the expense of maintaining the failing mining industry of the Donbass are two cases that have forced at least some Russian officials to resist expansionistic policies.[13]

In October 1994 the creation of the CIS Interstate Economic Committee (MEK), was announced. The committee, based on the model of the old Soviet industrial branch ministries, has been the option advocated by supporters of reintegration in Moscow. According to its designers, this supranational bureaucracy will be involved not only in regulation and economic planning, but also in direct investment and management of enterprises. Many Moscow officials toiling in this "new and improved" CIS-wide Gosplan are inimical toward the new market, and will do their best to regulate it out of existence.[14] At the October 1994 CIS summit, Russia imposed its own Ministry of Economics upon the CIS to act as the committee's coordinating staff.

The Russian military and the security services constitute by far the most resolute driving force behind the restoration of some form of Russian-led entity. The end of the Cold War and the collapse of the Berlin Wall terminated, at least temporarily, confrontation with the West, leaving the Red Army and especially its general staff, the GRU (military intelligence), and the ex-KGB desperately seeking new missions. Current Russian military doctrine calls for intervention in the former Soviet states in instances that are in clear violation of international law.[15] Adopted after the bloody events of October 1993, this doctrine was authored by the same military specialists who published it for the first time in Zhrinovsky's *Liberal*.[16] Furthermore, it was none other than Vladimir Zhirinovsky who in 1991 came up with a proposal to incorporate the then-Soviet military into the international peace-keeping process and thus earn hard currency through UN funding. At the time, the liberal Russian media rejected the idea as too cynical, but by 1993, Yel'tsin and Kozyrev were promoting it wholeheartedly.[17]

Russia evacuated its troops from the Baltic States only after the exertion of strong international pressure, but refused to withdraw troops from Moldova, which was ravaged by the Russian-supported separatist Dniestr Republic forces. There, the Russian Fourteenth Army has been acting as a purported peacemaker between Moldova and a force created by the Russian military. Meanwhile, at Ukraine's expense, Moscow has used its political and economic muscle to secure practically exclusive use of the Crimean peninsula and the Sevastopol port and naval base for the Black Sea Fleet. The former Soviet military played a key role in supporting the Georgian opposition to President Zviad Gamsakhurdia, who was replaced by Eduard Shevardnadze in May 1992. Later, the military also engineered the removal of Abkhazia from the independent state of Georgia. While Russian military leaders sold modern weapons to both sides in the Nagorno-Karabakh conflict, Russia was also behind the insurrection that deposed the democratically elected president of Azerbaijan, Abulfaz Elchibey.[18]

The successor to the KGB's First Chief Directorate, now known as the Foreign Intelligence Service of Russia (SVRR) and led by KGB general and Middle East expert Yevgeni Primakov, recently published a significant document on Russia's policies in the Near Abroad. The analysis *Russia—CIS: Does the Western Position Require Correction?* appeared in Moscow on the eve of Yel'tsin's visit to the United States.[19] It stresses that Russia is increasingly pursuing its national interests, including those encompassing its periphery. The document also claims to discover "objective" centripetal forces working to reintegrate the former Soviet Union.[20]

While declaring the sovereignty of the new independent states "irreversible," the SVRR document proceeds to drain that sovereignty of any meaning. The frontiers of the CIS states will remain "transparent," as were the borders of the USSR's union republics, while the external frontiers of the CIS will be protected by Russian border guards, currently led by the charismatic General Andrei Nikolayev. Supranational political bodies (dominated by Russia) will be created, and sovereign powers will be delegated to them. General Primakov's analysts-turned-economists argue that any integration of the CIS states into the global economy that is not carried out via Moscow is doomed to fail—as demonstrated by the failure, because of Russian pressure, of Kazakh and Azerbaijani joint ventures to export their oil without Russian participation. Moreover, any resistance to the postulated "centripetal tendencies," as well as any attempt to develop economic cooperation outside the CIS is ominously declared hopeless and "lacking perspective."[21]

The states of the CIS southern tier came under pressure from Russia even before they declared their independence from the USSR. Moscow incited local pro-Russian factions—be they ethnic Russians in eastern Moldova, Abkhazians in Georgia, or hard-line communist, pro-Russian clans in Tajikistan—to challenge the independence of the nascent states. The results were devastating, leaving hundreds of thousands dead, wounded, or homeless.

MOLDOVA

Populated by Romanian-speaking Moldovans (65 percent), Ukrainians (14 percent), and Russians (13 percent), Moldova was torn apart by a local war fought during 1991-92 in the Transdniestr (Pridniestrovye) region on the left bank of the Dniestr River. Only a third of Moldova's Russians live in the "Dniestr Soviet Socialist Republic." This Soviet-style, Russian-speaking republic on the left bank of the Dniestr yearns to be part of a future Greater Russia (although Ukraine separates it from the Russian Federation).[22] Most of these Russians are recent immigrants into the region, attracted by its warm climate and abundant food supply. As in the Baltic States, large numbers of the resettled Russians are retirees from the Soviet Army along with their families. The Russians comprise a minority among the population of the Transdniestr (25 percent). Few of them support the hard-line communist regime of the "exclave." A plurality in the Transdniestr consists of Romanian-speaking Moldovans, and the rest are Ukrainians.

In March 1992, and for many months thereafter, a small minority of Russian separatists supported by the Russian Federation, together with the former Soviet Fourteenth Army stationed in the area, engaged the weak Moldovan military in battles on the left bank of the Dniestr. In addition, the town of Bendery on the right bank was captured by the Dniestr forces. Lacking the Russians' heavy artillery and tanks, the Moldovans were routed.

The Dniestr Republic is important for Russian imperialists as it constitutes a Russian "bridgehead" in the rear of Ukraine and at the doorstep of the Balkans. The Dniestr Republic has the dubious distinction of being called the last socialist country in Eastern Europe.

The exclave has attracted some of the most sinister characters among Russian imperialists and nationalists. The commanders of the (formerly Soviet) special militia units, the OMON, from Riga, Latvia—Vladimir Antufeyev and Oleg Goncharneko—are operating in the Transdniestr under the assumed names of Vadim Shevtsov and Nikolai Matveev. Shevtsov is the Minister of State Security and Matveev is Deputy Minister of Internal Affairs of the Dniestr Republic. They were jointly responsible for the creation of the Dniestr Battalion, an elite special operations force that was sent to Moscow to defend the rebellious leaders of the former legislature in their October 1993 confrontation with President Yel'tsin. Many of its men fought with the Serbs against Croatia, and in Abkhazia against Georgia.[23]

Extreme Russian nationalists such as Vladimir Zhirinovsky, Aleksandr Rutskoi, Vladimir Barkashov, and Aleksandr Prokhanov have made pilgrimages to the area. The political support in Moscow for the Dniestr Republic, however, can be found beyond the nationalist camp. "Centrists" like Sergei Stankevich, Oleg Rumiantsev, and Yevgeni Ambartsumov were openly supportive of the region's right to join the Russian Federation. Andrei Kozyrev and Boris Yel'tsin, as well as the Russian liberal media (Ostankino Television Network, *Izvestiya,* and *Komsomol'skaya pravda*), supported these ethnic brethren even after their key role in the October 1993 attempt to overthrow the Yel'tsin administration.[24]

General Aleksandr Lebed', until recently commanding officer of the Fourteenth Army, was brought to Moldova to "install peace." His past as a fierce paratroop commander in Afghanistan and his dubious fame as the Butcher of Baku hardly prepared him for the job. Lebed' repeatedly has called for restoration of the Soviet Union and has attacked both President Yel'tsin and Defense Minister Pavel Grachev. Yet Lebed' apparently enjoys the support of both men despite the fact that his ideology is close to the rebellious leaders of the former legislature of the Russian Federation. He has declared that it would take him seven hours to take Bucharest and three days to reach the Adriatic Sea. He surpassed both Yel'tsin and Grachev in an October 1994 poll of Russian officers as the most popular leader of the armed forces.[25]

In its drive to overthrow Russian reformers, the Dniestr Republic has twice played a crucial and grim role as a hard-line stronghold. It provided support to the putschists in August 1991. Hundreds of fighters from the region converged on Moscow in the beginning of October 1993, participating in bloody attacks on the Moscow mayor's office and the television station, and providing guards and cannon fodder for the hard-liners. If not disbanded, the exclave not only violates Moldovan sovereignty and territorial integrity, but once again may play the role of a reactionary bridgehead.

THE TRAGEDY IN ABKHAZIA

After the collapse of the Soviet Union, post-communist Russia, in a move reminiscent of its bolshevik predecessor in 1920, decided to recapture the Transcaucasus and deny its peoples independence. For centuries this frontier area between Europe and Asia, and between Islam and Christianity, has been a hotbed of ethnic warfare. A large-scale war between the Armenians and Azeri Turks over the enclave of Nagorno-Karabakh has raged since 1988. The Soviet central regime and later the Russian leadership were either unwilling or unable to stop this conflict. The wars between the Georgians and the Abkhaz, as well as the civil war in Georgia between supporters of democratically elected nationalist president Zviad Gamsakhurdia and his opponents, had a much higher degree of Russian overt and covert involvement than did the Karabakh conflict.

Before the war, the population of the Abkhaz Autonomous Republic (legally a part of Georgia) numbered some 537,500 persons, with the ethnic Abkhaz comprising only 17.8 percent of the inhabitants of "their" autonomy. The plurality of the population was Georgian (45.7 percent), with Russians and Armenians numbering 16 and 15 percent, respectively. Abkhazia was under the rule of the Ottoman Empire from the sixteenth century, and was annexed to the Russian Empire in the nineteenth century. It was part of independent Georgia in 1918–21, and a union republic (but also part of the Georgian SSR) until 1931.[26] Abkhazia contains desirable stretches of Black Sea coast, monopolized by dachas of former Soviet leaders and military rest homes.

In 1978, the Abkhaz began an unsuccessful campaign to secede from Georgia and join the Russian Federation. On July 23, 1992, the Abkhaz Supreme Soviet suspended the autonomous republic's 1978 constitution and voted that the Abkhaz constitution of 1925, which declared Abkhazia a sovereign state, was in force.[27] On numerous occasions, the irredentist leaders of Abkhazia, led by the chairman of the Abkhaz Supreme Soviet, historian Vladislav Ardzinba, declared their intent to join Russia. Promises of prize real estate, including former Soviet Army rest homes and sanitaria, were generously doled out to the Russian generals in exchange for military support. Ardzinba was successful in securing assistance from hard-line leaders in Moscow such as Ruslan Khasbulatov and Aleksandr Rutskoi, as well as the generals of the defense ministry and senior Yel'tsin administration officials. Boris Pastukhov, the Russian Deputy Foreign Minister and Moscow's envoy, told the Georgian government in Tbilisi, "We will not let you win the war in Abkhazia."[28]

Ardzinba skillfully put together a coalition against Georgia's President Eduard Shevardnadze, including the Caucasus Mountain Moslem Confederation, the Russian military, "zviadist" Georgians, Cossacks, and the Pridniestrovye government. This diverse support is seen as stemming from hatred of former Soviet Foreign Minister Shevardnadze, who is viewed by Russian nationalists as one of the main "culprits" in the collapse of the Soviet Empire in Eastern Europe and within the USSR.

The bitter year-long war in Abkhazia, which claimed over 35,000 lives, was precipitated by Russian military involvement authorized by Defense Minister Grachev. The few Abkhaz separatists (numbering a mere 90,000 out of Abkhazia's population of more than 500,000) could never have created a modern fighting force of their own. The poorly trained and inadequately equipped Georgians were faced with Russian-supplied tanks, artillery, and modern communications equipment.

Russian pilots from bases in the North Caucasus military district flew sorties for the Abkhaz, and some were shot down by the Georgian troops. The Black Sea Navy shelled Georgian units in Abkhazia.[29] Cossacks from the Don region, well-paid "volunteers" from the hard-line Dniestr Republic, and bands of Chechen fighters allegedly connected to then Russian Supreme Soviet chairman Ruslan Khasbulatov fought against Shevardnadze's forces. In addition, Gamsakhurdia's personal friendship with the leader of Chechnya, General Dzhokhar Dudayev, secured the participation of a large (Moslem) Chechen force in the attack upon (Christian) Georgia. (Late in 1994, Dudayev received Russia's thanks for helping to subdue Georgia—in the form of Russian bombs on his capital, Grozny.) Conducting such a complex military operation required logistical and communications sophistication that only the Russian army possessed.

The cease-fire brokered by Pavel Grachev in August 1993 and guaranteed by Russia was immediately breached by the Abkhaz separatists and their Russian military supporters. The Georgians were duped. Russian "peacemakers" evacuated the Georgian force, including heavy equipment, to the port of Poti, south of Sukhumi, rendering the latter city defenseless. Immediately thereafter, the Russians returned to the Abkhaz rebels heavy artillery, which was being guarded by the Russians as part of their "peacekeeping duty." A parachute brigade, stationed in Abkhazia as a part of a "peacemaking" agreement, refused to intervene to stop the Abkhaz assault. After Shevardnadze called Grachev in desperation and asked him to stop the war, Grachev offered to introduce three Russian divisions numbering 30,000 troops, but Shevardnadze refused. As a result, Sukhumi, known as one of pearls of the Black Sea, fell into rebel hands, and 240,000 ethnic Georgian (and some Abkhaz) refugees were forced from their dwellings and left wandering in the snowy Caucasus Mountains, threatened by starvation.

From 1991 through the end of 1993 Georgia was in the midst of a bloody civil war that pitted supporters of President Shevardnadze and followers of ousted President Gamsakhurdia against each other. Political violence became chronic. Even after his victory over Gamsakhurdia, Shevardnadze's authority was challenged by politicians, warlords and militias, despite his victory in the October 1992 parliamentary elections. After Georgia's rout in Abkhazia in September 1993, Gamsakhurdia returned from exile in the neighboring republic of Chechnya to his political stronghold in western Georgia, and captured the key Black Sea port of Poti.

Moscow had orchestrated a media campaign against the autocratic Gamsakhurdia soon after his election in 1991. After Russia had engineered the fall of Sukhumi, it suddenly threw its support behind Shevardnadze, providing the crucial four T-72 tanks that defeated Gamsakhurdia's ragtag militia. In exchange, Shevardnadze was finally forced to join the CIS, a step he had previously bitterly opposed. When he attempted to read his press release announcing this step, Russian diplomats took it out of Shevardnadze's hands and gave him a Moscow-authored text to read. A defeated Gamsakhurdia died under mysterious circumstances at the end of 1993.

OSSETIA, INGUSHETIA, CHECHNYA

Another conflict—between Georgia and Ossetian separatists—has been on ice since a cease-fire in the spring of 1992. The residents of South Ossetia, which is part of Georgia, want to unite with their ethnic kin in the North Ossetian autonomous republic, which is part of the Russian Federation. The South Ossetians were supported by local Russian military commanders, who bear a grudge against the Georgians.

In the Russian Federation proper, the Ingush people, exiled by Stalin in 1944 and returned to the Northern Caucasus in 1956, claim a tract of land called Prigorodny Rayon, which was transferred to North Ossetia. Russian Deputy Premier Viktor Polyanichko and a Russian general were murdered in the area in late July 1993.

Recent events in the neighboring republic of Chechnya are too well-known to require much elaboration. Moscow sought over many months to subvert Chechnya's separatist government and to control the oil fields around Grozny. Russia created and supported diffuse centers of power in Chechnya to compete with President Dzhokhar Dudayev.[30] Russian weapons, including tanks, artillery and helicopters, were supplied to anti-Dudayev clan militias. Russian pilots flew sorties for the "opposition," and Russian "volunteers" were captured by the government troops.

The desperate Dudayev administration in Grozny, fighting for its physical survival, attempted to woo radical Islamic elements throughout the Middle East and Central Asia. In December 1994, when covert efforts to overthrow Dudayev failed, Yel'tsin suddenly resorted to a full-scale military assault upon Chechnya, with results that were dismal for the reputation of Russia's armed forces, for the lives of many thousands of Chechen civilians, and for Yel'tsin's own authority and popularity. It is too soon to assess the long-term effects.

THE KARABAKH CONFLICT

Populated by Armenians, Nagorno-Karabakh was put under Azerbaijan's jurisdiction in 1921, after Stalin negotiated a treaty in the Transcaucasus between communist Russia and Turkey. The strife between Armenians and (Turkic) Azeris escalated in 1988, and full-scale war broke out in 1992. Today, Karabakh is a self-proclaimed republic. Its battles are fought primarily by independent Karabakh forces, rather than by the Armenian army. Thus far, Azerbaijani political and military leadership has been poor. Baku has seen three changes of regime and had six defense ministers, losing one-fifth of its territory since the collapse of the Soviet Union.

Moscow has intermittently supported the Armenians, yet there are also reports of large-scale Russian weapons supplies to Azerbaijan. Russia suggested that it become a guarantor of peace in the region, but the idea of a "Pax Russica" was resisted by the other CSCE powers.[31] Under Russian pressure, oil-rich Azerbaijan joined the CIS. Moscow, until recently, was adamantly against allowing the CSCE to send peacekeepers to the region, attempting to secure an exclusive "peacemaking" role for itself in the conflict. However, under Western pressure it agreed to a multilateral force for Karabakh.

In 1993 Russia threatened to engage the Turkish army if it attacked Armenia, and Turkish and Russian troops exchanged fire on the Turkish-Armenian border. Russia and Iran are increasingly cooperating to keep Turkey and the West out of the region. However, the intransigence on the part of the Karabakh Armenians, the Azerbaijani government, and Russia frustrates a coordinated attempt by the CSCE to end the war.

AZERBAIJAN

Turkey supported Azerbaijan's democratically elected president Abulfaz Elchibey until he was overthrown in June 1993 by former KGB general and Brezhnev Politburo member Geidar Aliev, who later became president with 98.5 percent of the popular vote. Suret Huseinov, a warlord who enjoys good relations with the Russian military, and especially with Russian Defense Minister Pavel Grachev, was a key player in ousting Elchibey and engineering Aliev's return.[32] In September 1994, President Aliev and Huseinov (then prime minister) parted ways. A failed putsch attempt by Huseinov led to his ouster and arrest, and to a massive purge of his supporters. Two vice prime ministers, as well as the ministers of agriculture and security (relatives of the prime minister), were fired. Huseinov fled the country and currently resides in Russia.

The turmoil in oil-rich Azerbaijan is occurring against the backdrop of Azerbaijani defeat on the battlefields of Karabakh. Also at issue is the signing of a $6 billion Caspian Sea shelf petroleum deal between Azerbaijan and a consortium of large international oil companies. This deal was facilitated first by Elchibey and later by Geidar Aliev. Initially, it was planned that a pipeline from the Caspian Sea would extend to the Turkish port of Yumurtalik in the eastern Mediterranean.

According to Azerbaijani sources, Suret Huseinov was supported
by the Russian military and oil interests opposing the deal.[33] While the
Russian oil company Lukoil was part of the international consortium, other Russian oil interests felt excluded. Both the Russian foreign ministry and the
Russian defense ministry came out squarely against the deal. Moreover, Russia
attempted to reclassify the Caspian Sea as a lake, so that Moscow could
extend its jurisdiction beyond the 12-mile economic zone to which it is entitled according to international law.

Russia considered Aliev's policies too independent and supported
Huseinov in order to destabilize the country and torpedo the oil contract. As
in Chechnya, Georgia, and Tajikistan, an alternative power center was created with Russian support to challenge the central government. Azerbaijan
was supposed to recognize Russia's role as the chief peacekeeper and agree
to the posting of Russian border guards on the Azerbaijani-Iranian and
Azerbaijani-Turkish borders. It was planned that Huseinov eventually would
facilitate the return of the pro-Russian former first secretary of the Azerbaijani
Communist Party, Ayaz Mutalibov, as Azeri president.[34]

CENTRAL ASIA

The conflict in Tajikistan began brewing in November 1991, when hard-line
communists, led by the first secretary of the Brezhnevite Tajik Communist
Party, Rakhmon Nabiev, declared him winner in the Tajik presidential elections. A full-scale civil war in the mountainous republic broke out in June
1992. Neighboring Uzbekistan and former Soviet troops supported the pro-Russian communist hard-liners who controlled the government in Dushanbe.
The pro-Moscow politicians came from the clans traditionally associated
with the Soviet regime. Their main group was based in Khodzhent (Leninabad)
in the north, and led by Nabiev. A southern clan from the city of Kulyab
supplied most of the country's military leaders, many of whom were convicted criminals. The current leader of Dushanbe's pro-Russian government,
a Kulyabi named Imomali Rakhmonov (former chairman of the Tajik Supreme Soviet), was declared winner of the presidential election held on November 6, 1994. He was supported by the Russian military against a
Khodzhenti, Abdumalik Abdullodzhanov, a former prime minister and candidate endorsed by the Russian foreign ministry.

In 1992, the opposition consisted of the intellectuals in Dushanbe, the capital, led by a famous filmmaker, Davlat Khudonazarov, Sunni Moslem clergy led
by Hodzhi Akbar Turandzhonzoda, Ismaili tribes of the Pamir mountains, the
Garm clans from the center of the republic, and the southern clans of Kurgan-Tyube. Major atrocities were committed by both sides. Close to half a million
refugees fled across the former Soviet border into Afghanistan.[35]

Moscow supplied a Russian officer, Colonel Aleksandr Shishlyannikov, to serve as Dushanbe's minister of defense (but he is outranked by the Russian commander of the CIS troops in Tajikistan and is often not consulted on key issues). While the greatly expanded 201st Russian motorized division has supported the Tajik authorities, the opposition was at first reluctant to request assistance from the fundamentalist groups in neighboring Afghanistan. However, relentless pursuit and atrocities by the Dushanbe government forced the Tajik opposition to solicit help from Islamic fundamentalists in Afghanistan, Iran, and Pakistan. These links were facilitated by the fact that large numbers of ethnic Tajiks live in Afghanistan, and that the Iranians and Tajiks speak essentially the same language.

Russia, while militarily supporting the Dushanbe government, is currently advocating a political solution to this war. Russia, Afghanistan, Uzbekistan, the Islamic guerrillas, and Pakistan have expressed willingness to participate in peace talks. But the Tajik hard-liners in Dushanbe, led by president Rakhmonov, refuse to negotiate.

The "Lebanonization" of the CIS southern frontiers dates back to July 13, 1993, when 25 Russian guards on the Tajik-Afghan border were killed. The attack was launched by Tajik Moslem guerrillas (*mujaheddin*) operating from Afghanistan. In July 1993, Yel'tsin announced that the Tajik border with Afghanistan was effectively Russian, increasing Russia's military force there from 15,000 to almost 20,000. Raids into the Afghan territory were undertaken, but could not resolve the situation militarily. As with Afghanistan, the Russians are risking a costly long-term involvement.[36]

Tajikistan is falling apart. Military hostilities continue in the Pamir mountains. The Gorno-Badakhshan, Leninabad, and Gissar regions are distancing themselves from the government in Dushanbe. As mentioned earlier, different official institutions in Russia and Uzbekistan supported two rival presidential candidates, neither of whom was acceptable to the opposition. To date, the military pressure of Russian and opposition forces, as well as a slow diplomatic process, are part of the scene.[37]

The war in Tajikistan is the central conflict in the area. However, several potential confrontations in this region lie relatively dormant, waiting to be exploited when the time is deemed opportune. There are irredentist claims on the part of Russian minorities in northern Kazakhstan, clan tensions in Kyrgyzstan, and the Tajik territorial claims against the Uzbeks, especially regarding the historic cities of Bukhara and Samarkand.

PEACEKEEPING

Currently, "peacemaking" and "peacekeeping" in the southern tier are dominated by Russia. Moscow played a key role in exacerbating the conflicts by identifying the pro-Russian party and supporting it, while later marching in with the peacemaking contingent. The West, especially the CSCE countries, which, since 1992, have failed to supply ample peacekeeping troops for the conflict zones, cannot be absolved entirely from blame. Western countries have argued, sometimes convincingly, that peacekeeping is possible only when all warring factions are ready to end hostilities and are asking for a neutral force to step in, which has not often been the case in Eurasia.

The current peacekeeping force of 1,500 in Pridniestrovye is jointly administered by Russia, Moldova, and Pridniestrovye, and costs about $40 million per year. Moldova has requested that the UN and the CSCE play a role in the conflict. For three years, Russia refused to commit to a timetable to withdraw its forces, and currently promises to withdraw the Fourteenth Army "three years after the political solution of the conflict," which is hardly in sight.

The trilateral observer force in Abkhazia consists of about 500 Russian, Georgian, and Abkhazian soldiers. The current cost of the operation is estimated at $30 million per year. The CSCE has sent fact-finding missions and several observers into the area. In South Ossetia the cease-fire is administered by a Russian-Georgian-Ossetian peacekeeping force of about 500. The estimated cost of the force is $15 million per year. Intermittent negotiations were conducted to place this force under the authority of the CSCE. The CSCE also has sent a fact-finding mission to Karabakh. A proposed CSCE observer force would be 2,000- to 3,000-strong, and would cost $200 million per year to operate. So far, Russia, Italy, and Turkey have promised participation in this contingent.

Russia has requested that a 2,000-strong joint CIS peacekeeping force be dispatched to Tajikistan at the cost of $200 million per year. Moscow also suggested that the UN cover these costs, which is unrealistic, considering the financial strain on UN peacekeeping operations elsewhere. The UN was also asked to provide peacekeepers. While 150 were promised, the UN planned to send only 10 into the area during the fall of 1994. Finally, only an OSCE mediator arrived.

CONCLUSION

If the international community does not demand that Russia stop its overt and covert interference in the internal affairs of the newly independent states, Moscow will continue its attempts to install "Pax Russica" in the southern tier of the former Soviet Union. Russia should allow for CSCE and UN participation in peacekeeping efforts. At the same time these organizations must be ready to offer ample resources to undertake the challenging tasks the region is facing. Otherwise, Russia will continue playing the central role in the area's peacemaking efforts aimed at conflicts that are, in part, of its own fabrication.

Moscow's support of the Dniestr Republic indicates how strong the Greater Russian and imperialist elements in the Russian central foreign policy and military bureaucracies really are. Despite the active role the Dniestr

Russian fighters played in both the hard-line coup attempts to date, the Yel'tsin administration continues to tolerate and support their separatist exclave. The importance of the Transdniestr region is also defined by the geopolitics of a Russian presence in the gateway to the Balkans.

The wars in the Transcaucasus should be viewed in light of the increasing struggle for Russian control of Azerbaijan's oil reserves and the Black Sea coast. The growing destabilization of the Transcaucasus and the active involvement of Iran are definitely not in the West's or America's interests. The inability of Turkey to sustain a pro-Western influence in the Caucasus makes American participation in the search for solutions especially urgent.

Russia, by assaulting the Chechen government and the Islamic opposition in Tajikistan, may trigger further deterioration on its southern borders, making the area part of the global Islamic anti-Christian and anti-Western crusade. The Tajik war is complicated by the presence in Tajikistan of 300,000 Russian settlers. Moscow is concerned that if the Russian troops leave, Uzbekistan and Kyrgyzstan—with their population of 1.5 million Russians[38]—could become destabilized, creating an unbearable refugee problem for Russia. Still, current Russian policies, which serve only to exacerbate the conflict and activate the Islamic fundamentalist factor, may bring about the same result.

The Russian political elites have not risen above the imperialist ideology that inspired both pre-1917 and Soviet expansionism. In every case examined in this chapter, the Russian leadership has identified and supported the most pro-Moscow faction, be it the Transdniestrian ethnic Russians, the separatist Abkhaz, the Huseinovs and the Mutalibovs of Azerbaijan, or the pro-communist clans in Tajikistan.

Competing political interests often prompt local elites to challenge the faction in power and to seek Moscow's support. Russian military commanders and industrial chieftains on the ground are also interested in the continuation of links with the metropolis. This is a classic scenario for imperial expansion. What is common to all these instances is that, without Russian support, the pro-Moscow faction could not have dominated its respective region, and would have been forced to seek a negotiated and peaceful solution to conflict.

NOTES

1. For an excellent account of the early Soviet nationality policy, see Frantisek Silnicky, *Natsional'naya Politika KPSS (1917-1922)* (Washington, D.C.: Problems of Eastern Europe, 1990). Unless noted otherwise, all translations are by the author.

2. For a thorough analysis of the Soviet imperial collapse, see Ariel Cohen,

"The End of Empire: Russian and Soviet Imperial Development and Decline," (Ph.D. diss., The Fletcher School of Law and Diplomacy, Tufts University, 1993).

3. Ibid., chapter 1.

4. Nikolai Ryzhkov, "Kompass istorii snova ukazyvayet na Soyuz" (Compass of History Once Again Points Towards the Union), *Pravda* (Moscow), 28 September 1994, p. 1.

5. Aleksandr Solzhenitsyn, speech to the Duma, *Radio Free Europe/Radio Liberty Media Monitoring,* 28 October 1994.

6. Sergei Blagovolin, presentation at the National Defense University, Washington, D.C., June 1994.

7. Andrei Kozyrev in *Radio Free Europe/Radio Liberty Daily Report,* 22 November 1994.

8. Ibid.

9. *Radio Free Europe/Radio Liberty Daily Report,* 7 November 1994.

10. *Radio Free Europe/Radio Liberty Daily Report,* 22 November 1994.

11. *Radio Free Europe/Radio Liberty Daily Report,* 5 October 1994.

12. Author's interviews, Moscow, Tallin, Riga, June-July 1993, and Moscow, February and May 1994.

13. Yegor Gaidar gave the Belarus' affair as one of the reasons for his resignation. The Donbass was cited by him as another example of an "industrial albatross" that Russia should not hang on her neck.

14. Author's interviews with economic experts involved in the critique of the CIS integration proposals, Moscow, May-June 1994.

15. Uri Ra'anan, "Russia's New Doctrines and Operations," presentation at the conference "Russia: A Return to Imperialism?" Boston University, 9 November 1994.

16. Victor Yasman, "New Ideology Impacts on the Role of Military and Security in Foreign Policy," manuscript, Summer 1994, pp. 9-10. The specialists are Maj.-Gen. German Kirilenko of the Faculty of Strategy, General Staff Academy, and Col. Dmitrii Trenin of the Institute of Europe. First publication appeared in Zhirinovsky's *Liberal* (Moscow), nos. 8-9, 1992.

17. Ibid., p. 9.

18. Author's interviews with Arkady Dubnov, ethnic conflict correspondent for *New Times,* June 1993. Reportedly, Suret Guseinov, the warlord who led the revolt, is married to the daughter of a Russian general.

19. *Rossiya-SNG: Nuzhdayetsia li v korrektirovke pozitsia zapada* (Moscow: Sluzhba Vneshnei Razvedki Rossiyskoy Federatsii, 1994).

20. Ibid., pp. 4-6.

21. Ibid., pp. 8-10. "Creation of a unified economic space in the CIS is practically the only way to reduce tensions in inter-state relations because . . . 25 million Russians and the so-called Russian-speaking population . . . remain beyond the borders of Russia." Here the SVRR is threatening to utilize the Russian residents of uncooperative CIS states to destabilize them.

22. Another ethnic minority in Moldova, the Christian Turkish-speaking Gagauz, also gained the support of the Russian Federation. They claimed independence from Moldova and expressed willingness to join the Russian Federation.

23. Vladimir Socor, "Dniester Involvement in the Moscow Rebellion," *RFE/RL Research Report,* 19 November 1993, p. 25.

24. Vladimir Socor, "Moldova's 'Dniester' Ulcer," *RFE/RL Research Report,* vol. 2, no. 1, 1 January 1993, p. 15.

25. Lebed' is repeatedly mentioned as a presidential candidate capable of taking on both Yel'tsin and Zhirinovsky.

26. Elizabeth Fuller, "Abkhazia on the Brink of Civil War," *Radio Free Europe/Radio Liberty Weekly Report,* 4 September 1992, p. 3.

27. Ibid.

28. Akaky Mikadze, "Peace Remains a Distant Hope in Georgia," *Moscow News,* 23-29 September 1994, p. 4.

29. Author's interviews with Eduard Shevardnadze's national security advisors and Georgian parliamentary delegation, Washington, D.C., September-December 1993. Russian television monitoring, August-September 1993.

30. Author's interview with one of President Yel'tsin's advisors who asked to remain anonymous.

31. "Ethnic Violence in Transcaucasia," Hearing before the Conference on Security and Cooperation in Europe, 103 Congress, 8 March 1993, p. 8. Testimony of Ambassador Maresca, US Department of State.

32. Huseinov's patron was the former Azerbaijani defense minister Rahim Gaziev, closely connected to Grachev. Elizabeth Fuller, "Azerbaijan's June Revolution," *RFE/RL Research Report,* 13 August 1993, p. 27.

33. El'mira Akhundova, "I neft tomu prichinoi?" (And Oil is the Reason for It?), *Literaturnaya gazeta* (Moscow), 10 October 1994, p. 7.

34. Ibid. Also see Igor Rotar', "Bal pravit chelovek s ruzhyem" (A Man with a Gun is in Charge of the Ball), *Komsomol'skaya pravda* (Moscow), 19 October 1994, p. 4.

35. Some Tajik refugees were so ignorant of events that they asked a journalist,

"Why doesn't the Politburo in Moscow meet and do something about it?" They did not realize that the USSR had collapsed.

36. There was little, if any, debate in the Russian Supreme Soviet as to the goals, strategy, costs, and legality of this war. The situation in the Duma has not improved. Due to insufficient civilian control, the military executes an autonomous policy in Tajikistan, often competing with other branches of the Russian government, such as the Border Forces and the foreign ministry.

37. Sanobar Shermatova, "Tajikistan Elections Threaten Uncertainty," *Moscow News,* 7-13 October 1994, p. 13.

38. These population totals are steadily diminishing because of an outflow of Russian refugees and migrants.

6

NATO, Russia, and East European Security

Mark Kramer

This chapter will discuss the relationship between NATO and the East European countries that formerly belonged to the Warsaw Pact. The focus will be on the four members of the so-called Visegrad Group—Hungary, Poland, the Czech Republic, and Slovakia—which are the most likely candidates for future admission into NATO.[1] Some references to Bulgaria and Romania, and also to the three Baltic States (Latvia, Lithuania, and Estonia), will be included as well. Rather than simply dwelling on transient events, the chapter will place the recent debate about NATO and Eastern Europe into a broader historical perspective. It also will explore the various political and military issues that are likely to determine where the debate eventually leads.

THE EMERGENCE OF A SECURITY VACUUM, 1990–91

The collapse of communism in East Europe, the dissolution of the Warsaw Pact, and the demise of the Soviet Union removed the security framework that had been imposed on Eastern Europe for some 45 years. As auspicious as all those developments may have been, they left the region in a kind of security vacuum. The end of Soviet hegemony in Eastern Europe eliminated the chief source of the region's periodic crises in the post-war era, but other dangers soon emerged. The new East European governments found themselves having to contend with a number of serious threats without the benefit of a security framework to replace the one that had collapsed.

Initially, the most salient of the threats confronting the new East European regimes was the continued uncertainty about the political future of the Soviet Union. Even before the reformist trends in Moscow turned sour in late 1990 and early 1991, apprehension about Soviet political developments was readily apparent in most of the East European states. Hungarian Foreign Minister Géza Jeszensky consistently warned in 1990 that events could take a sharp turn for the worse in the Soviet Union, and that any such reversal would have ominous implications for the Warsaw Pact countries:

> Only recently has the Soviet Union become a trustworthy partner in efforts to truly liberate the Hungarian people.... But there are different trends in Moscow and they are in conflict with one another.... Our major problem is that it is difficult to predict the direction of processes in the Soviet Union.[2]

Polish officials had begun to speak in even gloomier terms by mid-1990 about "the threat of a conservative overthrow" in Moscow, which would cause

> the USSR to disintegrate into parts that would not only be riven by *internal* conflicts, but would also be prone to unleash some sort of *external* conflict, if only to provide the population with easy victories and conquests. [We cannot] assume there will automatically be peace [with the Soviet Union] in the future."[3]

The concerns expressed by these East European officials took on a new sense of urgency after the abrupt resignation of Soviet Foreign Minister Eduard Shevardnadze in December 1990, coupled with his warnings about "reactionary" elements who were pushing the Soviet Union toward a new "dictatorship."[4] This sense of urgency was heightened still further by the violent crackdown in the Baltic republics in January 1991, which prompted all the East European governments to condemn the Soviet Union and to threaten to withdraw immediately from the Warsaw Pact. (The Pact was not due to be abolished formally until July 1991.) A top aide to Polish President Lech Wałęsa warned at the time that the Polish government could "no longer rule out the possibility that Russian generals are thinking about regaining Eastern Europe."[5] Although most East European officials assumed that the Soviet High Command had grudgingly come to accept the demise of the Warsaw Pact, many were still uneasy about what would happen if the Soviet armed forces acquired a larger political role or, worse yet, launched a coup. Even the then Polish foreign minister, Krzysztof Skubiszewski, who had tried to defuse the most extreme speculation about Soviet policy in the region, admitted to a few misgivings about "the Soviet Army's Stalinist desire to win back territory, expand Soviet borders, and regain a military presence" in central Europe.[6]

In addition to concerns about a hard-line backlash in Moscow, the widespread feelings of uncertainty that followed the collapse of the Warsaw Pact induced all the East European governments to look for new security arrangements. The general perception, as voiced by the then Polish deputy defense minister, Janusz Onyszkiewicz, was that "we do not know what is going to happen in our part of the world once the straitjacket of the Soviet Army is removed."[7] In the days when the East European countries were strictly subordinated to Soviet control, the Soviet Union could set the whole political agenda for the region. Territorial and other disputes that were so common before 1945, such as those between Poland and Germany, Hungary and Romania, and Bulgaria and Romania, as well as the general phenomenon of "balkanization," ceased to be as important in an era of Soviet domination. But once Soviet hegemony was gone, most East European officials assumed that long-submerged tensions and conflicts would surface more easily, perhaps culminating in outright hostilities between two or more countries. Hungarian defense minister Lajos Für was among those who expressed this view:

> Aggressive reflexes have not disappeared from the European countries of various development levels. Unfortunately, wars have always been part of the human struggle for existence. . . . Eternal peace would be a good thing, but I do not believe in it, and I do not trust the infallible politicians who say that a lasting and holy peace will soon emerge in Europe.[8]

The particular concern among most officials was the possible spread of ethnic violence, which, they feared, might spill over into other countries or provoke outside intervention. Their fears seemed to be borne out by the escalating war in Yugoslavia in the spring and summer of 1991, when all the surrounding states put their military forces on high alert and Austria mobilized some 10,000 troops and dozens of combat aircraft to contain the fighting. Officials in the region were concerned that the situation might eventually induce most of the Balkan states to reopen their long-standing disputes over boundaries and the status of ethnic minorities.

The impending disintegration of the Soviet Union in 1991 raised further anxiety among officials in Poland, Hungary, and Czechoslovakia, who feared that newly independent republics might press irredentist claims. The concern expressed by a senior Polish military officer in late 1990 that the "current nationalist trends in Ukraine and Lithuania" might someday prompt one or both of those republics "to challenge [Poland's] eastern border" was indicative of this line of thought.[9] Indeed, the "possibility that territorial claims will be made against Poland by its neighbors or that nationality clashes will emerge in connection with national minorities and chauvinist groups in neighboring states" was taken seriously enough at the time by top Polish officials that they openly warned it could lead to "the involvement of our country in an armed conflict, and even in a war."[10]

In short, there were enough potential dangers around after 1989 to support the Hungarian government's contention that the "security situation [in East-Central Europe] is not firm enough" in the "completely new situation that is emerging."[11] Fears of a large-scale East-West war in Europe all but disappeared, but many East European officials believed that a series of smaller conflicts, over time, could be nearly as detrimental to European security. The end result, as Václav Havel put it in the spring of 1991, could be "chaos or even worse."[12] Although many officials initially hoped to contend with future security threats by relying on a pan-European organization like the CSCE, those hopes proved to be illusory.[13] All the East European governments soon realized that the use of the CSCE for most security functions would be viable only in the longer term, if ever. In the interim, some other arrangement was deemed essential to fill what top East European officials described as the "military vacuum" and "deep political void" created by the disintegration of the Warsaw Pact.

THE INCEPTION OF THE VISEGRAD GROUP

One option that Polish leaders tried to promote was a form of sub-regional security cooperation among Poland, Hungary, and the former Czechoslovakia. Polish officials even spoke hopefully about the possible establishment of an "organized alliance" over the longer term.[14] In April 1990 the leaders of the three (later four) countries held preliminary discussions at Bratislava, but those discussions were almost entirely symbolic and had no specific agenda. Five months later, the deputy foreign and defense ministers from the three sides met near the Czechoslovak-Polish border, in Zakopane, to consider the idea of a trilateral security framework. That session was followed in November 1990 by a higher-level meeting in Budapest, and by another gathering of the deputy foreign ministers in Prague in late December 1990. A fifth session, involving the foreign ministers of the three countries, took place in Budapest in mid-January 1991, and a climactic sixth meeting, which brought together the presidents and prime ministers of the three states, was held in the Hungarian city of Visegrad the following month.[15] That session marked the true beginning of what came to be known as the "Visegrad Triangle" (and then the "Visegrad Group" after the split of Czechoslovakia).

Shortly before the Visegrad summit, Bulgarian and Romanian officials expressed interest in joining a sub-regional organization if one were formed by the other three countries.[16] The Romanian overtures were promptly rebuffed by the Visegrad participants (led by Hungary), but the Bulgarian request encountered a somewhat more favorable response. Even so, Bulgarian leaders were too optimistic in concluding that "the 'troika' will eventually expand and become a 'group of four'."[17] The Visegrad participants were all well aware that trilateral cooperation on issues such as military strategy, defense planning, and weapons procurement would be difficult enough without bringing in other East European countries whose political stability and economic status were problematic at best.

Indeed, it soon became clear that even with the participation of just Poland, Hungary, and Czechoslovakia, no multilateral security arrangement was going to emerge. Although Hungarian leaders acknowledged the desirability of "some kind of closer [military] cooperation among the three countries when some kind of identity of interests can be shown," they were reluctant to undertake any major commitment, for fear that Poland would try to make the organization into an anti-German coalition.[18] To be sure, both Hungary and Czechoslovakia later displayed some interest in pursuing military cooperation with Poland, including joint air defense efforts and the possibility of a sub-regional military consultative group.[19] The appeal of such an arrangement increased as the domestic situation in the Soviet Union grew more turbulent. Moreover, the Hungarian and Czechoslovak governments signed a bilateral military treaty in January 1991, and both of them subsequently concluded similar bilateral treaties with Poland.[20] The three states also began joint air defense operations in early 1991 to make up for the integrated air-defense network they had formerly shared with the Soviet Union.[21]

Nevertheless, the Polish government's hopes of taking these arrangements much further by forming a full-fledged security organization went unfulfilled. The bilateral military agreements that the three states signed were limited in scope and contained no provisions for automatic assistance in the event of an attack. Moreover, at no point did either Hungary or Czechoslovakia express interest in merging the treaties into a broad, trilateral military agreement, much less a quadrilateral pact with both Poland and Bulgaria, or a pentagonal arrangement that included Romania as well. On the contrary, Czechoslovak and Hungarian leaders said explicitly at the time that they did not intend to form a "new alliance" or "bloc" at the sub-regional level.[22] Even Polish officials eventually conceded that it was premature to "conclude a military alliance," though they still hoped to "formulate a common approach to questions of security and regional stability."[23]

A further obstacle to military cooperation among the Visegrad countries came, ironically enough, when the Soviet Union broke apart. This development seemed to eliminate, or at least mitigate, the most exigent threat to the East European states, and hence it removed the main incentive for pursuing joint military efforts in the first place. Most East European officials argued that it made far more sense, in those circumstances, to press for membership in NATO rather than trying to make the Visegrad framework into a quasi-alliance.[24] The efficacy of the Visegrad arrangement was also attenuated by the split of Czechoslovakia. Under the leadership of Václav Klaus, the Czech government was wary of developing close ties with the other Visegrad countries, for fear of being held back in its drive to obtain membership in the European Community (now renamed the European Union) and NATO. The Czech Republic's shift after 1992 toward a "go-it-alone" approach did not obviate the prospects of sub-regional military cooperation altogether, but it certainly cast doubt on the longevity of the Visegrad Group.

Thus, even though officials in Hungary, Poland, the Czech Republic, and Slovakia were still concerned about the security vacuum in East-Central Europe, they all had concluded by 1994 that the only way to fill that vacuum was through an extension of NATO, not through the creation of a mini-alliance system.[25] This judgment was especially compelling in light of the military forces deployed by the Visegrad states. Even if the four governments had committed themselves wholeheartedly to a separate military alliance, their combined armies would have been unable to handle anything except relatively low-level threats (see Chart 1). Under the limits imposed by the Conventional Forces in Europe (CFE) Treaty signed in November 1990, the combined military strength of the then three Visegrad states was infinitesimal compared to the Soviet armed forces. This disparity was mitigated somewhat by the dissolution of the Soviet Union, but even now the Polish, Hungarian, Czech, and Slovak armies combined are still dwarfed by the Russian army (not to mention the Russian, Ukrainian, and Belarusian armed forces together).

The disproportion in Moscow's favor is even greater than it may seem, because the Russian Army has tens of thousands of weapons deployed east of the Urals that are not covered by CFE. Most of those weapons were initially relocated there by the Soviet government in 1990 to ensure that they would be exempt from the treaty's limits.[26] If a severe crisis were to erupt in Europe, much of this equipment could be shifted back to western Russia to augment Russian ground and air forces. The weaponry located east of the Urals thus could vastly magnify the force imbalance in East-Central Europe. Although the process of transporting such large amounts of hardware back to Europe would be very costly and might take as long as several months, the redeployments in 1990 showed that the task is eminently feasible.[27] Hence, so long as concern persists about the possible emergence of military dangers "to the east," the Visegrad states will have an incentive to look to the great powers, both inside and outside Europe, for protection.

INITIAL EAST EUROPEAN MOVES TOWARD NATO, 1990–91

Given the lack of satisfactory alternatives, the East European states have looked increasingly to NATO, both implicitly and explicitly, to fill the

Chart 1

ARMED FORCES DEPLOYED IN EUROPE: Russia and the Visegrad Group Countries

CFE Limits and Actual Holdings (12/93)

Country	Manpower		Tanks		ACV		Arty		Attack Hel		Combat Aircraft	
	Holding	Limit	Holding	Limit	Holding	Limit	Holding	Limit	Holding	Limit	Holding	Limit
Russia	1,110,578	1,450,000	7,493	6,400	13,466	11,480	6,069	6,415	954	890	3,921	3,450
Czech Republic	92,893	93,333	1,525	957	2,254	1,367	1,620	767	36	50	265	230
Hungary	75,294	100,000	1,191	835	1,645	1,700	991	810	39	108	171	180
Poland	269,670	234,000	2,515	1,730	2,232	2,150	2,151	1,610	70	130	446	460
Slovakia	54,223	46,667	912	478	1,169	683	931	383	19	25	146	115

NOTE: The limits and holdings for Russia apply only to forces based west of the Urals. Russian forces east of the Urals are not covered by CFE.

SOURCE: International Institute for Strategic Studies, *The Military Balance 1994-1995* (London: IISS, Autumn 1994), p. 267.

(Reprinted by permission of Oxford University Press.)

vacuum left by the Warsaw Pact. Even before the East European govern-ments started openly pursuing full membership in NATO, they set about establishing firm ties with the alliance and with individual member-states. By 1991, exchanges between top East European political and military officials and their Western counterparts had become so frequent and extensive that they rarely drew more than passing notice. Following the visit of the Polish foreign minister, Krzysztof Skubiszewski, to NATO's headquarters in Brus-sels in March 1990, Poland established formal diplomatic contacts with NATO.[28] All the other East European countries promptly followed suit. In addition, a Polish deputy was elected in November 1990 to be a special member of a political commission in the North Atlantic Assembly, the parliamentary body of NATO.[29] This marked the first time that a parlia-mentarian from a non-member state had been formally elected to partici-pate in the Assembly. That same month, a group of Bulgarian legislators and aides paid a special visit to NATO's headquarters in Brussels, where they informed Manfred Wörner, the secretary-general of the alliance, that "Bulgaria is in the process of shifting its foreign policy priorities" in fa-vor of NATO.[30] The extent of this shift became evident in January 1991, when 135 of the 400 members of the Bulgarian parliament, who had formed groups known as "Friends of NATO" *(Priyateli na NATO)* and the "Atlantic Club," sponsored a bill calling for Bulgaria to seek mem-bership in the Western alliance.[31]

Soon thereafter, in March 1991, Václav Havel became the first East European head of state to visit NATO's headquarters; a few weeks later, Lech Wałęsa became the second. During their visits the two presidents expressed strong interest in forging much closer ties with NATO, includ-ing the possibility of formal membership over the longer term if Western countries would agree. Havel emphasized that the alliance "should not be forever closed" to the East European states, and he expressed hope that Czechoslovakia would eventually become a "regular NATO mem-ber" even if it "cannot become one at the moment."[32] Similar comments were made by the Bulgarian prime minister, Dimitur Popov, during his visit to NATO headquarters in April and May 1991. All these political contacts, and numerous others, were indicative of what the Bulgarian foreign minister described as a widespread desire for "new forms of co-operation between [Eastern Europe] and NATO."[33]

Equally noteworthy was the expansion of direct military contacts between the East European countries and the Western alliance. Even before the upheavals of 1989, Hungary tentatively began to establish military-diplomatic exchanges with NATO countries.[34] After 1989, such contacts multiplied exponentially and became much more wide-ranging, not only for Hungary, but for all the East European states. The Hungarian and

Romanian defense ministries began preparing as early as the fall of 1990 to send officers for training at military academies in Great Britain, Germany, France, Italy, and the United States.[35] (The actual training for Hungarian officers began in the fall of 1991.) In turn, officers from those five Western countries were invited to study at military institutions in Hungary and Romania. Poland established similar exchanges with Western military academies, and sought to broaden its military cooperation and "unconventional contacts" with all the major NATO countries.[36] By mid-1991, the Polish government had arranged to send officers to the Royal Naval Academy and Sandhurst military college in Great Britain, to the two main war colleges in France, to a number of Bundeswehr academies in Germany, to West Point and other military colleges in the United States, and to advanced military schools in Italy. Poland also set up exchanges with Austria and with the Higher Land Army Officer School in Sweden.[37]

Czechoslovakia, for its part, arranged to send 20 army officers to Germany's Bundeswehr training academy in Koblenz and a smaller group of officers to the Bundeswehr's university in Neubiberg-Munich.[38] The Czechoslovak government established similar arrangements with other Western countries, including the United States, France, Great Britain, and Italy, and assigned a permanent military representative to NATO. In addition, Czechoslovak leaders proposed formal cooperation with NATO on anti-aircraft defense and civil defense when the chief of NATO's Military Committee, General Vigleik Eide, visited their country in April 1991.[39] Czechoslovakia also sought close bilateral military relations with some of the smaller NATO members, notably Spain, Belgium, and the Netherlands. Bulgaria did the same with Greece, including the signing of a formal pact enabling the two countries to "undertake joint [military] action to remove a threat to peace in the Balkans or to the security of either party."[40] The Bulgarian government also sought cooperative military links with the larger NATO countries, including exchanges and sharing of data with the United States, Britain, Germany, and Italy. The first group of Bulgarian officers to be trained in the United States received full access to military academies and training facilities upon arriving in June 1991. Other Bulgarian officers were enlisted at NATO's own military schools.

Furthermore, virtually all the East European governments began approaching the United States, Germany, Great Britain, and France about the possibility of obtaining weapons and support equipment in the future. By purchasing Western-made arms, they hoped to eliminate, or at least reduce, their logistical dependence on the former Soviet Union and establish greater commonality with NATO. As early as May 1990 the French government expressed tentative support for French-Polish military coproduction ventures, including joint development, engineering, and manufacturing arrangements, as

well as exchanges of technical knowledge. Later that year the French government also indicated its readiness to "set up arms cooperation and sell
military technology" to Hungary.[41] Polish and Hungarian officials received
nearly as favorable a response when they visited the United States, from
which Poland was particularly eager to obtain F-16 fighters.[42] Similar overtures (albeit only of an exploratory nature) were made by the other East
European governments. Despite severe constraints imposed by shortages of
hard currency and lingering export controls, the East European states, by
early 1991, had made clear their desire to shift away from former Soviet
arms manufacturers toward greater ties with the West.

Equally important, the East European governments sought to establish
concrete military cooperation with NATO and to "side with the West" as
much as possible on key international issues.[43] During the Persian Gulf war
in early 1991, all the East European states contributed military personnel
and equipment to the American-led multinational force, in contrast to the
Soviet Union, which refrained from taking part at all.[44] The East European
units were placed under direct American and British command (except for
some personnel primarily under Saudi command), and they served alongside
American soldiers. In addition, several of the East European countries provided use of their air space and air fields to NATO for military purposes
before, during, and after the war. Both Hungary and Czechoslovakia gave
Germany permission to fly combat aircraft over their territory in early 1991,
something that would have been inconceivable when the Warsaw Pact still
existed. Those same two East European countries, plus Bulgaria and Romania, allowed the United States to send many hundreds of military transport
and cargo flights through their air space during the war itself.[45] Hungary also
permitted the American planes to land and refuel at Hungarian air bases.

Poland, for its part, provided crucial intelligence support for the war
effort. Because Polish construction and engineering firms had done extensive work in Iraq for many years, by 1990 Polish officials were able to supply
detailed information about Iraqi military facilities and precise maps of Baghdad
to the United States.[46] Poland also turned over valuable technical data about
Iraq's air defense systems, tanks, fighter aircraft, and other weaponry, which
had been bought mainly from Warsaw Pact countries. Most dramatically of
all, Polish intelligence officials masterminded the escape of six key US intelligence agents who had been inadvertently trapped behind Iraqi lines when
the crisis broke. The success of this operation, as a senior Polish diplomat
later exclaimed, "proved to the Americans that we [in Poland] are a reliable
partner who can carry out sensitive, delicate missions on behalf of the American government."[47]

As significant as all these military links between NATO and the East
European states had become by mid-1991, they were destined to grow both

in number and in scope over the next few years, as the Warsaw Pact and the Soviet Union disappeared from memory.

SOVIET PRESSURE AND EAST EUROPEAN RESISTANCE

The rapid expansion of NATO's political and military ties with Eastern Europe in 1990 and 1991 raised the prospect that one or more of the former Warsaw Pact countries would eventually be ready to move further. Havel had already broached the idea of Czechoslovak membership in NATO during his visit to Brussels in March 1991, and the outgoing Hungarian foreign minister, Gyula Horn, was even more explicit in proposing the same status for Hungary. Other countries soon followed suit.

The growing indications by the first half of 1991 that some or all of the East European states might pursue outright membership in NATO provoked dismay in the Soviet Union, where many officials were still not fully reconciled to the loss of Eastern Europe. (Support in Moscow for a tougher stance vis-à-vis Eastern Europe had been growing in any case after the sudden resignation of Soviet Foreign Minister Eduard Shevardnadze in December 1990.) As early as January 1991, the leadership of the CPSU approved a secret report drafted by the CPSU Central Committee's International Department, which called for "vigorous action to oppose the entry of our former military allies into other military blocs or groupings, above all into NATO—and also possibly into the West European Union (WEU), the nascent military arm of the European Union (EU)—as well as their participation in arrangements that would enable foreign troops to be deployed on their territory."[48] The report, which was published in full in the Central Committee's main journal in March 1991, stressed that "no matter what, these countries *must* remain free of foreign bases and armed forces," and that "under no circumstances must a real or potential threat to the military security of the Soviet Union be permitted to arise in the East European region."[49] Both points were repeated, for special emphasis, in the CPSU leadership's resolution of approval.

These instructions were quickly translated into action. During the first several months of 1991, senior officials from the CPSU International Department published a series of articles in major Soviet newspapers warning of "dire consequences" if the East European states acted in ways "detrimental to vital Soviet interests."[50] Soviet embassies in the Warsaw Pact countries were instructed to bring all such articles to the attention of their host governments. Following up on this campaign, the Soviet leadership tried to conclude a series of bilateral military treaties that would have explicitly committed the East European states "not to participate in a military-political alliance directed against [the Soviet Union], and not to permit a third country to use the transport and telecommunications systems or the infrastructure of one [party to the treaty] against the other."[51] Soviet foreign ministry officials acknowledged that these provisions were intended to prevent the East European countries from joining NATO.[52]

Officials in Hungary, Poland, Czechoslovakia, and Bulgaria immediately rejected the proposed clauses as an "infringement of sovereignty" and an "unacceptable restriction" of their countries' "freedom to choose to join security alliances."[53] Hungarian leaders were particularly insistent that "an approach toward NATO is unavoidable," and that the bilateral agreement with the Soviet Union "must not impede Hungary's gradual integration into the existing Western security systems," especially NATO and the WEU:

> Hungary will not take upon itself to refrain from joining any other organization. NATO and the Western European Union are now changing. . . . The Hungarian-Soviet agreement must not hinder us in negotiating and consulting with these organizations, and in joining them.[54]

Hungarian leaders also warned that if the offending clauses were not omitted, they would abrogate their existing state treaty with the Soviet Union and would refuse to sign a new one because "having no treaty at all is better than concluding a bad one."[55] Hungary's rejection of the Soviet proposal—and the equally firm rejections by Czechoslovakia, Poland, and Bulgaria—demonstrated, as clearly as anything could, the extent of Eastern Europe's realignment following the collapse of the Warsaw Pact.

The only partial exception to this trend was in Romania. Although Romanian officials in 1990 and 1991 praised NATO for its "stabilizing influence" in Central Europe and called for the Western alliance to play a "greater role" in "guaranteeing the security of the whole of Europe," Romania's ties with NATO were inherently limited by the continued political instability and repression under the post-Ceausescu government. The Romanian authorities were therefore less inclined to push for a formal status in the Western alliance. Moreover, in April 1991 Romania agreed, at Soviet behest, to declare that it would not join a "hostile alliance" in the future, a pledge that all the other East European countries had found unacceptable.[56] To be sure, Romanian leaders denied that the pledge was directed against NATO, saying that it referred to "offensive" alliances, whereas NATO has always been "defensive." Romanian foreign ministry officials insisted that "Romania retains complete freedom to participate in alliances of a defensive nature," including NATO.[57] From Moscow's perspective, however, such distinctions were meaningless. The Soviet government left no doubt that it construed the pledge to be aimed against NATO, regardless of the Romanian interpretation.

Aside from Romania, all the East European states did their best to preserve maximum flexibility vis-à-vis NATO. The Hungarian, Czechoslovak,

Polish, and Bulgarian governments also made clear that even if they could not formally join NATO in the near term, they still hoped to receive security commitments from the alliance, similar to the implicit commitments that non-members like Sweden and Switzerland have long enjoyed. East European leaders were especially eager to receive such commitments from the United States. In early 1991 the then prime minister of Hungary, József Antall, declared that "Hungary and the United States may as well consider each other allies without an alliance," and he urged the US government to "*increase* its military role in Europe," arguing that this would be the "best guarantee of Hungary's security."[58] Without a strong American military presence, Antall warned, "there can be no assurance of security in Europe."[59]

The other East European countries echoed Hungary's support for a continued US military presence in Europe, and also sought to promote the idea of security commitments from NATO. In addition, they began referring more explicitly and more frequently to the possibility of joining NATO. This was especially the case in Czechoslovakia, where Havel and other officials broached the topic as often as they could. For the time being, the East European governments were willing to accept close but informal ties with NATO rather than making a bid for full membership, but they emphasized their hopes of soon joining the alliance outright "if NATO wants us" and "if an expansion of the alliance is needed to preserve a firm American commitment to Europe's security."[60] Even officials who were wary of seeking a formal role in NATO expressed strong backing for solid commitments from the alliance.

NATO's Ambivalent Response

Despite the steadily increasing contacts between the former Warsaw Pact states and NATO, overtures from the East European governments about the possibility of full membership got a mixed reception in allied capitals. On the one hand, the NATO states welcomed East European participation in many of the alliance's activities, and in the spring of 1991 NATO leaders granted the former Warsaw Pact countries "associate" membership in the North Atlantic Assembly. Western governments also agreed to extend "indirect" security commitments to the East European states. On the other hand, the NATO countries quietly discouraged the East European governments from seeking formal membership in the alliance, warning that a drastic realignment of this sort could spark a backlash in the Soviet Union. In June 1991 the then secretary-general of NATO, Manfred Wörner, publicly stated that "granting NATO membership to former Warsaw Treaty members would be a serious obstacle to reaching mutual understanding with the Soviet Union."[61] Although Western leaders were willing to consider East

European membership in the political councils of NATO, they did their best to dissuade the East European states from trying to join the military organs. As the political situation in the Soviet Union took a turn for the worse in late 1990 and early 1991, concerns about the effect of East European admission into NATO were cited ever more frequently.

Following the rebuff of the hard-line coup attempt in Moscow in August 1991 and the disintegration of the whole Soviet state four months later, many of NATO's earlier inhibitions and reservations about its dealings with the East European states ceased to be relevant. Moreover, although the threat from the Soviet Army to the East European countries effectively collapsed along with the Soviet state itself, the former Warsaw Pact governments spoke even more openly in late 1991 and 1992 about their hopes of joining NATO. As a result of these two factors—the demise of the Soviet Union, and the continued East European interest in NATO membership—the alliance recast its policy to take somewhat greater account of the East European states' security concerns. The new approach was evident as early as December 1991, when the North Atlantic Cooperation Council (NACC) was established with a membership comprising all the NATO countries, all the former Warsaw Pact countries, and all the former Soviet republics.[62] NACC was designed as a post–Cold War multilateral security forum that would enable the East European governments to feel they had a direct cooperative partnership with NATO. Some East European officials initially were wary of joining NACC, believing that the organization was little more than a ploy by NATO to avoid offering full membership, but in the end all the former Warsaw Pact states did enroll.

Despite this new arrangement, the NATO countries still discouraged the East European states from seeking full membership in the alliance. Although all the East European governments and several of the former Soviet republics (the Baltic States and Ukraine) by mid-1992 had openly proclaimed their hopes of joining NATO, the West's reluctance to admit them seemed, in some respects, even greater than before. The hesitation among Western governments stemmed chiefly from lingering concerns about the effects such a move would have on Russia. Although the Russian government itself occasionally expressed interest in joining NATO, the option of membership was usually discussed in terms of the five (six, after 1992) East European states, and particularly Poland, Hungary, and the Czech/Slovak Republics. US officials were concerned that admitting the East European states into NATO would be construed by Moscow as a step directed against Russia and possibly Ukraine. Because US leaders wanted to avoid giving ammunition to the hard-line opponents of Boris Yel'tsin's reformist government, they sought to avoid even the appearance of a Western security arrangement aimed at surrounding or containing Russia. The emphasis, both then and ever since, has been on strictly equal treatment of the East European states and the former republics of the Soviet Union.[63]

In that sense, the relationship between the former communist countries and NATO has been quite different from the relationship between those countries and the EU. So far, NATO has treated all the former Warsaw Pact states equally, admitting each of them into NACC and the Partnership for Peace and declining to speculate about precisely when one or more might become full members. By contrast, the EU has given unambiguous preference to the East European countries, especially the Czech Republic, Hungary, and Poland. The Visegrad states were granted associate membership in the early 1990s, a status that is not envisaged for any of the former Soviet republics other than the three Baltic States. The EU subsequently indicated that the East European countries could be eligible for full membership by the year 2000 if reforms stayed on track, a goal that has been ruled out even more firmly for the former Soviet republics (again, excepting the Baltic States).[64] Although some EU member-states, notably France, have tried to back away from any firm commitment on East European accession to the EU until well into the next century, even the French government has conceded that the Visegrad countries, and perhaps the Baltic States, could eventually be admitted, something that is not under consideration for Russia, Ukraine, or any other members of the CIS.[65]

The different approaches of NATO and the EU can be explained by the simple fact that NATO is a security organization and must act accordingly, whereas the EU is concerned, above all, about the economic and political standing of prospective members. The preferential treatment that the EU has accorded to the East European states merely indicates that the potential for sustained economic growth and political stability in Eastern Europe is much greater than in the former Soviet Union. If NATO were to behave in a similar manner—that is, if it were to treat the former communist states unequally—the implications would be very different. Some officials in the West, especially in Germany, have argued that NATO *should* treat the ex-Warsaw Pact countries unequally, but at least for now, concerns about a potential backlash in Russia have induced the allied governments and NATO as a whole to abide by a strictly egalitarian approach.

How long this egalitarian approach can be maintained is a different matter. Developments by mid-1994 suggested that the notion of equal treatment might be unviable for more than another year or two. In May 1994 the foreign and defense ministers from all ten member-states of the WEU issued a declaration granting "associate partnership" in the WEU to the four Visegrad countries, the three Baltic republics, Romania, and Bulgaria.[66] This status, according to the WEU's declaration, was intended to prepare the nine ex-communist countries "for integration into and eventual membership in the European Union."

Although the declaration did not provide any formal security guarantees to the new partners, it did encourage them to participate in the WEU's formal meetings and in its peacekeeping and humanitarian activities.

The Western European Union's decision not to extend associate partnership to any CIS countries (including Russia) was in line with the EU's earlier decision not to confer associate status on any of the former Soviet republics other than the three Baltic States. In the case of the WEU, however, this unequal approach was more significant because the WEU handles military affairs, and all its members belong to NATO. The organization is identified under the Maastricht Treaty as the future defense mechanism of the EU's "common foreign and security policy," but the WEU is also widely regarded as an emerging European "pillar" of NATO[67] To the extent that the WEU continues to bridge the gap between NATO and the EU in the future, the unequal treatment it has accorded to the former communist countries is bound to affect NATO's policy as well. This, indeed, is precisely what many East European officials are hoping, as the Polish defense minister explained in March 1994, shortly before the WEU's action:

> Our chances for integration into the WEU are much greater than our chances for direct entry into NATO, but the WEU is a component of NATO and therefore this will be a means of entering the European defense system by the back door rather than the front entrance. It's a very tempting proposition, which we will certainly take up 100 percent.[68]

Although WEU officials went out of their way in May 1994 to stress that the declaration on associate partnership was not directed against Russia or any other country, the implications of the move did not go unnoticed in Moscow. The Russian Ministry of Foreign Affairs promptly issued a statement alleging that the WEU was trying to "create a new model of a military-political alliance in a limited space in Europe."[69] Subsequently, Russian military commentators accused the WEU of seeking to "repartition Europe" and of engaging in nefarious "diplomatic ploys" aimed at promoting the "eastward expansion of the North Atlantic bloc."[70] These complaints, at such an early stage, adumbrate the tensions that may ensue in the latter half of the 1990s, when NATO will have to make firmer decisions about East European membership.

Lingering Western Concerns

Russia's continued opposition to East European membership in NATO has not been the only factor driving Western policy. An expansion of the alliance would raise a host of other thorny security issues that Western governments would prefer not to have to address. In particular, NATO would have to rethink its whole policy vis-à-vis the conflict in the Balkans, something that will be particularly difficult after the fiasco in Bosnia-Herzegovina in late 1994. For now, the only major border between a NATO member and the former Yugoslavia is the border between Greece and Macedonia.[71] If Hungary were to become a member of NATO, the alliance's frontline would suddenly be extended to the border with Serbia, Croatia, and Slovenia.[72] Similarly, if Bulgaria were admitted into NATO, the alliance would be far more directly involved in any potential fighting in Macedonia, an issue that is complicated enough already in light of Greece's firm—and, many would say, highly obstructive—stance. NATO's reluctance to take on a greater role in the former Yugoslavia was one of the reasons that Albania's formal application to join the alliance in December 1992—the first formal application by any former communist country—was quickly rejected. Western leaders sensed, correctly, that Albanian officials were hoping for a reliable guarantee in case the Serbian government tried to crush ethnic Albanians in Kosovo province and the Albanian government felt compelled to intervene on their behalf.

Even if no problems emerged with the former Yugoslavia, East European membership in NATO could give rise to a number of other highly contentious issues, such as conflicts between Hungary and one or more of its neighbors, notably Romania, Ukraine, or Slovakia (not to mention Serbia).[73] When bloody clashes erupted between ethnic Romanians and Hungarians in the Transylvanian region of Romania in March 1990, Hungary came under pressure to intervene in some way.[74] Such pressure would be likely to re-emerge in the future if the plight of the Hungarians in Transylvania were to deteriorate severely, or if civil war were to engulf Romania. Hungarian leaders would face a similar dilemma if Ukraine were to dissolve into widespread turmoil and the ethnic Hungarians there became scapegoats. Tensions between Hungary and Slovakia abated after Vladimir Mečiar's government fell from power in March 1994, but Mečiar's electoral success in October 1994 raised concerns in Budapest that Hungarian-Slovak relations might again be marked by acrimony.[75] If both countries were members of NATO, the potential for conflict between them would be nearly as disruptive for the alliance as the long-standing tensions between Greece and Turkey have been. At the very least, the NATO governments would be averse to admitting Slovakia and Hungary unless there was good reason to expect that serious internecine disputes could be avoided. Hungarian Defense Minister György Keleti recently acknowledged that long-standing problems with both Slovakia and Romania, if left unresolved, might thwart Hungary's chances of getting into the alliance:

> We should not only establish cooperation with NATO members and evince our determination to do so, but should also demonstrate this intention in our relations with neighboring countries. For I am convinced that NATO would not admit countries between whom there is a conflict situation or lack

of understanding, or between whom the level of military trust is not high enough to permit them to be admitted into a joint military organization.[76]

The extension of NATO membership to Hungary might also raise political hackles unless Hungarian leaders pledged—at least tacitly—not to try to prevent other East European countries like Romania from joining the alliance in the future.[77]

More generally, the entry of the Visegrad states into NATO would bring to the fore some of the dilemmas that have long bedeviled the alliance. The security guarantee that members of NATO receive under Article 5 of the North Atlantic Treaty is, ultimately, a nuclear guarantee.[78] Although it is difficult at this point to envisage any European conflicts that would risk the use of nuclear weapons, an unforeseen turn for the worse in the former Soviet Union might change that in the future. If nothing else, the NATO governments, especially the United States, will have to think through what extended nuclear deterrence might mean in an alliance of twenty or more members. The NATO countries also will have to consider the types of forces that will be needed to ensure the fulfillment of allied security guarantees, well short of the use of nuclear weapons. It is unclear, for example, whether that task might require the deployment of NATO troops or pre-positioned equipment on East European soil and, if so, whether political difficulties might arise. For example, would Poland and the Czech Republic accept the presence of German troops on their territory if NATO deemed that appropriate? Who would pay for the deployments? Questions of this sort, though by no means intractable, are bound to be used by opponents of NATO enlargement to halt or at least hinder the process.

The admission of several former Warsaw Pact countries into NATO would also raise serious questions about the future of the CFE Treaty. The treaty, as originally conceived during the Cold War, was designed to impose equal limits on heavy weapons deployed by NATO and the Warsaw Pact. By the time the treaty was signed in late 1990, the Warsaw Pact had been gravely weakened, and by the time the document entered into force in July 1992, the Pact had ceased to exist. Before the treaty could be signed, the Soviet Union and the six East European states had to engage in protracted and bitter negotiations to allocate weapons shares.[79] The basic apportionment that they finally devised in the fall of 1990 has been preserved in subsequent years, even as major adjustments in other areas have been needed to compensate for the dissolution of the Soviet Union and the split of Czechoslovakia. The status of the treaty's allocations could be undermined, however, if the Visegrad countries formally joined NATO. Even if commensurate reductions were made by existing alliance members to keep the aggregate force levels below CFE limits, there is little doubt that the entry of the East European states into NATO would require yet another series of adjustments in a treaty that has already undergone drastic and often painful changes.

As important as these other concerns may be, they pose far less of an obstacle to East European membership in NATO than does the Russian government's opposition. Although Russian President Boris Yel'tsin seemed to drop his objections to NATO expansion when he visited Poland in late August 1993, he backed away from that position the following month in a letter to the US, British, and French heads of state warning against any attempts to expand the alliance "at Russia's expense."[80] Russian officials followed up on Yel'tsin's retraction with a barrage of articles and interviews claiming that the admission of the Visegrad states into NATO would leave Russia "dangerously isolated" and "keep Russia out of its rightful place in Europe."[81] Even the Russian Foreign Intelligence Service (SVRR) was called into the act to provide a lengthy public analysis of "The Prospects for NATO Expansion and the Interests of Russia." Although the SVRR's report was much less shrill than other pronouncements by the Russian government, it warned that the expansion of NATO could lead, if only inadvertently, to the creation of a new *cordon sanitaire* in Europe and the disruption of "interstate borders that were fixed by the results of the Second World War."[82]

The intense Russian campaign against NATO enlargement in the late summer and early fall of 1993, which was reminiscent of the program devised in early 1991 by the CPSU International Department, posed obvious difficulties for Western leaders. The Clinton administration's willingness to challenge Yel'tsin's position on this matter was not great to begin with, and it diminished even further after two crucial events in Russia in the last few months of 1993: the violent suppression of a hard-line rebellion in early October, and the strong showing of ultranationalist and communist forces in the parliamentary elections in December. Both events confirmed how tenuous and fragile the roots of democracy in Russia still are, and both events seemed to instill Yel'tsin's personal role with even greater importance. Faced with the possibility that virulently anti-democratic forces could take power in Russia if the political situation were to deteriorate, Western leaders were even more inclined to err on the side of caution. The last thing they wanted was to provide an additional grievance for Yel'tsin's hard-line opponents to use. Not until a meeting of the NATO foreign ministers in early December 1994 and a CSCE summit four days later was the United States willing to challenge Russia's opposition to East European membership in NATO (see below). Even then, the differences between the two sides were mainly—though not entirely—over rhetoric, rather than a fundamental clash of policy.

THE PARTNERSHIP FOR PEACE

Concerns about Russia were instrumental in NATO's decision in January 1994 to establish the Partnership for Peace (PfP).[83] Instead of setting a timetable for the admission of the Visegrad states into the alliance, NATO leaders agreed to defer the matter and to create a new body that would enable individual East European countries to prepare themselves for full membership by taking part in NATO's military exercises, by promoting transparency of military planning, by strengthening civilian control over military forces, and by coordinating their military doctrines, force structures, and operational capabilities and planning with the alliance. In accordance with a "Framework Document," the PfP was open not only to all the East European countries, but to the former Soviet republics and to West European states outside NATO. It thus was based, once again, on the principle of egalitarianism.

The formation of the PfP was controversial in several respects, not least because it came as a bitter disappointment to many East European officials, who had been hoping that they would receive a more clear-cut assurance of future membership in NATO. Polish President Lech Wałęsa was especially critical of the West's "timidity" in devising such a "totally inadequate" and "almost useless" response to the "resurgence of imperialist thinking in Moscow."[84] Czech President Havel was more discreet, but he, too, criticized the West's actions as "cautious, slow, and perhaps too pragmatic," and warned that a "new Munich" might be in the offing. Havel renewed his earlier calls for the Visegrad states to be admitted promptly into NATO as a hedge against the "chauvinistic, Great Russian, crypto-Communist, and crypto-totalitarian forces" that might someday gain ascendance in Moscow.[85] Despite these criticisms and many other complaints, all the East European states promptly joined the PfP.

The other major controversy surrounding the PfP in the first half of 1994 was caused by Russia's reaction. Although the Russian government finally agreed in principle to join the PfP in June 1994 (a decision that was temporarily reversed in December 1994), Russian officials persistently tried to secure formal recognition of a special "great-power" status for their country.[86] By seeking a pre-eminent spot in the PfP, the Russians apparently hoped to gain some sort of veto over NATO's actions. This same goal was evident in the Russian government's statements in the first half of 1994, which consistently sought to downgrade NATO's status as a European security mechanism in favor of CSCE and NACC. Russia's tentative decision to sign onto the PfP seems to have been motivated less by any real warming toward the organization than by a recognition of how isolated Russia would be if it did not join.[87] Officials in the Russian foreign ministry warned Russian leaders that, without Moscow's participation, the PfP might even become a direct means for the East European states to obtain full membership in NATO.

Hence, Russia's chief aim when agreeing to take part in the PfP was to prevent the organization from becoming a vehicle for the East European countries to join the alliance. In all other respects, Moscow obtained relatively little of what it had been seeking. Although Russia was granted recognition of its "unique" status as a "great European, world, and nuclear power," that designation was conferred in a largely meaningless protocol, rather than in the Partnership agreement itself.[88] Moscow received no veto over NATO's decisions or over any of its formal consultative mechanisms, nor did it succeed in downgrading NATO's status relative to the CSCE's.

In spite of the widespread dissatisfaction with the PfP, the Partnership began to function as planned in 1994. The first large-scale military exercises involving NATO and East European ground and air forces were held in Poland in September 1994.[89] Russian military observers attended the exercise, but did not actually take part. That was also the case during a follow-up exercise aimed at planning for and coordinating peacekeeping missions, staged at the Harskamp Military Training Ground in the Netherlands. The exercise involved platoon- and company-size units from Canada, the Czech Republic, Estonia, Germany, Great Britain, Lithuania, the Netherlands, Poland, Slovakia, Sweden, Ukraine, and the United States. In the first large-scale naval exercise sponsored by the PfP, which was held near a NATO base at Stavanger, Norway in late September and early October 1994, Russian troops did finally participate. Two ships from Russia's Baltic Fleet, the *Neustrashimyi* and the *Druzhnyi*, operated alongside vessels and aircraft from Sweden, Poland, Lithuania, and ten NATO countries, including the United States.[90] The Russian navy also took part in another major naval exercise, Maritime Partner-94, on the Black Sea in late October.[91] This exercise, which included vessels from Bulgaria, Romania, Turkey, Greece, the United States, and Ukraine as well as Russia, was designed to simulate the enforcement of UN-mandated economic sanctions.

In addition to these four large joint exercises, many other PfP-sponsored military and political activities got underway in 1994 on both a bilateral and a multilateral basis, and a program of eighteen multinational and twenty bilateral military exercises was adopted for 1995. Even Albania, which had never before conducted military exercises with foreign countries, began taking part in PfP maneuvers in early 1995, contributing six naval vessels to a joint operation involving the United States, Germany, Italy, and Great Britain.[92] The growing scope and quantity of activities caused some East European officials who had initially been skeptical about the PfP's merits to begin looking more favorably on the organization. In late 1994 the chairman of Hungary's parliamentary committee on defense, Imre Mecs, declared that, contrary to his earlier expectations, "it has now become clear that NATO partnership is not an empty phrase or an attention-diverting maneuver, but is a series of real joint endeavors through which we can achieve full membership in NATO within the foreseeable future."[93] Other East European officials were not willing to go that far, but they did acknowledge that the PfP had proven somewhat more useful than they initially had anticipated.

Increasingly, though, it seemed clear that the PfP's ventures, no matter how worthwhile, would not be enough to meet East European concerns. In the fall of 1994, officials in the Clinton administration acknowledged that the PfP was "inadequate and was oversold when it was first proposed. . . . Much of the rhetoric that was used in the past was empty of substance."[94] According to a senior Defense Department official, Joseph Kruzel, the administration belatedly "recognized that we were making a tactical mistake by emphasizing Partnership for Peace almost to the exclusion of NATO's expansion."[95] This growing sense of the PfP's shortcomings prompted the US government to begin exploring ways to accelerate the entry of the Visegrad states, and perhaps other countries, into NATO. The aim, at least at the outset, was to come up with a viable set of proposals by the end of 1995.

The Clinton administration presented its initial findings in early December 1994 to a meeting of the NATO foreign ministers in Brussels and a summit of CSCE leaders in Budapest. Although the preliminary ideas were extremely modest (no timetable for expansion was specified, and no candidates for membership were mentioned) and included a plan to increase the powers and functions of the CSCE, the very fact that NATO was reconsidering the status of the East European countries was enough to spark a hostile reaction in Moscow. Russian Defense Minister Pavel Grachev immediately warned that "if new members are admitted into NATO, Russia will have to take additional security measures" to compensate.[96] He did not specify what these additional security measures might be, but other commentators in Moscow suggested that Russia might have to begin redeploying large quantities of ground-based tactical nuclear weapons (which were supposed to be eliminated under a pledge adopted by Mikhail Gorbachev in 1991, and later reaffirmed by Yel'tsin) and might even have to consider bringing back some intermediate-range nuclear forces (INF), which were banned under the 1987 INF Treaty.[97]

Similar warnings were voiced by Russian Foreign Minister Andrei Kozyrev at the NATO meeting, where he denounced what he claimed was the "hasty expansion of NATO" and the movement toward "setting an explicit schedule for this process."[98] He declined to give Russia's final signature to a cooperation agreement with the PfP that had been tentatively approved several months before. That same day, Kozyrev delivered a speech before the WEU's parliamentary assembly in which he asserted that "the aspirations of the countries of Central Europe to be admitted into NATO should be regarded as nothing more than capriciousness."[99] He called instead for the "establishment of a new 'architecture' for European security" that would eclipse existing institutions, and he implied that the United States was trying to force the idea of NATO enlargement on its allies. "We, the Europeans," he declared, "must in the first instance look after ourselves."[100] Kozyrev pledged that Russia was ready to pursue far-reaching military cooperation with the WEU (as opposed to NATO) if the member-states joined Russia in "giving a firm rebuff to violators of UN Security Council resolutions," a clear reference to the recent US decision to cease enforcing the UN-sponsored arms embargo against Bosnia-Herzegovina.[101] At the CSCE meeting a few days later, President Yel'tsin voiced even harsher criticism of the Clinton administration's new approach to the question of NATO enlargement, accusing the United States of "sowing the seeds of mistrust" and of "threatening to plunge Europe into a cold peace." Yel'tsin maintained that the "alleged expansion of stability," as proposed by the United States, was really targeted at "undesirable developments in Russia."[102]

Faced with these criticisms, US officials insisted that "no outside country will be allowed to veto NATO's expansion," and they expressed hope that Kozyrev's and Yel'tsin's comments were intended largely for domestic audiences. Even so, the Russian statements could not help but take their toll. Even before the meetings in Brussels and Budapest, few members of the Clinton administration were inclined to give high priority to the expansion of NATO, in part because of strong resistance within allied councils, especially from France. The increased vehemence of the Russian government's opposition to proposed moves beyond the PfP merely reinforced the administration's caution. After Vice President Albert Gore traveled to Moscow and met with Russian leaders in mid-December, the Russian government expressed satisfaction with his "clarifications" of US policy on NATO and Eastern Europe.[103] With parliamentary elections in Russia scheduled for the end of 1995 and presidential elections in both Russia and the United States scheduled for 1996, the US government was clearly averse to taking any steps that might trigger a reaction beneficial to hard-line, xenophobic candidates in Russia. Even when Western leaders protested the widespread bloodshed that Russian troops caused in Chechnya in early 1995, there was no hint that NATO would begin rethinking its policy on near-term expansion.[104] The only concrete form of retaliation taken by the West against Russia was the postponement of expanded trade and economic ties and the deferral of some joint military and political activities.

DISSENTING WESTERN VIEWS

NATO's cautious approach to the issue of enlargement has not won universal approval in the West. A few highly influential commentators outside

Western governments, such as Zbigniew Brzezinski, Leslie Gelb, and Samuel Huntington, have strongly advocated the near-term expansion of the alliance.[105] Even within official NATO circles, pro-enlargement views have by no means been entirely absent. Before the Russian parliamentary elections in December 1993, the German government, especially the defense minister, Volker Rühe, had repeatedly argued that "NATO should not be a closed shop" and that "the time has come to open a more concrete prospect for those countries of Eastern Europe that want to join and that we may consider eligible."[106] More recently, some German leaders, including Prime Minister Helmut Kohl, have sought to downplay that theme, but most officials and non-governmental experts in Germany have continued to advocate the eastward expansion of NATO.[107] Indeed, in August 1994 Defense Minister Rühe went well beyond his previous statements in calling for NATO to make clear that it intended to accept the Visegrad states (and perhaps Bulgaria, Romania, and the Baltic republics) as full members, and did not intend to admit Russia under any circumstances:

> Integration and cooperation are necessary for stability for Europe as a whole. Our policy must be clear. It would be wrong to pursue a policy based on the imperative of maintaining "the highest possible degree of ambiguity." Our neighbors in the East, too, are aware that it is part of the logic of the European processes that only future candidates for membership of the European Union are genuine candidates for membership of the Western alliances. Here, I am thinking primarily of the four Visegrad states. It is clear, however, that *Russia cannot be integrated—neither into the EU nor into NATO.*[108]

Rühe's professed aim was not to isolate Russia from Europe; on the contrary, he urged that NATO "deepen its cooperation with Russia," a process that he believed would expedite rather than impede East European entry into NATO. "The more concrete the content of the strategic partnership between NATO and Russia becomes," he argued, "the more Russia will be prepared to accept the integration of our eastern neighbors."[109]

The goal of near-term membership for the Visegrad states also has been championed by a few prominent American officials, notably the Republican senator from Indiana, Richard Lugar, who previously served as chairman of the Senate Foreign Relations Committee. Since 1992, Lugar has consistently argued that the alliance will disintegrate unless it is willing to admit new members. In June 1993 he warned that "if NATO is not able to respond to situations such as Yugoslavia . . . NATO will die. Simply, the rationale for it will not be there."[110] He emphasized that the first step for the alliance in "adjusting to the post–Cold War era" must be to consider "immediate membership" for Hungary, Poland, and the Czech Republic. His views were given extensive and laudatory coverage in the media of the Visegrad states.[111] Although many other members of the US Congress viewed the matter very differently—claiming that they would oppose any extension of NATO into regions of potential instability and ethnic turmoil—Lugar's statements carried a good deal of weight because of his expertise and reputation for sound judgment. His position was given a further boost by the decisive victory of the Republican party in the November 1994 Congressional elections, which brought to power a number of legislators who share Lugar's doubts about the existing value of NATO and who are less willing to defer to Russia's objections.

Even so, skepticism about the wisdom of enlarging the alliance anytime in the near future still prevailed in 1993 and 1994 in most of the NATO countries, not least the United States. This skepticism hardly seemed likely to diminish in light of the Russian government's volte-face on the matter in the fall of 1993. If the statement President Yel'tsin made during his visit to Poland in August 1993 had been allowed to stand—with the gloss put on it by Polish officials—it would have been much harder for the NATO governments to discourage the Visegrad states from seeking to join the alliance. But Yel'tsin's letter of retraction lent new impetus to the arguments of Western experts and policymakers who believed that the expansion of NATO would be incompatible with a "cooperative security" framework for dealing with Russia.[112] Those arguments have loomed ever larger in the wake of the controversial statements made by Yel'tsin and Kozyrev in late 1994. If the Clinton administration's preliminary and highly circumscribed steps toward the enlargement of NATO could provoke such a harsh reaction, the notion of pressing ahead at a faster pace—as Volker Rühe advocated—was bound to run into stiff opposition in Washington.

Combined with the views of French leaders, who have been firmly opposed all along to the idea of bringing new members into the alliance, US anxieties about Russia and the Clinton administration's desire not to be seen as having compounded the "Zhirinovsky factor" will be a significant obstacle to any prospective enlargement of NATO, regardless of official pronouncements that "no outside country will be allowed to veto expansion." Concerns about Russia also are likely to ensure that most Western leaders will adhere, at least for now, to NATO's official line of "not automatically excluding any country [that is, Russia] from joining" the alliance.[113] Rühe's blunt denial that Russia can ever become a member of NATO may be more realistic, but it is doubtful that NATO will explicitly embrace that position unless circumstances in Moscow take a disastrous turn in the future (for example, if a Zhirinovsky-type figure seizes power).

EAST EUROPEAN INTERESTS AND CONCERNS

From the outset, East European officials have cited two key benefits they expect to gain from full membersh`ip in NATO: a reliable military guarantee against

external threats, and a vehicle for promoting internal political and economic stability and democratization. The first benefit is seen as a crucial
hedge against the uncertainties of post–Cold War Europe. Most officials
in the region do not perceive any serious military threats to their countries at present, and are hopeful that no such threats will arise in the
future. They are concerned, however, that an unforeseeable turn of events,
especially in the former Soviet Union, could drastically alter the situation. They also believe that the only way to provide their countries with
concrete insurance against these sorts of unexpected developments is
through full membership in NATO.[114] Security commitments that are left
vague and ambiguous—the way most officials in the region view the commitments accompanying NACC, PfP, and other forms of association with
NATO short of full membership—may well go unfulfilled when the critical moment comes. By contrast, the formal guarantees that would result
from full membership in the Western alliance would almost certainly be
upheld in time of need. It makes sense, in their view, to hedge against a
possible threat well before the threat materializes, since it may be too
late to do anything once the danger is at hand, as the Hungarians learned
in November 1956 when confronted by a Soviet invasion.

The other benefit of NATO membership often cited by East European officials has been less prominent in recent debates, but is at least as
important. More than just a military alliance, NATO has served as a vi-
brant community of democratic states, helping to nourish and sustain
democratic values and institutions among its members.[115] It played an
important role in bolstering democratic systems in Spain, Portugal, and
Greece after those countries emerged from many years of dictatorship.[116]
Officials in East-Central Europe now hope that the alliance can serve as
an equally effective stabilizer for the democratic changes and sweeping
economic reforms under way in their own societies. Leading experts in
all four of the Visegrad countries, especially the Czech Republic and
Hungary, cite this potential benefit of NATO membership long before
they mention any of the military gains.[117]

To the extent that East European hopes of relying on NATO as a stabilizing influence are well-founded, the implications for European security may
be broader—and, from the West's standpoint, more valuable—than they first
seem. The well-established notion that democratic states have never (or almost never) gone to war with other democratic states suggests that NATO
membership, by bolstering democracy in individual East European countries, would contribute to peace and stability throughout the region.[118] This
view has been strongly endorsed by the chairman of the Hungarian
parliament's defense committee, Imre Mecs, when he explained why he supported NATO membership not only for Hungary, but for Romania as well:

Hungarian-Romanian relations and the question of joining NATO are of fundamental importance from the standpoint of regional security. . . . If a country wants to become a member of NATO, it will have to ensure that all its policies conform with European norms. These European norms do not permit the use of the army to solve internal ethnic problems. That is why Romania's rapprochement with the European Union and NATO must be supported. With such a step, the Romanian government's alleged and unacceptable plans [to have the army intervene against unrest in Transylvania] could no longer be prepared, and the [Hungarian] minority would no longer have to fear that the army would be deployed against them. Those kinds of plans would be incompatible with the image and norms of Europe.[119]

Echoing that position, leaders of the Hungarian community in Romania have vigorously supported "Romania's membership in NATO [because it] would be a guarantee that the army would never be used against the civilian population."[120] They acknowledge that democracy alone would not remove ethnic tensions, but they claim it would greatly increase the likelihood that all sides would confront their differences peacefully. This, in turn, they argue, would effectively eliminate the risk of an armed conflict between Hungary and Romania and the potential for a broader regional "spillover."

NATO's reluctance to expand its membership has done little to deter the East European states from seeking to join the alliance. All the East European governments, from Albania to Poland, have set NATO membership as the official goal of their countries. Poland, Hungary, and the Czech Republic even have included explicit provisions to this effect in their national security legislation.[121] Since 1990, all the East European governments have been designing their military doctrines and restructuring their armed forces with an eye to facilitating eventual membership in NATO. Political and military cooperation between the alliance and the former Warsaw Pact states has been steadily increasing, as evidenced by the joint combat operations they have undertaken in the Persian Gulf and in regions contiguous with the former Yugoslavia. Moreover, even before the PfP was established, the Visegrad states had been taking a direct part in NATO's high-level military and political deliberations. In June 1993, Hungary became the first non-NATO country to host the alliance's annual meeting on military security issues and crisis management. Hungary was also the first East European country to establish a bilateral military working group with the United States to deal with all aspects of security issues that might confront NATO. Poland and the Czech Republic quickly followed suit. By now, the military and political ties between NATO and the Visegrad countries have become so close that one can almost begin to speak about de facto membership. Although the de jure role of the East European states in NATO has been limited primarily to membership in NACC and the PfP, the de facto role that these countries have been taking on is already more important than the contributions of at least a few existing members of the alliance.

Non-governmental experts in Poland, Hungary, and the Czech Republic have been overwhelmingly supportive of their countries' efforts to join NATO, and the same result is evident in public opinion surveys. In Poland, for example, public support for NATO membership has consistently been around 80 percent (with some 5 to 10 percent opposed and the rest undecided) and at times has approached 90 percent.[122] Nearly as strong support is evident in Hungary and the Czech Republic.[123] A few experts in Prague argue that the Czech government's bid for NATO membership is more of a "quick-fix" gimmick than a well-conceived policy, and some specialists in Slovakia maintain that public support for NATO is only lukewarm and the benefits of membership are unclear. Aside from this small number of skeptics, however, experts and ordinary citizens in all the Visegrad states believe that admission into NATO should be the chief foreign policy goal for their countries. The public support for NATO has often been adduced by Polish, Czech, and Hungarian leaders, who contrast these sentiments with the anti-NATO feelings that crop up from time to time in some allied countries, such as Greece. Polish officials also cite opinion surveys showing that most Poles regard NACC and the PfP as little more than vehicles for NATO to dodge the question of expansion.[124] Even ordinary citizens, they argue, understand that the main benefits of establishing ties with NATO can come only through full membership.

East European leaders acknowledge that the entry of their countries into NATO would entail certain risks, but they offer two arguments in response to the points advanced by Western governments: first, that there are even greater risks in keeping their countries out of the alliance; and second, that the effects on Russia would not be as clear-cut as the NATO governments have implied. East European officials maintain that if appropriate guarantees are offered to Russia, it would be possible to enlarge the alliance without creating even the appearance of an anti-Russian grouping.[125] This line of argument has been advanced in its most elaborate form in Poland, where officials point out that since 1993 their country has been surrounded by seven new and potentially unstable (and even hostile) neighbors in an uncertain post–Cold War order.[126] Such factors, they argue, could induce Polish military planners to err on the side of caution by undertaking a military buildup and seeking local alliances, notably with Ukraine.[127] But if Poland could be admitted into NATO, the Polish government would feel much less threatened by Russia (and Germany) and could instead scale back its armed forces and proceed much further with the demilitarization of Polish society.[128] Both results, they add, would be highly favorable to Russia as well as to other neighboring countries. This same reasoning could be applied to all the East European states, whose membership in NATO would enable them to make drastic, permanent cuts in their armed forces and thus (at least south of the Carpathian mountains) be perceived as less of a potential threat by their neighbors. In that sense, an enlargement of NATO can be seen as a way of forestalling the competitive renationalization of armed forces and military policy in Eastern Europe and the instability that would accompany it.

ISSUES TO BE RESOLVED

Even if Russia's concerns can be assuaged and the other obstacles to NATO's eastward expansion can be overcome, the Visegrad governments are aware that their countries will be expected to meet certain stiff criteria, which in some cases may be used by NATO to slow down their bids for membership. These criteria were touched upon at the NATO meeting in Brussels and the CSCE summit in Budapest in late 1994.

Political Compatibility

All the East European governments recognize that democratic political systems will be a prerequisite for future NATO membership. Some nettlesome problems in this regard have persisted in Slovakia, especially under the Mečiar governments; but overall, the Visegrad states have made dramatic progress in consolidating democracy. The Czech Republic, Poland, and Hungary are at least as far along as, say, Spain was when it was admitted into NATO. Much the same is true of the three Baltic republics, especially Estonia. The outlook is a good deal more problematic in Bulgaria and particularly Romania, where, despite some impressive gains, democratic institutions are still rudimentary at best. Several more years may be needed before it is clear whether the limited progress in these two countries can be sustained.

It is possible that a few additional complications will emerge for countries like Poland and Hungary, where former communists have been voted back into power. (The same is true of Lithuania and Bulgaria, not to mention Romania, where many top communists never really left power.) This trend need not pose any grave obstacles for Hungary, where the socialists have aligned themselves with the strongly pro-Western Alliance of Free Democrats and have pursued NATO membership even more vigorously than did the nationalist governments under the Hungarian Democratic Forum.[129] In Poland, however, the situation is not quite as clear-cut. Although the leftist coalition government in Warsaw has continued to seek membership in NATO with nearly the same vigor that its Solidarity-led predecessors did, it remains to be seen whether the presence of so many former communists in top political and national security posts will affect

Poland's chances of getting in.[130] Gaffes like the one committed in August 1994, when a notorious communist-era spy, Marian Zacharski, was nominated to direct Poland's foreign intelligence service, certainly will not inspire confidence about the trustworthiness of some of the "post-communist" leaders. Zacharski's nomination was quickly withdrawn, but the episode raised questions both inside and outside Poland about the damage it would do to the country's quest for NATO membership.[131] Similar questions were raised in January 1995 when the Polish prime minister, Waldemar Pawlak, proposed that a hard-line communist ideologue, Longin Pastusiak, who had opposed NATO membership, become the new Polish defense minister. The nomination in this case was motivated by political skirmishing between Pawlak and Lech Wałęsa and was not intended to be taken seriously, but the episode caused adverse political fallout nonetheless. The outgoing Polish foreign minister, Andrzej Olechowski, denounced Pawlak's action and publicly asked him: "Do you want to join NATO or not?"[132]

Finally, some glitches may arise from the difficulty that most of the East European states are having in asserting clear-cut civilian control over their military establishments. After 1989 all the Visegrad states appointed civilians as defense ministers (an action reversed by the Slovak government after the split of Czechoslovakia), but the defense ministries in those countries remained predominantly under military control, as they always had been in the past. The process of civilianizing the defense ministries (as opposed to the *ministers*) is proving to be a good deal slower than expected, in part because of the exiguity of civilians who are well-versed in military affairs. In some countries, notably Hungary, complaints have even arisen that the continued "militarization" of the defense ministry is "weakening civilian control of the army" and thwarting military reform.[133] Somewhat different problems have arisen in Poland, where ambiguous lines of authority in civil-military relations have been the subject of intense political dispute.[134] Lech Wałęsa's efforts to consolidate presidential control over the Polish military establishment, and the periodic challenges he has confronted from parliament and other quarters, have contributed to the country's political turmoil. Many of these problems will disappear if appropriate constitutional mechanisms are adopted and applied by the courts, but the obstacles to orderly civilian control over military establishments in Eastern Europe may well persist for years to come.

Military-Technical Compatibility

At present the armies in the Visegrad states and other former Warsaw Pact countries are equipped almost entirely with weapons of Soviet manufacture or design. Economic constraints will make it extremely difficult in the near to medium term for them to obtain Western-made armaments that are compatible with NATO's forces, but some efforts to this end have been under way. The Polish Navy, for example, is seeking Western command and fire-control systems for the four new frigates it will be procuring, and the Czech national defense ministry recently selected the Rockwell Aerospace Corporation to design and integrate a new avionics system for the Czech air force's 72 L-159 multi-role fighter aircraft.[135] The three Baltic countries received fast patrol boats and other naval equipment from Norway in 1994, allowing them to operate better alongside NATO vessels.[136] In early 1995 the United States indicated that it would help establish an integrated airspace management system for Eastern Europe and the Baltic States. The radars and control stations in the proposed network will allow for full compatibility with NATO forces.[137] This initiative was inspired by a deal that Hungary struck with the United States in late 1992 to buy 118 APX-100 advanced IFF (identification friend or foe) transponders to modernize its MiG fighters, the first time US military equipment had ever been sold to a former Warsaw Pact country. As part of the same deal (known as "Peace Pannon"), Hungary also received TPX-54 interrogators, GPA-28 antennas, modern surveillance displays, and computerized work stations to upgrade the four main Hungarian ground-based surveillance facilities.[138]

The US-sponsored modernization of Hungary's military air control system was offset to some extent by the Hungarian government's decision in June 1993 to accept a squadron of MiG-29 fighters from Russia to help pay off Russia's large hard-currency debt to Hungary. Subsequently, Moscow arranged a similar transfer of MiG-29s to Slovakia and tried, unsuccessfully, to do the same with the Czech Republic.[139] One of the main factors cited by Czech leaders when turning down the Russian offer was the danger of remaining too dependent on Soviet-made arms. They sought instead to obtain F-16s or F-18s from either Belgium or the United States, a move that, they hoped, would underscore the Czech Republic's commitment to NATO.

Despite the Czech government's hopes of steadily increasing its reliance on Western-made arms and components, its efforts in this particular instance may prove to be an aberration, at least in the near term. Purchases of major weaponry from NATO countries will require economic tradeoffs that may not be feasible anytime soon for any of the East European states, including the Czech Republic itself. Moreover, it is not clear that the receipt of the MiG-29s will necessarily be a major step backward for either Hungary or Slovakia. A leading member of NATO, Germany, has been operating three mixed squadrons with 24 MiG-29s since 1990, when it inherited them from the former Nationale Volksarmee.[140] The aircraft have been adapted to make them interoperable with NATO forces, and the experience that the Bundeswehr has gained can easily be transferred to the East European countries, as the German defense ministry has promised. In other cases, too, the East European armed forces can seek to achieve greater interoperability with NATO units by relying on modifications, upgrades, and new communications systems, rather than by scrapping all their existing weapons and purchasing an array of costly new equipment.

In the future, the Visegrad states will do their best to procure weapons that can be standardized with NATO, but progress on this matter is bound to be slow and faltering. Even upgrades and modifications can often prove excessively costly.[141] The US decision in February 1995 to lift all remaining restrictions on arms exports to Eastern Europe and the Baltic States is thus likely to have only a minor effect, at least for some time to come.[142] It is worth pointing out, however, that repeated attempts by NATO itself to achieve technical compatibility almost always have fallen well short of the mark, without irreparable damage to the alliance. Hence, this criterion may not be as important a barrier to East European membership as some NATO officials have made it out to be.

Military-Organizational Compatibility

The former Warsaw Pact countries will have to be able to operate effectively alongside NATO units. Progress in this area has been far greater than in the previous category. The Hungarian armed forces already have shifted over to a unified corps-brigade command system, which is eminently suitable for NATO; and the other Visegrad militaries are in the process of doing so.[143] Moreover, the armies in the region have been getting solid experience by taking part in joint military exercises with NATO through PfP and even by cooperating in actual combat, as during the 1991 Persian Gulf War. More recently, Hungary allowed NATO Airborne Warning and Control System (AWACS) aircraft to use Hungarian airspace and refueling bases while monitoring the conflict in the former Yugoslavia, and Hungarian MiG fighters were deployed as escorts for the AWACS aircraft to ward off any potential interference by Serbian planes. The Czech, Polish, and Hungarian governments also have cooperated with NATO countries in peacekeeping efforts in Croatia, Kurdistan, Liberia, and elsewhere, and have shown keen interest in contributing troops to other peacekeeping missions that NATO might organize in the central Eurasian region.

Economic Compatibility

Unlike many public goods, the protection afforded by voluntary membership in an alliance does not come cost-free. Prospective applicants for NATO will have to devote substantial funding to allied operations and activities, as the chairman of the Hungarian parliament's defense committee, Imre Mecs, recently pointed out:

> We must accept that membership in NATO will involve considerable extra expenditures. . . . This is in the interest of the entire country, and it is in the

interest of the government overall. If we become NATO members within two, three, or four years, as we hope, then we will need an army with fewer soldiers but with modern equipment, an army that can adapt to Western standards and is able to fulfill minimum requirements, and we surely will have to devote money to this.[144]

The East European governments have indicated a willingness to bear the financial costs of allied membership, in part because they sense that over the long run "it would end up being far more expensive for [them] to organize [their] defense independently" of NATO.[145] For now, though, resource stringency already has limited the Visegrad states' scope of action. The pursuit of military-technical compatibility, for example, has clearly been hindered by economic constraints. Military spending has declined precipitously in all the East-Central European countries since 1989, and funds for weapons procurement have been particularly hard hit.[146] Hence, purchases of F-16s and other advanced weaponry may be out of reach for a long time to come. On a more mundane level, budgetary pressures were one of the factors that induced the Hungarian government to forgo participation in the three major PfP-sponsored joint military exercises in 1994. This omission caused widespread apprehension in Budapest that the NATO countries might "hold a grudge" against Hungary and be less enthusiastic about its bid for full membership in the alliance.[147]

Similar economic constraints may arise for the East European states in the future, particularly if they become full members of NATO and are expected to contribute to allied military and peacekeeping operations. Funding issues will be especially controversial if NATO troops or pre-positioned equipment are deployed on East European soil. The existing allied states will not want to admit free-riders into NATO, but at the same time they must take account of economic realities in Eastern Europe. A considerable period may still be needed before any of the Visegrad states are able to claim true economic compatibility with the alliance.

Alluding to these criteria of political, military-technical, military-organizational, and economic compatibility, numerous officials in the Visegrad region have maintained that their countries are already suitable, or nearly suitable, candidates for membership in NATO. The most outspoken has been Prime Minister Václav Klaus of the Czech Republic, who has frequently argued that his country is at least as qualified to be a member of NATO as some existing members are (Luxembourg and Canada, for example, not to mention Iceland, which does not even have an army).[148] Czech leaders also point out that even an important member like France still has not returned to NATO's integrated military command, and that Spain has never been a part of it. Hence, they argue, there should be no real obstacle to Czech membership.[149] Officials in the other three Visegrad countries are not quite as outspoken as their Czech counterparts, but most of them strongly agree that their countries should be eligible in the near term for NATO membership. A senior Polish official, for example, recently emphasized that "NATO was willing to accept Portugal, Greece, and Turkey, whose armies, at the time they were admitted into the alliance, were much further from Western norms than our army is today."[150] The WEU's decision to grant "associate membership" to the East European states and the three Baltic republics in May 1994, with the expectation of eventual membership, has lent further weight to the arguments of the East European governments that their countries should receive analogous treatment from NATO.

A key issue that must still be resolved, however, is just how far the prospective expansion of NATO will actually go. This matter is especially sensitive in Bulgaria, Romania, and the three Baltic republics, where officials are uncertain whether the entry of the Visegrad states into NATO would expedite their own countries' admission or whether, on the contrary, it would be accompanied by tacit Western assurances to Russia that NATO would be expanded no further.[151] If the latter were to happen, Romania and Bulgaria would be kept permanently on a "second tier" in central Europe, and the Baltic States would perceive themselves to be even more firmly relegated to Russia's sphere of influence and isolated from the very governments—above all in Poland, Germany, and the Scandinavian countries—that they had hoped would serve as their "bridge to Europe." Thus, the key issue in Romania, Bulgaria, and the Baltic States is not whether NATO should be expanded eastward, but whether the expansion will go far enough.

The situation is even more complex for Ukraine. Until mid-1994, when Ukraine's relations with Russia were still acrimonious, some Ukrainian officials had supported the prompt admission of the Visegrad states into NATO even if Ukraine were not admitted, because they believed that Russia would oppose any expansion of the alliance. This view became much less prevalent in the latter half of 1994 as a result of the dramatic improvement in Russian-Ukrainian relations following the electoral victory of Leonid Kuchma, an advocate of close ties with Russia. During a visit to Washington in November 1994, Kuchma explicitly warned that "the speeding up of the process [of NATO expansion] would not enhance the security of Europe" because Russia "would not just stand by."[152] Although Kuchma said that the admission of new countries into NATO was needed, he emphasized that the process "must be prolonged in time." At a press conference during the CSCE summit two weeks later, Kuchma warned that "the rapid admission of East European countries into NATO" would "divide Europe into two halves again" and provoke "discord with Russia."[153] These statements heralded a growing consensus in Kiev that a limited expansion of NATO would be undesirable. Some who espoused this view, including Kuchma, were mainly concerned about preventing a backlash in Russia, whereas others were worried that Ukraine would end up being left outside NATO indefinitely. For whatever reason, the general view of NATO expansion was far more ambivalent in Ukraine by the end of 1994 than it had been earlier in the year.

CONCLUSION

Unless the East European states are granted full membership in NATO, they will have to make do with indirect security commitments from the alliance. The credibility and value of these commitments were temporarily bolstered in early 1991 by the overwhelming military success that the United States and its coalition partners achieved in the Persian Gulf war.[154] Kuwait had no formal military links with any of the Western countries at the time of the Iraqi invasion, but that did not prevent allied leaders from undertaking extreme measures to restore Kuwaiti independence. Although some East European officials, such as Gyula Horn, had predicted that NATO would be reluctant to aid countries outside the alliance, the successful resolution of the Persian Gulf crisis seemed—at least briefly—to prove otherwise. The allies' decisive stance against Iraq provided temporary reassurance to East European leaders that even if things in Moscow were to go disastrously awry, "the West, especially the United States, would not tolerate Soviet military action against Poland, Czechoslovakia, or Hungary."[155]

Despite this favorable precedent, the confidence of the East European governments quickly faded. For one thing, they were well aware that their own countries, unlike Kuwait, do not possess large oil reserves, and that Western leaders therefore would have less incentive to come to their aid. More important, they witnessed how little the NATO governments were willing to do about the conflict in Yugoslavia. The dismay that East European leaders felt as they watched the fighting in the Balkans escalate prompted many of them to question whether NATO could truly adjust to the post–Cold War world.[156] Although NATO's eventual enforcement of a no-fly zone over Bosnia-Herzegovina provided a brief ray of hope for the East European governments, NATO's apparent indifference to a Bosnian Serb victory in late 1994 was clearly a chastening experience for officials who might have hoped that they could rely on indirect commitments alone.

Mindful of such problems, NATO leaders have done their best to persuade the Visegrad governments that regardless of what happens in Moscow, closer East European ties with both NATO and the WEU will "deter any idea" Russian leaders may have of "using force [against an East European country] to gain an advantage."[157] As early as June 1991, the Western allies were willing to pledge that their "own security is inseparably linked to that of all other states in Europe," and that NATO will oppose "any form of coercion or intimidation" directed against the East European countries.[158] As with previous Western statements, however, the allied declaration failed to specify precisely what NATO would do if events deteriorated and a major threat to East European security actually arose. Statements issued by NATO in subsequent years have done little to clarify the matter.

Although a certain degree of ambiguity has been viewed as necessary in some Western official circles, it has left many East European leaders uneasy. The experience of 1956, when some Hungarians mistakenly assumed they could count on Western military support, illustrates the dangers that ambiguous commitments (or non-commitments) can sometimes create. The hazards of ambiguity were just as evident in the spring of 1991, when the United States openly encouraged the "people of Iraq" to rise up against Saddam Hussein, but then refused to assist the Kurdish and Shiite rebellions, for fear that Iraq would split apart. Given the magnitude of the threat that most of the East European countries would face in a worst-case scenario—an attack by a regional hegemon equipped with nuclear weapons—it is understandable why they are so intent on gaining the concrete security guarantees that full membership in NATO would bring. The mere existence of these guarantees, as a form of credible commitment by the alliance, would probably be enough to deter any threats of external aggression, no matter what direction events in Moscow take.

Even if the worst-case threats never materialize and the allied security guarantees prove unnecessary, membership in NATO will be a vital stabilizing influence for the new democracies in Eastern Europe. In the past, the alliance was crucial in helping to sustain and consolidate democratic institutions in countries like Spain and Portugal, and it can now perform this same function in the former Warsaw Pact countries. The preservation of democratic systems in Eastern Europe will be immensely beneficial for European security as well as for Western values and traditions. Up to now democratic countries have not gone to war with other democratic countries, and there is little reason to expect that this pattern will change in the future. Hence, the likelihood of interstate conflict in Eastern Europe is bound to diminish if democracy takes firm root. The stabilizing role of NATO membership for individual countries will therefore yield much wider security benefits.

There is obviously some risk that the entry of former Warsaw Pact countries into NATO will antagonize Russia and provoke a backlash in Moscow; but these concerns may not be as acute as often thought. An analogous situation from the recent past is instructive to recall here. From the mid-1950s until the late 1980s, most Western analysts assumed that the Soviet Union would never permit Germany to be reunified as a noncommunist state. Soon after the East German communist regime collapsed in late 1989, Soviet leaders realized they could no longer forestall eventual German reunification, and the main question was whether Moscow would permit a reunified Germany to be a member of NATO.[159] Once again, many Western observers predicted that no such thing would ever be tolerable for the Soviet leadership. Those predictions corresponded with Moscow's own position in the first half of 1990, when Soviet officials repeatedly declared that "any attempt to resolve the problem of German reunification by including Germany solely within NATO is out of the question because it would severely disrupt the military-strategic balance in Europe."[160] For several months, even the staunchest proponents of "new thinking" in Soviet foreign policy, such as Soviet Foreign Minister Eduard Shevardnadze and Gorbachev himself, warned that the inclusion of a reunified Germany within NATO would be "unacceptable to the Soviet people" and would inspire a hard-line backlash. Then suddenly, in July 1990, Gorbachev agreed that Germany could remain a member of NATO after reunification, and the thing that had long seemed inconceivable came to be regarded as natural and perfectly routine. The public in the Soviet Union barely took any notice of the outcome, and no hard-line backlash resulted.[161]

It is possible, though by no means certain, that Russia's opposition to the entry of the Visegrad states into NATO could prove equally ephemeral. Proposals for the admission of the Central European states have sparked vehement objections from the Russian government. If the proposals were actually put into effect, however, and concrete reassurances were offered to Moscow (in the form of close political and military cooperation with NATO and an increased peacekeeping and security role for the renamed CSCE), the whole matter might quickly fade and the expansion of NATO into Central Europe might eventually seem as logical and proper as Germany's status in NATO now does.

If this scenario is at all plausible, the trick in achieving it will be a carefully designed policy on the part of the NATO countries, especially the United States. US persistence in backing German reunification in 1990 while taking account of legitimate Soviet concerns was crucial in persuading Gorbachev to change course. Much the same will be true in the future with regard to the expansion of NATO. In addition to offering stronger NATO ties with Russia (so long as democratization continues) and a much-enlarged role for the CSCE, the NATO countries might agree to consider some of Russia's demands for modifications to the sub-regional limits of the CFE Treaty. The treaty, in its current form, prevents the Russian Army from redeploying most of its ground forces from the Central European part of Russia to the turbulent areas along the country's southern flank. Russian military officials have frequently called for the elimination of the treaty's "flank" limitations so that Russia can have greater flexibility to cope with large-scale disturbances in the Caucasus.[162] The NATO governments have been unwilling to go along with Moscow's request, in part because it would require significant changes in the treaty that might give other states a wedge to press for adjustments of their own, and in part because Turkey has strongly opposed Russia's efforts to establish a greater presence in the Caucasus. The massive Russian incursion into Chechnya in December 1994 has made the whole issue even more sensitive.

Nevertheless, the entry of the Visegrad countries into NATO is bound to raise questions about the CFE Treaty anyway, and thus the Western governments may have considerable leeway to make some sort of tacit exchange with Russia by allowing greater flexibility on the flanks. NATO will have to avoid any deal that would leave the three Transcaucasus republics (Azerbaijan, Armenia, Georgia) under permanent Russian military sway, and will have to ensure that armed intervention by the Russian Army against separatist groups within Russia does not become a regular practice. These two goals may prove to be infeasible, but if there is any hope of achieving them, delicate trade-offs will be needed, and close coordination with Turkey and Norway (the two NATO countries on Russia's flanks) will be essential throughout. Despite the many obstacles, NATO should at least be willing to consider the possibility of easing the flank limitations in return for Moscow's acquiescence in the admission of East European states into the alliance.

There is no guarantee that such steps will be enough to overcome Russian objections, but that in itself should not be a cause for paralysis. Ultimately, NATO's policy vis-à-vis the East European states must be based on its own merits, without interference from outside. As Václav Havel recently stated:

> If East and West live in proper harmony, it should not bother anyone when a country becomes a NATO member. The Commonwealth of Independent States, too, is a security structure, and it would be absurd if anyone [outside the CIS] were to decide who should or should not belong to it. Similarly, Russia cannot impose anything on NATO. . . . Everyone has the right to decide on which side to stand. This right, which is based on individual nations' will and is not imposed by some powerful nation, must be respected.[163]

Havel affirmed the need for a "permanent dialogue at several levels with Moscow" to ensure that Russian leaders "understand that NATO's eastward expansion does not threaten their interests," but he emphasized that "Russia does not have the right to dictate to other countries which alliances they can belong to."[164] Assuming that political reforms stay more or less on course in Russia—which may be a dubious assumption—the multi-level dialogue that Havel recommended and the other steps mentioned above will go as far as possible toward alleviating Russian concerns.[165]

NATO should not act with undue haste, but neither should it delay indefinitely. Unless Western governments adopt a clear-cut policy soon, additional pretexts for doing nothing are bound to arise. The alliance's failure in August 1993 to welcome and take prompt action on Yel'tsin's comments to Lech Wałęsa enabled the hard-line anti-NATO forces in Moscow to regroup and consolidate their influence over the policy debate. Moderate Russian officials who would have been willing to accept the enlargement of NATO under certain conditions were put on the defensive, and they are likely to be even more isolated if NATO continues to defer taking action. Once a new policy has been enunciated, some tensions with the Russian government may persist for a while; but over time, as any lingering doubts in Moscow are removed about the West's desire to bolster prosperity and democratic change in Russia, the controversy surrounding the admission of the East European states into NATO should rapidly abate. If so, an expanded alliance not only would guarantee Western military security, but would help ensure democracy and stability throughout Europe.

NOTES

1. Although the large majority of NATO governments and outside observers regard the Visegrad states as the most plausible candidates for near-term membership in the alliance, a few dissenting views have been expressed. Officials in both Italy and Greece have maintained that highest priority should be given to southeastern Europe—and specifically to Bulgaria and Romania—to ensure greater stability for the Balkans in the wake of the Yugoslav tragedy. Turkey, by contrast, has been very leery of suggestions that Bulgaria be admitted anytime in the near future. Within the alliance, the greatest opposition to accepting new members has come from France. The French government has not ruled out the possibility of expansion, but has sought to discourage it as much as possible.

2. Interview in *Magyar Nemzet* (Budapest), 13 October 1990, p. 7. Unless noted otherwise, all translations are by the author.

3. "Zmierzch bloków," *Żołnierz rzeczypospolitej* (Warsaw), 6 September 1990, p. 3 (emphasis in original).

4. See, for example, Waldemar Gontarski, "Odejście Eduarda Szewardnadze: Sprzeciw wobec dyktatury," and Jadwiga Butejkis, "Może za wczesnie śpiewać requiem?" both in *Rzeczpospolita* (Warsaw), 21 December 1990, pp. 1, 7. See also the interview with Czechoslovak Foreign Minister Jiří Dienstbier in "Vstupujeme do dramatického období" *Lidové noviny* (Prague), 4 January 1991, p. 7.

5. Statement by Andrzej Drzycimski, cited in Kazimierz Groblewski, "OKP u prezydenta: Wybory parlamentarne jesienią?" *Rzeczpospolita* (Warsaw), 18 January 1991, p. 1. On this same point, see "Prezydent Havel nie odwiedzi republik bałtyckich," *Słowo powszechne* (Warsaw), 29 January 1991, p. 2.

6. "Nic o Polsce bez Polski: Rozmowa z ministrem spraw zagranicznych prof. Krzysztofem Skubiszewskim," *Gazeta wyborcza* (Warsaw), 24 January 1991.

7. Cited in Ruth Graber, "Poland Revises Defense Strategy," *The Christian Science Monitor,* 26 June 1990, p. 3.

8. Interview with Lajos Für in *Népszava* (Budapest), 7 December 1990, p. 4.

9. Colonel Michal Glinski, "Ku przyszłości—realnie i z wyobraźnia," *Żołnierz rzeczypospolitej* (Warsaw), 14-16 September 1990, p. 4.

10. Jan Parys, "Siła wojska i ekonomii," *Rzeczpospolita* (Warsaw), 10 January 1991, Ekonomia i prawo, p. 3. Parys, who later became a controversial defense minister, was a senior official in the defense ministry at the time.

11. Interview with Hungarian Defense Minister Lajos Für in *Népszabadzag* (Budapest), 20 October 1990, p. 1.

12. "Setkáni V. Havla," *Občanský deník* (Prague), 23 March 1991, pp. 1-2.

13. In December 1994 the CSCE was renamed the "Organization for Security and Cooperation in Europe," or OSCE. The more familiar acronym will be used here unless otherwise noted.

14. See, for example, the comments of Janusz Onyszkiewicz in Dariusz Fedor, "Nowa armia," *Gazeta wyborcza* (Warsaw), 16 November 1990, p. 1. See also Miroslaw Cielemęcki, "Manewry pod giewontem: Być może wojskowym udalo sie to, co do tej pory nie wyszło politykom," *Przegłąd tygodniowy* (Warsaw), no. 40, 7 October 1990, p. 6.

15. Kazimierz Woycicki, "Szansa dla Europy Środkowej: Zbliżenie polsko-czechosłowacko-węgierskie," *Życie warszawy* (Warsaw), 16-17 February 1991, pp. 1, 4; Jan Kunc, "Třistranný summit ve Visegrádu," *Občanský deník* (Prague), 15 February 1991, p. 1; Lt.-Col. Marek Sieniawski and Capt. Apolinary Wojtys, "Wojsko—to sprawa nas wszystkich: Konferencja prasowa ministra obrony narodowej RP," *Polska zbrojna* (Warsaw), 16-18 November 1990, pp. 1-2; Cielęmecki, "Manewry pod giewontem," p. 6; and Yu. Gatselyuk, "Bez uchastiya SSSR," *Izvestiya* (Moscow), 21 September 1990, p. 3.

16. See "Prezidentite Zhelyu Zhelev i Vatslav Khavel razgovaryakha v Praga," *Duma* (Sofia), 5 February 1991, p. 1. See also the interview with Bulgarian Foreign Minister Viktor Vulkov in "Varshavskiyat dogovor ostana bez mundir i pagoni: Iztochna likvidira blokovata kolektivna sigurnost," *Otechestven vestnik* (Sofia), 26 February 1991, p. 1.

17. Interview with Bulgarian president Zhelyu Zhelev in "Sudurzhatelno sutrudnichestvo," *Zemedelsko zname* (Sofia), no. 29, 19 April 1991, pp. 1, 4.

18. Budapest Domestic Service, 10 October 1990.

19. Interview with Czechoslovak Foreign Minister Jiří Dienstbier in "Táto cesta nie je na preteky," *Národna obrodá* (Bratislava), 23 January 1991, p. 5.

20. On the Czechoslovak-Hungarian military agreement, see "Smlouva mezi armádami: Vojenské vztahy s Maďarskem," *Lidové noviny* (Prague), 22 January 1991, p. 2. See also "Schůzka ministrů v Budapešti," *Občanský deník* (Prague), 22 January 1991, pp. 1, 7; and the interview with Czechoslovak Defense Minister Luboš Dobrovský in "Nová vojenská doktrina státu," *Verejnosť* (Bratislava), 29 January 1991, p. 6. On the Polish-Hungarian agreement, see "Minister obrony narodowej zakończyłoficjalną wizyte na Węgrzech," *Polska zbrojna* (Warsaw), 21 March 1991, p. 1. On the Polish-Czechoslovak agreement, see "Minister obrony CSRF z roboczą wizyta," *Polska zbrojna* (Warsaw), 28 February 1991, pp. 1-2.

21. Interview with Piotr Kołodziejczyk, then-minister of defense in Poland, in "Wojsko ma mniej tajemnic," *Rzeczpospolita* (Warsaw), 29 March 1991, pp. 1, 2.

22. Interview with Hungarian foreign ministry state secretary Tamás Katona in *Népszava* (Budapest), 15 March 1991, p. 9.

23. "Warszawa-Praga-Budapeszt: Jesteśmy dopiero u progu współpracy," *Rzeczpospolita* (Warsaw), 18 April 1991, p. 7.

24. See, for example, "Rozhovory s NATO," *Pravda* (Bratislava), 30 September 1993, p. 2.

25. Barbara Sierzula, "Grupa Wyszehradzka nie istnieje," *Rzeczpospolita* (Warsaw), 15-16 January 1994, p. 23; "Václav Havel: Dobá velkých společných gest pominula," *Mladá fronta dnes* (Prague), 3 November 1994, p. 7; "Česko, Polsko a Maďarsko jsou na stejne urovni," *Lidové noviny* (Prague), 2 December 1994, p. 7; "Imrich Andrejčak: Západní orientace Slovenska je nezpochybnitelná," *Hospodářské noviny* (Prague), 20 November 1994, p. 4; and the interview with Hungarian Foreign Minister László Kovacs in *Magyar Nemzet* (Budapest), 10 December 1994, p. 7.

26. Army-General V. N. Lobov, "Puti realizatsii kontseptsii dostatochnosti dlya oborony," *Voennaya mysl'* (Moscow), no. 2, February 1991, p. 16. See also the interview with the military economist V. Litov in "Nasha bezopasnost' i parizhskii dogovor," *Sovetskaya Rossiya* (Moscow), 9 January 1991, p. 5; the interview with then-Soviet Foreign Minister Eduard Shevardnadze in "Edouard Chevardnadze: 'Notre problème, le votre, c'est de reussir la perestroïka. . . .'," *Le Figaro* (Paris), 22-23 December 1990, esp. p. 4; the interview with Col.-General Nikolai Chervov, deputy chief of the Soviet General Staff, in "Kam sa podeli tanky?" *Verejnosť* (Bratislava), 8 January 1991, p. 4; and the interview with Army-General Mikhail Moiseev, chief of the Soviet General Staff, in "Oborona: Korni i krona," *Pravitel'stvennyi vestnik* (Moscow), No. 9, February 1991, pp. 10-11.

27. The swift redeployments in 1990 were an extremely impressive logistical feat, but they absorbed so much of the USSR's rolling stock during the harvest season that they were one of the main factors behind the near-breakdown of Soviet food distribution in 1990-91. See "Nasha bezopasnost' i parizhskii dogovor," p. 5.

28. "Zmierzch bloków," p. 3; and interview with Jerzy Nowak of the Polish foreign ministry, in "Drogą ku bezpieczeństwu," *Żołnierz rzeczypospolitej*

(Warsaw), 12 September 1990, p. 3.

29. "Minister Skubiszewski na forum NATO: Bezpiecznie, bez zagrożeń" *Rzeczpospolita* (Warsaw), 30 November 1990, p. 5.

30. "Bulgarski parlamentaristi posetikha glavnata kvartira na NATO," *Duma* (Sofia), 21 November 1990, p. 3. See also "Bulgaria: NATO Visit," in US Department of State, *Focus on Central and Eastern Europe,* no. 29, 19 December 1990, p. 1.

31. "Varshavskiyat dogovor: A posle?" *Narodna armiya* (Sofia), 23 January 1991, p. 4. See also the interview with the then-Bulgarian Defense Minister, Col.-General Iordan Mutafchiev, in "Zad paradniya stroi na bulgarskata armiya," *Vecherni novini* (Sofia), 29 January 1991, p. 1.

32. "Náš prezident byl první" and "Přijimáme podanou ruku: Z projevu prezidenta ČSFR Václava Havla v bruselském sidle NATO," both in *Občanský deník* (Prague), 22 March 1991, pp. 1-2.

33. Cited in Maksim Bozhilov, "Bulgariya ofitsialno se sreshchna s NATO," *Duma* (Sofia), 16 January 1991, p. 3.

34. Zolton D. Barany, "The Western Contacts of the Hungarian Army," RAD Background Report No. 231 (East-West Relations), *Radio Free Europe Research,* 29 December 1989.

35. Interview with Hungarian Defense Minister Lajos Für in *Népszabadsag* (Budapest), 10 September 1990, p. 5; interview with Ernö Raffay, then-deputy defense minister in Hungary, in "Pożegnania," *Przegląd tygodniowy* (Warsaw), no. 42, 21 October 1990, p. 8; and interview with Romanian National Defense Minister Victor Stănculescu in Adevărul (Bucharest), 13 October 1990, p. 1.

36. "Drogą ku bezpieczeństwu," p. 3; "Sprzet z ZSRR, wiedza z Ameryki," *Gazeta wyborcza* (Warsaw), 9 April 1991, p. 2; and "Delegacja MON zakończyła oficjalną wizyte w RFN: Wracamy z precyzyjnym planem dalszego działania," *Polska zbrojna* (Warsaw), 30 November-2 December 1990, pp. 1-2.

37. Interview with Col. Józef Jura, then-deputy chief of Poland's military educational directorate, in "Odgórna rewolucja," *Żołnierz Polski* (Warsaw), no. 4, 27 January 1991, p. 5.

38. "Aus der Bundeswehr: Studium," *Wehrtechnik* (Bonn) 23:1, January 1991, p. 69.

39. "Hoste z NATO v Brne: Nová bezpečnost," *Lidové noviny* (Prague), 25 April 1991, p. 2.

40. "Zavurshi poseshchenieto na Grutskiya ministur-predsedatel v Bulgariya," *Duma* (Sofia), 13 January 1991, pp. 1-2. See also the interview with the Greek national defense minister, Ioannis Varvitsiotis, in "Bulgariya-Gurtsiya: Edinstvo po mnogo problemi," *Narodna armiya* (Sofia), 29 January 1991, p. 3. Although Bulgaria's diplomatic efforts were aimed mainly at improving military ties with Greece, some attempt

was also made to shore up relations with Turkey. See, for example, "Sutrudnichestvo s Turtsiya na vuzdukh, susha i more: Dvete strani se integrirat evropeiskite transportni strukturi," *Otechestven vestnik* (Sofia), 28 February 1991, p. 1; and the interview with Army General Mehmed Yonder, first deputy commander of the Turkish General Defense Staff, in "Mezhdu Bulgariya i Turtsiya nyama vuprosi, koito da ni razdelyat," *Otechestven vestnik* (Sofia), 22 February 1991, p. 3.

41. Interview with General László Borsits, chief of the Hungarian General Staff, in *Népszabadsag* (Budapest), 17 December 1990, pp. 1, 5.

42. "Biało-czerwone F-16—jesz nie teraz" and "Format krótkiej wizyty: Temat naśdzi ," both in *Polska zbrojna* (Warsaw), 6 December 1990, pp. 2 and 1, respectively.

43. Interview with Hungarian Deputy Foreign Minister Tamás Katona in *Népszabadsag* (Budapest), 10 January 1991, p. 1.

44. Hungary sent a military medical unit of 37 people to Saudi Arabia; Poland contributed two military vessels with a total of 150 people, plus another 150 medical specialists for two military hospitals in Saudi Arabia; Czechoslovakia sent a regiment of nearly 200 anti–chemical warfare specialists; Romania dispatched a military medical team of 360 specialists and a chemical warfare decontamination unit of 180 people; and Bulgaria agreed to provide two chemical warfare decontamination units with a total of 278 personnel (though Bulgaria's units were held up because of a delay in receiving a formal invitation from Saudi Arabia, and, therefore, were not actually deployed before the war ended).

45. "Bez munice nad ČSFR," *Zemědělské noviny* (Prague), 14 February 1991, p. 2; and "Popov, Mutafchiev i Danov otgovaryat na deputatski vuprosi," *Duma* (Sofia), 22 February 1991, p. 1.

46. Witold Beres, *Gliniarz z "Tygodnika": Rozmowy z byłym ministrem spraw wewnętrznych Krzysztofem Kozłowskim* (Warsaw: BGW, 1991), esp. pp. 73-78.

47. Cited in John Pomfret, "Escape from Iraq," *The Washington Post,* 17 January 1995, p. A-27.

48. "O razvitii obstanovki v Vostochnoi Evrope i nashei politike v etom regione: Postanovlenie Secretariata TsK Kommunisticheskoi Partii Sovetskogo Soyuza," no. St-15/2 (SECRET), 22 January 1991, in *Tsentr khraneniya sovremennoi dokumentatsii* (Moscow), Fond 89, Opis'45, Delo 63, List 9.

49. Ibid., Ll. 1, 7, 8 (emphasis added). The published version, under the same title, was in *Izvestiya TsK KPSS* (Moscow), no. 3, March 1991, pp. 12-17. According to an inscription at the back of the journal, the issue was sent to press on 27 February, roughly a month after the then secret report was adopted.

50. For a typical article, see V. Musatov, "Vostochnaya Evropa: 'Taifun' peremen," *Pravda* (Moscow), 13 March 1991, p. 3. Valeri Musatov was the deputy head of the International Department and one of the main authors of the January 1991 report for the CPSU leadership.

51. F. Luk'yanov, "My ne khotim byt' neitral'nymi, zayavil vengerskii prem'er," *Izvestiya* (Moscow), 1 May 1991, p. 4.

52. Interview with Soviet Deputy Foreign Minister Yuli Kvitsinski in *Népszabadsag* (Budapest), 29 April 1991, p. 1. See also the interview with Sergei Karaganov, deputy director of the USSR's European Studies Institute, in *Magyar Hírlap* (Budapest), 15 June 1991, p. 8.

53. "My ne khotim byt' neitral'nymi," p. 4; "Zayavlenie prezidenta ChSFR," *Izvestiya* (Moscow), 30 April 1991, p. 1; and "Podpishet li Bolgariya dogovor?" *Izvestiya* (Moscow), 1 May 1991, p. 1.

54. Interview with István Kormendi, head of the European department of the Hungarian foreign ministry, in *Magyar Hírlap* (Budapest), 28 February 1991, p. 3.

55. Interview with Foreign Minister Géza Jeszensky in *Beszelö* (Budapest), 25 May 1991, p. 9.

56. See the text (or partial text) of the treaty in *Romania Libera* (Bucharest), 12 April 1991, p. 1. See also Vladimir Socor, "The Romanian-Soviet Friendship Treaty and Its Regional Implications," *Radio Free Europe Research Report on Eastern Europe* (Munich) 2:17, 3 May 1991, pp. 25-33.

57. B. Rodionov, "Nakhodit' vzaimopriemlemye formuly: Kakimi budut dogovory SSSR s sosedyami v Vostochnoi Evrope," *Izvestiya* (Moscow), 4 June 1991, p. 5.

58. "Un entretien avec le premier ministre hongrois," *Le Monde* (Paris), 21 May 1991, p. 4.

59. "Le premier ministre hongrois au '*Figaro*': 'Notre armée quittera le Pacte de Varsovie en 1991,'" *Le Figaro* (Paris), 24 September 1990, p. 3.

60. Interview with Ognyan Avramov, secretary for the Bulgarian president, in "Ne e shega—ot purvi april Varshavskiyat dogovor mozhe da bude razpusnat," *Otechestven vestnik* (Sofia), 13 February 1991, p. 3.

61. TASS report, 16 June 1991.

62. "Declaration of the Heads of State and Government Participating in the Meeting of the North Atlantic Council Held at NATO Headquarters," Brussels, 18 December 1991. For an assessment of NACC's aims and activities, see André Dumoulin, "Le Conseil de cooperation nord-atlantique (CCNA)," *Défense Nationale* (Paris) 48:6, July 1992, pp. 103-115.

63. This statement applies only to NATO, not to the Western European Union (WEU). The four Visegrad states, the three Baltic republics, Romania, and Bulgaria were made "associate partners" of the WEU in May 1994, an arrangement that will not be extended to Russia or other members of the Commonwealth of Independent States (CIS). See the discussion below.

64. See "Family Frictions: A Survey of the European Union," *The Economist*

(London), 22 October 1994, esp. pp. 16-19.

65. Daniel Vernet, "Impatience a l'Est," *Le Monde* (Paris), 3 December 1994, pp. 1, 8. See also "Předseda Evropské komise proti plánům USA na rozšíření NATO," *Hospodářské noviny* (Prague), 8 December 1994, p. 23.

66. "Kirchberg-Erklärung der Westeuropäischen Union: Tagung des Ministerrates der WEU am 9 Mai 1994 in Luxemburg," *Presse- und Informationsamt der Bundesregierung Bulletin* (Bonn), no. 46, 20 May 1994, pp. 405-409.

67. Marc Rogers, "WEU Edges Toward a European Defence," *Jane's Defence Weekly* (London) 22:20, 26 November 1994, p. 11. For background, see Michael Brenner, "Multilateralism and European Security," *Survival* (London) 35:2, Summer 1993, pp. 138-155; Jonathan Dean, *Ending Europe's Wars: The Continuing Search for Peace and Security* (New York: Twentieth Century Fund Press, 1994), pp. 265-287; Catherine McArdle Kelleher, *A New Security Order: The United States and the European Community in the 1990s,* Occasional Paper (Pittsburgh: European Community Studies Association, June 1993); Trevor Taylor, "West European Security and Defence Cooperation: Maastricht and Beyond," *International Affairs* 70:1, January 1994, pp. 1-16; and US Congress, House of Representatives, Committee on Foreign Affairs, Subcommittee on International Economic Policy and Trade/Subcommittee on Europe and the Middle East, *Europe and the United States—Competition and Cooperation in the 1990s: Study Papers,* 102nd Cong., 2nd Sess., June 1992.

68. Cited in Jerzy Czarnecki, "Polska w europejskim systemie bezpieczeństwa," *Polska zbrojna* (Warsaw), 3 March 1994, p. 1.

69. ITAR-TASS, 12 May 1994. See also Vladimir Katin, "Na vsyakii sluchai: Devyat' vostochnoevropeiskikh stran assotsiirovannymi chlenami ZES," *Nezavisimaya gazeta* (Moscow), 13 May 1994, p. 4.

70. Manki Ponomarev, "I nevinnost' soblyusti, i kapital priobresti—vot chem ozabocheno rukovodstvo ZES i NATO," *Krasnaya zvezda* (Moscow), 25 November 1994, p. 3.

71. A much smaller and less significant border exists between Italy and Slovenia.

72. The issue would become even more delicate if Serbia feared that Hungary's admission into NATO would increase the Hungarian government's willingness to support ethnic Hungarians in Vojvodina.

73. Ernö Raffay, a former top official in the Hungarian defense ministry, has even warned that Romania, Slovakia, and Serbia might join in a combined military effort against Hungary. See the interview in *Új Demokrata* (Budapest), 15 December 1994, pp. 8-9.

74. Judith Pataki, "The Hungarian Authorities' Reactions to the Violence in

Tirgu-Mures," Vladimir Socor, "Forces of Old Resurface in Romania: The Ethnic
Clashes in Tirgu-Mures," and Michael Shafir, "The Romanian Authorities' Reac-
tions to the Violence in Tirgu-Mures," all in *Radio Free Europe Report on Eastern
Europe* (Munich) 1:15, 13 April 1990, pp. 23-35, 36-43, and 43-47, respectively.

75. Interview with Hungarian Prime Minister Gyula Horn in "Ein NATO-Ungarn
wäre keine Bedrohung Russlands: SZ-Interview mit dem ungarischen
Ministerpräsidenten," *Süddeutsche Zeitung* (Munich), 30 November 1994, p. 12.
For background, see Alfred A. Reisch, "The New Hungarian Government's Foreign Policy," *RFE/RL Research Report* (Munich) 3:33, 26 August 1994, pp. 46-57,
esp. 50-54.

76. György Kelety, interview on Duna Television, Budapest, 20 November 1994.
Similarly, in late 1994 the acting Slovak defense minister, Imrich Andrejčak, emphasized that "a prerequisite for NATO membership will be the dependability, security, and *neighborly cooperation* of the applicants" ("Západní orientace Slovenska
je nezpochybnitelná") p. 4 (emphasis added).

77. On this very point, see the news conference with Ambassador Traian
Chebeleu, a top aide to Romanian President Ion Iliescu, in *Dimineata* (Bucharest),
13 December 1994, p. 2.

78. Article 5 affirms that "an armed attack against one or more of [the signatories]
in Europe or North America shall be considered an attack against them all, and consequently they agree that, if such an armed attack occurs, each of them . . . will assist the
Party or Parties so attacked by taking forthwith . . . such action as it deems necessary, including the use of armed force, to restore and maintain the security of the
North Atlantic area."

79. For different perspectives on these negotiations, see the interview with István
Gyarmati, chief Hungarian delegate to the CFE talks, in "Unzer Ziel ist ein
kooperatives Sicherheitssystem in Europa," *Die Presse* (Vienna), 24 October 1990,
p. 4; the interview with then Czechoslovak defense minister Luboš Dobrovský in
"Za šestatřicet měsícu nová armáda," *Mladá fronta dnes* (Prague), 13 December
1990, p. 3; "Na nachalakh razumnoi i nadezhnoi dostatochnosti dlya oborony,"
Krasnaya zvezda (Moscow), 6 July 1990, p. 2; and "Na Blaasstrasse 34 se finišuje:
Puvodni rozhovor HN s vedoucim delegace CSFR na vídenském jednáni o
konvenčnich ozbrojených silách," *Hospodářské noviny* (Prague), 15 October 1990,
p. 4. For another useful account of these talks, see Douglas L. Clarke, "The CFE
Talks: One Against Twenty-Two," *Radio Free Europe Report on Eastern Europe*
(Munich) 1:40, 5 October 1990, pp. 41-44.

80. Anna Wielopolska and Zbigniew Lentowicz, "Muzyka przeszłości: Jelcyn
kwestionuje polską drogę do NATO," *Rzeczpospolita* (Warsaw), 2-3 October 1993,
pp. 1-2. See also "Deklaracje Jelcyna były tylko gestem: Moskwa przeciw
rozszerzeniu NATO," *Rzeczpospolita* (Warsaw), 2-3 October 1993, p. 19. The
Russian government neglected to send a letter to Poland explaining why Yel'tsin
had changed his mind; see, for example, Andranik Migranyan, "Vneshnyaya
politika Rossii: Katastroficheskie itogi trekh let," *Nezavisimaya gazeta* (Moscow),

10 December 1994, p. 1; and Mikhail Karpov, "Voskhod NATO, zakat SBSE? Na dueli rossiiskogo i amerikanskogo prezidentov iz-za Evropy pobeda dostalas' Klintonu," *Nezavisimaya gazeta* (Moscow), 7 December 1994, p. 1.

81. Sergei Karaganov, "Rasshirenie NATO vedet k isolyatsii Rossii," *Moskovskie novosti* (Moscow), no. 38, 19 September 1993, p. 7.

82. Sluzhba vneshnei razvedki Rossii, *Perspektivy rasshireniya NATO i interesy Rossii* (Moscow), November 1993. The report was divided into two main sections: one focusing on the prospects for NATO's expansion, and the other dealing with the implications of such a development for Russian interests. Lengthy excerpts were published in many of Russia's leading newspapers. See, for example *Krasnaya zvezda* (Moscow), 30 November 1993, p. 3 and *Nezavisimaya gazeta* (Moscow), 26 November 1993, pp. 1, 3.

83. Stanley Sloan, "Transatlantic Relations in the Wake of the Brussels Summit," *NATO Review* 42:2, April 1994, pp. 27-31. For an overview of the PfP, see North Atlantic Assembly, International Secretariat, "NATO Enlargement and Partnership for Peace," Information Document AL GEN (94)-5, February 1994.

84. "Brak wizji Europy budzi demony: Udzielone w ostatnim tygodniu wywiady prezydenta Lecha Wałęsy na temat polityki zagranicznej," *Rzeczpospolita* (Warsaw), 8-9 January 1994, p. 20; "Prezydent i rząd o NATO: Zbyt krótki krok we właściwym kierunku," *Rzeczpospolita* (Warsaw), 11 January 1994, p. 1; and "Bez alternatywy: Kontrowersje wokół amerykańskiej propozycji," *Rzeczpospolita* (Warsaw), 12 January 1994, p. 23.

85. "Walka o wejście do sojuszu: Przed szczytem NATO," *Rzeczpospolita* (Warsaw), 8-9 January 1994, p. 21; and "Chci Evropu evropskou, Evropu všech jejích národů a státu," *Hospodářské noviny* (Prague), 2 December 1994, pp. 1, 23. At times, Havel has been more pointed in his criticisms, as in the fall of 1993 when he accused the West of resurrecting the "ghosts of Munich" and of "betraying" the East European states. See "Politycy przepowiadają długi marsz do NATO," *Rzeczpospolita* (Warsaw), 23-24 October 1993, pp. 1-2; "Drogą wstecz nie istnieje," *Rzeczpospolita* (Warsaw), 22 October 1993, pp. 1, 23; and "Havel w Warszawie: NATO nie jest wrogiem Rosji," *Rzeczpospolita* (Warsaw), 22 October 1993, p. 23.

86. For an overview of this controversy, see Michael Mihalka, "European-Russian Security and NATO's Partnership for Peace," *RFE/RL Research Report* (Munich) 3:33, 26 August 1994, pp. 34-45. See also US Congress, Commission on Security and Cooperation in Europe, *Russia and NATO: Moscow's Foreign Policy and the Partnership for Peace,* 103rd Cong., 2nd Sess., May 1994. For the Russian government's perspective, see Boris Kazantsev, "Pervye shagi k partnerstvu Rossii s NATO," *Mezhdunarodnaya zhizn'* (Moscow), no. 10, October 1994, pp. 22-29. Kazantsev was a senior foreign ministry official responsible for dealings with NATO.

87. P. E. Smirnov, "Dreif Vostochnoi Evropy na zapad i interesy Rossii," *SShA: Politika, Ekonomika, Ideologiya* (Moscow), no. 12, December 1994, p. 29.

88. "Protokol po itogam obsuzhdeniya mezhdu ministrom inostrannykh del Rossii Andreem Kozyrevym i Severoatlanticheskim sovetom," *Diplomaticheskii vestnik* (Moscow), nos. 13-14, July 1994, p. 31.

89. In mid-1993, before the PfP was formed, Poland took part in joint naval maneuvers in the Baltic Sea with the United States, Germany, and other NATO countries, but the exercises in September 1994 were the first exercises involving ground and air units.

90. Sergei Anisimov, "'Koopereitiv vencher-94': Rossiiskii i Andreevskii flagi—vpervye na sovmestnykh voenno-morskikh ucheniyakh s NATO," *Rossiiskie vesti* (Moscow), 19 October 1994, p. 3. For a valuable first-hand assessment of the exercise in the Russian Navy's main journal, see V. Ivanov, "Sovmestnoe deistvie-94," *Morskoi sbornik* (Moscow), no. 11, November 1994, pp. 39-43.

91. For a detailed analysis of this exercise, see Captain V. Pasyakin, "'Meritaim partner-94': Partnerstvo ili demonstratsiya prevoshodstva?" *Morskoi sbornik* (Moscow), no. 1, January 1995, pp. 35-38.

92. "Albania, U.S. Hail Their Joint Exercise," *The Washington Post,* 30 January 1995, p. A-12.

93. Imre Mecs, interview on Duna Television, Budapest, 20 November 1994.

94. Cited in Elaine Sciolino, "U.S. Wants to Expedite Entry of Eastern Nations Into Alliance," *The New York Times,* 27 October 1994, p. A-5.

95. Cited in Marc Rogers and Barbara Starr, "NATO: Ministers to Decide in '95 on New Members," *Jane's Defence Weekly* (London) 22:21, 3 December 1994, p. 6.

96. ITAR-TASS Newswire Report (Moscow), 1 December 1994.

97. Aleksandr Konovalov, "K novomu razdelu Evropy? Rossiya i Severoatlanticheskii al'yans," *Nezavisimaya gazeta* (Moscow), 7 December 1994, p. 5.

98. Mikhail Pogorelyi," Dvoinoi podkhod Rossiyu ne ustraivaet," *Krasnaya zvezda* (Moscow), 3 December 1994, p. 2; Mikhail Karpov, "Nesostoyavsheesya torzhestvo: Posle otkaza Rossii ot programmy sotrudnichestva s NATO uspekh Budapeshtskogo foruma SBSE stanovitsya problematichnym," *Nezavisimaya gazeta* (Moscow), 3 December 1994, p. 1; and "Zavtra ozhidaetsya podpisanie programmy 'Rossiya-NATO': No dlya etogo Sovet NATO dolzhen izyskat' 'okno' v svoem raspisanii," *Segodnya* (Moscow), 1 December 1994, p. 3.

99. Mikhail Karpov, "'My, evropeitsy…' Vchera Andrei Kozyrev vystupil na Parlamentskoi assamblee Zapadnoevropeiskogo soyuza v Parizhe," *Nezavisimaya gazeta* (Moscow), 2 December 1994, p. 1.

100. Ibid.

101. Throughout the speech Kozyrev played up the recent intra-NATO disputes

over the Balkans and other matters, and he emphasized that, in contrast to the "illegal" US position, the "Russian and WEU approaches to the Bosnian crisis are virtually identical." Although Kozyrev claimed that he was not seeking to split Western Europe from the United States, he clearly hoped to use the WEU itself as a wedge against NATO expansion. Among other things, he proposed "a more active search for common [Russian-WEU] approaches to the key problems of security in Europe," and called for the establishment of "joint groups of experts from Russia and the WEU to handle all problems of European security." With regard to specific areas of military cooperation, Kozyrev claimed that Russia wanted to pursue "joint military exercises" with the WEU (rather than through NATO mechanisms), "the joint development of a European anti-tactical ballistic missile defense" (implicitly omitting the United States), and the sharing of Russian satellite and aerial reconnaissance information with the WEU, a crucial function that the United States has long performed for the West European countries via NATO. The speech as a whole was reminiscent of Soviet attempts in the 1960s, 1970s, and 1980s to sow dissension within NATO, and as such it was likely to do little for the Russian cause. Still, to the extent that Kozyrev could stir up even a few extra doubts about the wisdom of admitting the East European states into NATO (as opposed to admitting them into a "new all-European security institution"), he might simply have been hoping to prevent the alliance from reaching a consensus in favor of enlargement.

102. Vladimir Kuzar', "Vstrecha SBSE na vysshem urovne ischet puti k Evrope XXI veka—kontinentu mira i bezopasnosti," *Krasnaya zvezda* (Moscow), 6 December 1994, p. 1; Aleksandr Gol'ts, "V dekabre nastupil 'kholodnyi mir'?" *Krasnaya zvezda* (Moscow), 7 December 1994, p. 2; and Dmitri Gornostaev, "Rossiya rasschityvaet na uchet svoikh interesov: Boris El'tsin schitaet, chto bloki i koalitsii ne dadut Evrope polnykh garantii bezopasnosti," *Nezavisimaya gazeta* (Moscow), 6 December 1994, pp. 1-2. For East European reactions to the Russian statements, see Maria Wągrowska, "Rosja grozi zerwaniem współpracy z NATO," *Rzeczpospolita* (Warsaw), 2 December 1994, p. 13; "KBSE: panovala shoda, ale s výhradami," *Lidové noviny* (Prague), 6 December 1994, p. 6; and "Budapesht videl bolee svetlye dni nashei diplomatii," *Izvestiya* (Moscow), 7 December 1994, pp. 1, 3.

103. Steven Erlanger, "Gore Upbeat After Talks with Top Russian Leaders," *The New York Times,* 17 December 1994, p. 7.

104. In Eastern Europe, by contrast, vigorous condemnations of Russia's actions in Chechnya were often accompanied by renewed appeals for the prompt enlargement of NATO. See, for example, Jiří Doubrava "Postsovětská dvanáctka má propletené kořeny," *Mladá fronta dnes* (Prague), 31 December 1994, p. 10; and Centrum Badania Opinii Społecznej, *Polską-Rosja-NATO* (Warsaw: CBOS, January 1995). Concern about the implications of Russia's policy in Chechnya was evident even before the conflict escalated. See, for example, Wojciech Jagielski and Bartosz Weglarczyk, "Propagandowa wojną o Czecznię," *Gazeta wyborcza* (Warsaw), 30 August 1994, pp. 6-7.

105. See, for example, Zbigniew Brzezinski, "A Plan for Europe," *Foreign Affairs* 74:1, January-February 1995, pp. 26-42 (condensed in "NATO—Expand or Die?" *The New York Times,* 28 December 1994, p. A-15); Leslie Gelb, "Quelling the Teacup Wars: The New World's Constant Challenge," *Foreign Affairs* 73:6, November-December 1994, pp. 2-7, esp. 3-4; and Samuel P. Huntington, "America's Changing Strategic Interests," *Survival* 33:1, January-February 1991, pp. 3-17, esp. 13. For an opposing view by another prominent expert, see Fred C. Ikle, "How to Ruin NATO," *The New York Times,* 11 January 1995, p. A-21.

106. Cited in "Komu otworzyć drzwi do Paktu," *Rzeczpospolita* (Warsaw), 8 October 1993, p. 23.

107. See, for example, Walter L. Bühl, "Gesellschaftliche Grundlagen der Deutschen Aussenpolitik," in Karl Kaiser and Hanns W. Maull, eds., *Deutschlands neue Aussenpolitik,* Band 1: *Grundlagen* (Munich: R. Oldenbourg Verlag, 1994), pp. 175-201, esp. 199.

108. Volker Rühe, "NATO in the Post–Cold War World," in *U.S. Relations with Central and Eastern Europe: Fifteenth Conference, August 23-27 1994,* Dick Clark, ed. (Queenstown, MD: The Aspen Institute, 1994), p. 26 (emphasis added). For an equally unambiguous statement by another senior German military official, see the interview with General Henning von Ondarza in "Rogatywka w NATO," *Polityka* (Warsaw), no. 50, 10 December 1994, p. 13.

109. Ibid.

110. German Press Agency wire report, 21 June 1993. Lugar presented these same remarks in his address before the Overseas Press Club, "NATO: Out of Area or Out of Business," Washington, DC, 24 June 1993.

111. See, for example, Ewa Szymańska, "Minister Onyszkiewicz w Waszyngtonie," *Rzeczpospolita* (Warsaw), 26-27 June 1993, p. 17. See also Sylwester Walczak, "Spór, który podzielił sojusz: Amerykańska dyskusja o członkostwie państw Europy Środkowo-wschodniej w NATO," *Rzeczpospolita* (Warsaw), 22 October 1993, p. 22.

112. On the concept of "cooperative security," see Janne E. Nolan, ed., *Global Engagement: Cooperation and Security in the 21st Century* (Washington, DC: Brookings Institution, 1994). A related concept that is even more germane in this context is "mutual security," as developed in Richard Smoke and Andrei Kortunov, eds., *Mutual Security: A New Approach to Soviet-American Relations* (New York: St. Martin's Press, 1990). Some experts in the Visegrad countries claim that certain NATO countries, especially the United States, may have actively encouraged Yel'tsin to retract his initial statements. The rationale, in their view, was to get a suitable pretext for deferring consideration indefinitely of full East-Central European membership in NATO. The evidence for these assertions is inconclusive.

113. "KBSE se vraci do politiky USA," *Lidové noviny* (Prague), 5 December 1994, p. 6.

114. "Echa Brukseli w Europie Środkowej" and "Żyrinowski grozi III wojną," both in *Rzeczpospolita* (Warsaw), 11 January 1994, p. 23; "Zieleniec: Definovat bezpečnostní struktury," *Lidové noviny* (Prague), 12 December 1994, p. 1; Andrzej Olechowski, "Ku jednej bezpecznej Europie," *Rzeczpospolita* (Warsaw), 28 November 1994, p. 28; the interview with Olechowski in "La Pologne dans l'Union européenne en l'an 2000," *Libération* (Paris), 14 December 1994, p. 13; Barbara Sierzula, "Zgoda na Partnerstwo," *Rzeczpospolita* (Warsaw), 13 January 1994, p. 1; and "Olechowski o bezpieczeństwie Polski: Dziś lepiej niz wczoraj," *Rzeczpospolita* (Warsaw), 19 January 1994, p. 23.

115. The record in this regard is not perfect—the breakdown of democracy in Greece in 1967 is the obvious exception—but it comes very close. Although numerous problems remain in Turkey today, those problems are undoubtedly much less severe than they would be if Turkey were not a member of NATO.

116. This argument also applies to the sustenance of democracy in postwar Germany. See Jeffrey J. Anderson and John B. Goodman, "Mars or Minerva? A United Germany in a Post–Cold War Europe," in Robert O. Keohane, Joseph S. Nye, and Stanley Hoffmann, eds., *After the Cold War: International Institutions and State Strategies in Europe, 1988-1991* (Cambridge, MA: Harvard University Press, 1993), pp. 23-62.

117. See, for example, the interview with then-Czech Defense Minister Antonin Baudys in "Čim driv budeme v NATO, tim lépe," *Lidové noviny* (Prague), 12 October 1993, p. 8. See also Andrzej Olechowski, "Lepsza historia kontynentu: Europa według ministra spraw zagranicznych," *Polityka* (Warsaw), no. 50, 10 December 1994, pp. 1, 13.

118. The view that democratic states do not go to war with one another was first put forth by Immanuel Kant in *Perpetual Peace* and has recently been developed in more elaborate form, albeit often with strongly Kantian overtones, by several Western political theorists and specialists in international relations. See, for example, the two-part essay by Michael Doyle: "Kant, Liberal Legacies, and Foreign Affairs," *Philosophy and Public Affairs* 12:3, Summer 1983, pp. 205-235 (Part 1) and 12:4, Fall 1983, pp. 323-353 (Part 2). The empirical evidence for the proposition may not be ironclad, but it is very strong. The only "exceptions" to the rule (for example, the Anglo-American conflict in 1812) depend on highly questionable definitions of "democracy." See James Lee Ray, *Democracies and International Conflict* (Columbia, SC: University of South Carolina Press, 1994); Spencer R. Weart, "Peace Among Democratic and Oligarchic Republics," *Journal of Peace Research* 31:3, August 1994, pp. 299-316; Nils Petter Gleditsch, "Democracy and Peace," *Journal of Peace Research* 29:4, November 1992, pp. 369-76; Steve Chan, "Mirror, Mirror on the Wall . . . Are The Democratic States More Pacific?" *Journal of Conflict Resolution* 28:2, Spring 1984, pp. 617-48; and Charles Kegley, "The Long Postwar Peace During the Cold War," *Jerusalem Journal of International Relations* 14:4, December 1992, pp. 1-18.

119. Imre Mecs, interview on Duna Television, Budapest, 20 November 1994.

120. Comments by Csába Takacs, national executive chairman of the Hungarian Democratic Union of Romania, op. cit.

121. See, for example, "Polityka bezpieczeństwa i strategia obronna Rzeczypospolitej Polskiej," *Polska zbrojna* (Warsaw), 12 November 1992, pp. 1-2; and "Założenia polskiej polityki bezpieczeństwa," *Polska zbrojna* (Warsaw), 3 November 1992, p. 2.

122. Centrum Badania Opinii Społecznej (CBOS), *Polska-Rosja-NATO,* pp. 3-8; "Partnerstwo dla Pokoju i przystapienie Polski do NATO," *Serwis Informacyjny* (Warsaw), July 1994, pp. 11-17; and CBOS, "Miejsce Polski w Europie, pozadani partnerzy gospodarczy i polityczni," *Serwis Informacyjny* (Warsaw), August 1994, pp. 28-34. See further results from the CBOS surveys in "Polacy o NATO i 'Partnerstwie dla Pokoju'," *Przegląd Rządowy* (Warsaw), no. 39, September 1994, pp. 41-42.

123. "Veřejné mínĕni k NATO," *Hospodářské noviny* (Prague), 9 December 1994, p. 2.

124. CBOS, "Partnerstwo dla Pokoju i przystapienie Polski do NATO." It should be noted, however, that public views of the PfP in Poland have become substantially more favorable over time, though still only a minority regard it positively.

125. "Václav Havel: Dobá velkých společných gest pominula," p. 7.

126. See, for example, "Nie drażnić Moskwy: W Kopenhadze o NATO," *Rzeczpospolita* (Warsaw), 12 October 1993, pp. 1, 21.

127. This point has been explicitly mentioned in one of the most insightful Russian analyses of the subject. See Smirnov, "Dreif Vostochnoi Evropy na zapad i interesy Rossii," op. cit., p. 30. In pointing out that Ukraine had earlier proposed the formation of a "Central European Zone of Security" to surround Russia, Smirnov argues that it would be better for Russia if Poland were to join NATO and put an end to any such ideas.

128. Polish experts began raising these arguments at a very early stage; see, for example, Waldemar Piotrowski, "Wojska NATO w Polsce? Szansa w nowej roli," *Życie Warszawy* (Warsaw), 1 June 1990, p. 5; and Jan Rylukowski, "Nowe wyzwania, stare odpowiedzi—remanenty polskiej polityki zagranicznej," *Tygodnik Solidarność* (Warsaw), no. 37, 14 September 1990, p. 5.

129. Reisch, "The New Hungarian Government's Foreign Policy," pp. 46-57.

130. On this point, see "Sprawa NATO testem dla postkomunistow," *Rzeczpospolita* (Warsaw), 8 October 1993, p. 22.

131. See, for example, "Zacharski to ja: Minister Andrzej Milczanowski broni kontrowersyjnej nominacji," *Gazeta wyborcza* (Warsaw), 24 August 1994, p. 1; and Jacek Kalabiński, "Pastusiak, Zacharski—szlaban do NATO," *Gazeta wyborcza* (Warsaw), 12 January 1995, p. 7.

132. Cited in Edward Krzemień, "Boks zagraniczny: Koalicja atakuje, Olechowski odpiera ataki," *Gazeta wyborcza* (Warsaw), 6 January 1995, p. 3.

133. Imre Mecs, cited in *Heti Világgazdaság* (Budapest), 12 November 1994, pp. 103-104.

134. For a useful survey of the ambiguities in Poland's civil-military relations, see the interview with the Deputy Minister of National Defense Danuta Waniek in "Logika demokracji czyli o cywilnej kontroli nad armia," *Polska zbrojna* (Warsaw), 2-4 December 1994, pp. 1-2. For additional background, see Andrzej Korbonski, "The Polish Military at a Time of Change," *RFE/RL Research Report* (Munich) 3:30, 29 July 1994, pp. 17-22. For a critical perspective on the latest dispute, see the interview with Janusz Onyszkiewicz in "Akcja generałów była wywołana przez Wałęsę," *Życie Warszawy* (Warsaw), 6 October 1994, p. 2.

135. Joris Janssen Lok, "Naval Forces: Polish Update Studies Western Systems," *Jane's Defence Weekly* (London) 22:17, 22 October 1994, p. 20; and "Letoun L-159 nemuši mit pouze americkou techniku, mini Dlouhy," *Mladá fronta dnes* (Prague), 3 December 1994, p. 2.

136. John Berg and Johan Rapp, "Naval Forces: Baltic States Receive Storm Patrol Boats," *Jane's Defence Weekly* (London) 23:2, 14 January 1995, p. 9.

137. "NATO ATC Proposed for Former Pact Countries," *Jane's Defence Weekly* (London) 23:2, 14 January 1995, p. 2.

138. The motivation for the "Peace Pannon" deal, from the US perspective, was simply to ensure that NATO's E-3 Airborne Warning and Control System (AWACS) aircraft, which were using Hungarian airspace to monitor the conflict in the former Yugoslavia, would be able to distinguish Hungary's MiG fighters from those flown by Serb and Croat forces.

139. "S MiGy-29 nechce armáda riskovat," *Mladá fronta dnes* (Prague), 19 November 1994, p. 5.

140. Hans-Werner Jarosch and Gero Schachthofer, "Die Luftwaffe in den kunftigen NATO-Streitkräftestrukturen," *Europäische Sicherheit* (Munich) 41:5, May 1992, pp. 280-84.

141. Grzegorz Lubczyk, "Kosztowne 'Partnerstwo'," *Rzeczpospolita* (Warsaw), 15-16 January 1994, p. 23. See also Ian Anthony, "International Dimensions of Industrial Restructuring," in Ian Anthony, ed., *The Future of the Defence Industries in Central and Eastern Europe,* SIPRI Research Report No. 7 (Oxford: Oxford University Press, 1994), p. 101.

142. Dana Priest and Daniel Williams, "U. S. Allows Arms Sales to 10 in Ex-East Block: Barrier to Offensive Weaponry is Removed," *The Washington Post,* 18 February 1995, pp. A-1, A-12. Most restrictions had been eliminated a few years earlier, but this decision cleared the way for the sale of tanks, artillery, combat aircraft, missiles, and other weapons useful for offensive operations. The decision did not apply to the CIS member-states.

143. As of late 1994, one of the Czech Army's mechanized divisions had been converted into a mechanized brigade, and its infantry division had been disbanded. Further moves to a brigade basis were underway. The Polish Army had disbanded one mechanized division and converted another. See the interview with General Stanisław Koziej, director of the defense system department in the Polish National Defense Ministry, in "Gry wojenne," *Gazeta wyborcza* (Warsaw), 15 December 1994, p. 10.

144. Interview on Duna Television, Budapest, 20 November 1994.

145. Interview with General Stanisław Koziej, in "Gry wojenne," p. 11.

146. Evamaria Loose-Weintraub and Ian Anthony, "Military Expenditure in Transition," in Anthony, ed., *The Future of the Defence Industries in Central and Eastern Europe,* pp. 37-57.

147. See the interview with the deputy secretary-general of NATO, Sergio Balanzino, in *Népszava* (Budapest), 11 November 1994, pp. 1, 9.

148. "Bezpečnost všech a pro všechny," *Hospodářské noviny* (Prague), 8 December 1994, p. 3. See also Václav Klaus, "Rozpočet a věčné levicové vábeni," *Lidové noviny* (Prague), 5 September 1994, p. 5.

149. Vilěm Holan, "Zisk a cena vstupu do NATO," *Lidové noviny* (Prague), 19 November 1994, p. 5. Holan became Czech defense minister in September 1994, replacing Antonin Baudys.

150. Interview with General Stanisław Koziej in "Gry wojenne," p. 11. See also "Możemy liczyć na pomoc: Olechowski i Pawlak po powrocie z Pragi," *Rzeczpospolita* (Warsaw), 14 January 1994, pp. 1, 23.

151. See, for example, the interview with Ambassador Traian Chebeleu, a senior aide to Romanian president Ion Iliescu, in *Dimineata* (Bucharest), 13 December 1994, pp. 2-3; the interview with General Gheorghe Rotaru, director of political analysis and international relations in the Romanian National Defense Ministry, in *Jane's Defence Weekly* (London) 23:2, 14 January 1995, p. 32; the interview with Radu Timofte, chairman of the Committee on Defense in the Romanian Senate, on the Bucharest Radio Network, 21 November 1994; and Maja Narbutt, "Własną drogą ze Wschodu na Zachód: Zgłoszenie przez Litwę akcesu do NATO jest dla Zachodu nieprzyjemną niespodzianką," *Rzeczpospolita* (Warsaw), 11 January 1994, p. 21.

152. Interview with Leonid Kuchma in "Danger Is Seen in Rapid NATO Expansion," *The Washington Post,* 23 November 1994, p. A-16.

153. Vladimir Skachko, "Iz mira vrazhdy—v mir problem: Kuchma v Budapeshte popytaetsya razblokirovat' pomoshch' Zapada Kievu," *Nezavisimaya gazeta* (Moscow), 6 December 1994, p. 3; and Vladimir Skachko, "V Budapeshte poverili Kievu," *Nezavisimaya gazeta* (Moscow), 9 December 1994, p. 3.

154. Vanya Encheva, "Edin ochakvan i zhelan razvod," *Zemedelsko zname* (Sofia), 2 April 1991, p. 4.

155. Interview with Polish Foreign Minister Krzysztof Skubiszewski in "Nic o Polsce bez Polski," p. 10.

156. Interview with Václav Havel in "On doit s'opposer au mal des le debut," *Libération* (Paris), 2 December 1994, p. 7.

157. Comments by the late NATO Secretary-General Manfred Wörner, cited in "Die Tschechoslowakei will eng mit der NATO zusammenarbeiten," *Die Welt* (Hamburg), 10 July 1993, p. 2.

158. "Partnership with the Countries of Central and Eastern Europe," statement issued by the North Atlantic Council's Ministerial Session in Copenhagen, 6-7 June 1991, Point 9.

159. For first-hand perspectives on these events, see A. S. Chernyaev, *Shest' let s Gorbachevym: Po dnevnikovym zapisyam* (Moscow: Progress-Kultura, 1993), pp. 304-310, 346-347; Sergei Akhromeev and Georgii Kornienko, *Glazami marshala i diplomata* (Moscow: Mezhdunarodnye otnosheniya, 1992), pp. 213-259; Valentin Falin, *Politische Erinnerungen* (Munich: Dromer Knaur, 1993), pp. 437-442, 451-493; Igor Maksimychev and Hans Modrow, *Poslednii god GDR* (Moscow: Mezhdunarodnye otnosheniya, 1993); and Yuli Kvitsinski, *Vor der Sturm: Erinnerungen eines Diplomaten* (Berlin: Siedler, 1993), esp. pp. 419-448.

160. Maj.-General M. Monin, "Politizatsiya OVD i NATO: Real'nost' i perspektivy," *Krasnaya zvezda* (Moscow), 4 May 1990, p. 3. Among countless other high-level Soviet statements condemning the prospect of German membership in NATO, see the interview with defense minister Dmitri Yazov in "Ot protivostoyaniya—k sisteme bezopasnosti," *Izvestiya* (Moscow), 13 May 1990, p. 3; interview with Yazov in "Zashchishchaya bezopasnost' naroda," *Pravda* (Moscow), 23 February 1990, p. 2.; interview with Marshal Sergei Akhromeev in "My dolzhny borot'sya za pravdu," *Krasnaya zvezda* (Moscow), 24 April 1990, pp. 1-2; interview with deputy foreign minister Anatoli Adamishin in "Po formule '2 plyus 4'," *Literaturnaya gazeta* (Moscow), no. 17, 25 April 1990, p. 15; comments of Valentin Falin in "Dve Germanii, odna Evropa?" *Pravda* (Moscow), 12 March 1990, p. 5; interview with Falin in "Sicherheitsbalance—Kern der deutschen Frage: Gespräch mit Valentin Falin, Leiter der Internationalen Abteilung des ZK der KPdSU," *Neues Deutschland* (East Berlin), 9 February 1990, p. 6; and interview with Falin in "'Für militärische Neutralität': Gorbatschows Deutschland-Experte Walentin Falin über die deutsche Einheit," *Der Spiegel* (Hamburg), no. 8, 19 February 1990, pp. 168-172.

161. "Gorbatschow und die deutsche Einheit," *Frankfurter Allgemeine Magazin* (Frankfurt), 17 June 1994, p. 23. Some recriminations about the "loss" of Eastern Europe arose well before Gorbachev's volte-face on the German issue, and the bickering continued until the aborted coup of August 1991; but the specific question of German membership in NATO had almost no effect on the exchanges one way or the other.

162. "Russia Seeks Greater CFE Vehicle Allowance," *Jane's Defence Weekly*

(London) 23:1, 7 January 1995, p. 5. For background on this matter, see Douglas L. Clarke, "The Russian Military and the CFE Treaty," *RFE/RL Research Report* (Munich) 2:42, 22 October 1993, pp. 38-43.

163. "Gefahr eines neuen Jalta," *Der Spiegel* (Hamburg), no. 7, 13 February 1995, pp. 136-138.

164. Ibid., p. 136.

165. For a more pessimistic appraisal, see Konovalov, "K novomu razdelu Evropy?" op. cit., p. 5.

III

THE
WESTERN
RESPONSE:

NATO;
THE UNITED STATES (DESCRIPTIVE);
THE UNITED STATES (PRESCRIPTIVE)

7

Decline, in Character:
Muffing NATO's Opportunity

Angelo M. Codevilla

> *"What happens when a determinedly impotent consensus wrests leadership from a supine superpower?"*
> —William Safire

Safire's question regarding the contemporary relationship between the United States and the rest of NATO is well-framed, except that Europe did not "wrest" leadership from the United States. In fact, the "determinedly impotent" politicians on the eastern shores of the Atlantic and the "supine" ones on the banks of the Potomac have regarded the former communist world from similar perspectives. Because they simultaneously shun leadership in military matters, their reaction to the opportunity to expand NATO eastward has been equally feckless. So, though the future of Western Europe has passed from America's hands, it is not in any other set of hands, either.

This chapter argues that the desire of various former communist countries—but especially Poland, Hungary, the Czech Republic, and Slovakia (the so-called Visegrad states[1])—for membership in NATO has embarrassed the governments of NATO Europe possibly even more than it has the government of the United States. It is customary to view NATO's dilemma as fear of a security vacuum on its eastern borders countered by fear that filling it would anger Russia. However when, in August 1993, President Boris Yel'tsin seemed to withdraw Russia's objection to NATO's inclusion of the Visegrad states, NATO did not quickly foreclose the vacuum. This is wholly unremarkable. Indeed, the unseriousness of subsequent acceptances and rejections has been consistent with the way in which Western foreign policy had been developing during the later part of the Cold War.

By 1989, Western Europe had long since ceased to hope for victory. In all but a purely formal sense, the overall effort to safeguard Europe's freedom had become the responsibility of the United States, and US military plans were becoming less realistic by the year. Hence, when victory came, there was no pent-up desire, and no backlog of plans to make something of it—certainly not in any military sense. In Europe even more than in the United States the events of 1989-91 were taken as a release from military worries forevermore. Modern West European regimes, absorbed by the business of parceling out the burdens and benefits of the welfare state, have accustomed themselves to discussions of defense so abstract as to be essentially means to avoid confronting military problems. Thus the defense section of the Maastricht Treaty, a masterpiece of abstraction by proceduralism, is actually an agreement to defer discussing the subject.

The European consensus to avoid military questions is remarkable also because it has waxed while Yugoslavia's war of dismemberment has been raging and Franco-British troops have been in the line of fire. That the European governments considered the Yugoslav situation a further incentive to remain unserious about military matters is important also as an indication of how they would react to graver challenges.

Finally, this consensus was surely shaped by the fact that in the early 1990s Americans were coming to Europe with questions rather than suggestions—and that they were happier than ever to receive fuzzy answers. So long accustomed to looking up to America's policy as the standard of military responsibility, NATO Europe had no difficulty adjusting to a lower American standard that now more nearly matched its own. President Bill Clinton's proposal of a contentless Partnership for Peace that would circle the globe—from the Bering Straits to the Bering Straits—fits perfectly the desire of many West Europeans simply not to deal with the whole subject of security against the secular troubles of the East, now compounded by three generations of totalitarianism.

German Defense Minister Volker Rühe's statements since September 13, 1994 that he expects the Visegrad states to become full members of NATO soon,[2] is not taken in Moscow, Washington, or apparently anywhere else, to mean that NATO's European members are willing to wage conventional war to defend Visegrad's eastern borders. Nor does anyone take the subsequent heartfelt statements in favor of NATO's expansion by Richard

Holbrooke, US Assistant Secretary of State for European Affairs, to mean that the United States is ready to wage nuclear war for those borders. Indeed the NATO governments' most pro-expansion statements clearly underline the theme of this chapter, namely the desire—almost as strong and widespread in Western Europe today as it was in 1950—somehow to keep the United States pledged to defend the eastern frontier, which most Europeans are very glad has shifted eastward. Nevertheless, though Europeans are more or less eager to see Poland and the other Visegrad countries defended, they want this to be accomplished by some sort of international arrangement, or by America, or perhaps by magic. The notion that *they* might do it has not entered public discourse. Americans too are glad that freedom has moved eastward in Europe, and lately have come around to the notion that a power vacuum between NATO and Russia is bad. But more than ever they believe that Europe's defense is Europe's business. Neither Holbrooke nor anyone else has told them otherwise, or why.

The heart of the matter is what has not happened: No West European country has made any commitment to the defense of any former communist country, or done anything to cause the United States to make such a commitment. Democratic countries make real commitments only after public discussions of serious proposals by serious leaders. There have been no real commitments because there have been no discussions, because there have been no serious proposals. All that is because the leaders do not speak a language in which such proposals could be formulated and debated. To make serious proposals one would have to sweep away fashionable talk of the end of history, recognize the character of the political forces that are reassembling the Russian Empire, and understand the ethical, economic, and military dimensions of the problem.

AN INSTANCE OF IMPOTENCE

After World War II a majority of Western Europe's political class yearned to liberate the east from Soviet tyranny and to build a Europe stronger and truer to its principles than ever. Konrad Adenauer, Charles de Gaulle, and Alcide de Gasperi made careers by looking forward to the day when Russia would retreat and resume its normal identity, and East-Central Europe could be reabsorbed into Christian civilization. To bring that day closer, they roused their poor, war-shattered countries to considerable military efforts. They and their immediate successors welcomed American nuclear weapons without reservation. Their leadership cast into the wilderness politicians like Kurt Schumacher and Pietro Nenni, who regarded military matters and especially nuclear ones as obscenities, who saw no enemy to the east or to the left, and who proposed a secular, collectivist cultural agenda.

By 1989, however, the tables had turned, and secularism, collectivism, and antimilitarism had become the order of the day. Far from regarding the East as an abomination to be guarded against, Western Europe's new leaders wanted to accommodate it. Schumacher's successors at the head of the West German Social Democratic Party (SPD) had been conducting a dialogue with East Germany's ruling communist party. Out of this had come agreement not just that Europe should be denuclearized, but that the socialist movement on both sides of the iron curtain shared a love of peace and goodness that set it apart from America. The German socialists actually got the British Labour Party to "support the principles worked out between the SPD and the SED [Socialist Unity Party]"[3] on these matters. Even though left-wing parties had been out of office in Germany and much of the rest of Europe during the 1980s, their ideas on security matters had become the standard for conservative politicians and, of course, for opinion leaders. Consider Britain's (and Europe's) foremost Germanist, Sir Ralf Dahrendorf, who wrote that "the GDR [German Democratic Republic] is the first modern society on German soil," that it had established its legitimacy by providing multiple channels of social mobility, and that to regard it as a mere creature of Soviet power would be a dangerous delusion.[4]

The official position of the SPD, uncontested by the Christian Democrats much less by the press and intellectual circles, was that the "Adenauer conception" (East Germany is illegitimate and will eventually be absorbed by the West) had been tragically wrong, that anticommunism had contributed to the division of Europe, if indeed it had not been its prime cause, and that the path to peace and progress now was more or less what it should have been in the late 1940s—heartfelt recognition of the legitimacy of the East European communist regimes, and transcendence of the senseless rivalry between the United States and the Soviet Union. Vestiges of the "Adenauer conception" were pathological. In 1988, when the GDR's dictator, Erich Honecker, visited Bonn and his birthplace in the Saarland, Helmut Kohl's conservative government treated him not as the Gauleiter of the "Soviet Occupied Zone," but as a long-misunderstood brother. Right up until the summer of 1989, the leading shaper of Europe's foreign policy, Germany's Foreign Minister Hans Dietrich Genscher, was steering a course between East and West. Genscher's Europe would build a privileged position for itself by brokering American concessions to the Soviet Empire, and by financing its communist regimes. This strategy had predictable effects, among them that, by 1989, European public opinion had come to regard Soviet dictator Mikhail Gorbachev as the harbinger of peace, and Ronald Reagan as dangerously obsessed with military matters.

Nor did America's foreign policy discourage this *Ostpolitik* (Ronald Reagan's occasional speeches of 1981-83 to the contrary notwithstanding). In 1981, when Reagan told the graduates of Notre Dame that communism was a "bizarre chapter in human history whose last pages are even now being written," Strobe Talbott reported—accurately—that this view was "idiosyncratic, extremist, and very much confined to the fringes of the government."[5] Later, Talbott rightly noted about a similar Reagan speech to the British parliament that "very few in the West took it seriously *as a statement of policy. . . .* There was little follow up in the form of cables from the State Department, Pentagon, or Central Intelligence Agency."[6] Real US policy, again ably chronicled by Strobe Talbott,[7] was to help a faltering Soviet Union to survive, help it to reform, and together with it to establish a peaceful, progressive world order. In this perspective, to enhance the United States' or its allies' preparedness for military defense would strengthen the hand of "hard-liners" in the Soviet Empire, while weakening Western military forces would strengthen Eastern reformers. Genscher could not have said it better.

This had been the entirety of US policy between 1941 and 1945. Not even between 1948 and 1961 was it completely extinguished. Thereafter it gradually regained prominence until, in President George Bush's Kiev speech, August 31, 1991, it was expressed more forthrightly than Henry Wallace would ever have dared to do.

According to this view, the Cold War was ending because reform-minded people "at the highest levels" on both sides had decided to strengthen each other by mutual concessions. Hence in 1990, as East Europeans were trying to rid themselves of all Soviet troops and were overthrowing every vestige of Soviet suzerainty, the US government was trying to negotiate equal, stable levels of Soviet and American troops on each side of a rapidly disappearing line. Also according to this view, the reunification of Germany occurred not because ordinary persons walked away from rotten communist regimes, but because a generation of Genschers had created a climate of rapprochement and because Secretary of State James Baker III conceived a diplomatic negotiating formula beyond his predecessors' ken known as "Four" (the victorious allies of World War II) "plus Two" (East and West Germany).

Meanwhile, of course, East Germans had entirely abandoned their government and, the moment guns ceased preventing them, were effectively incorporating themselves into the one Federal Republic, just as Adenauer had envisaged. Even as George Bush and the State Department were talking of a "New World Order" based on the UN's original conception of Soviet-American condominium, their Soviet interlocutor was disappearing.

Lifelong habits of thought and action endure in the people they shape, even through changing circumstances. Hence, the European and American foreign policy classes reacted to the end of the Cold War by attempting to carry on, as much as possible, as if events had gone as they had desired. They have treated

Russia as though it were the practical equivalent of the Soviet Union for which they had always wished. Thus *Time* magazine named Mikhail Gorbachev "Man of the Decade" for 1990, as if he had succeeded rather than failed, and the theme of its presentation essay was: "The doves in the great debate of the past 40 years were right all along." Whereas this point of view was hotly debated in the United States, in Europe it well-nigh monopolized policymakers.

Persons thus habituated, on both sides of the Atlantic, had become accustomed to thinking of the NATO alliance as at worst an unwarranted provocation, but usually as one more means of cooperation with the Soviet Empire or with whatever threat might come along. For them the end of the Cold War is an excuse to do what they really wanted to do all along, namely to forget about differences between nations and the burdens of national existence. The Visegrad states, however, come to NATO's door with entirely different mentalities. Their overriding priority, to re-establish national existence (so as never again to have to follow Moscow's will), clashes with the dominant passion of NATO's elite, to live as if history had ended. Moreover, because Visegrad's agenda hearkens back to NATO's original purpose and calls forth NATO's original emphasis on military commitment, it embarrasses those whose ends and means had changed.

In an article written as the hammer and sickle was coming down the Kremlin's flagpole Stephen Flanagan, a member of the State Department's Policy Planning Staff, described this mindset: "A rush by NATO now to forge closer ties to a few [East European] states could not only alarm defense officials in Russia and other republics but, more important, could undercut . . . reformers who are arguing for more cooperative security relationships with the West."[8] But no one in power in the West was proposing to rush. On the contrary: "A number of NATO states," reports Flanagan, "were at first reluctant" to have anything to do with the Poles, Czechs, and Hungarians, beyond information exchanges; but, he noted, the American side was bolder. At the June 1991 meeting of the North Atlantic Council, Secretary Baker offered a *dramatic* five-point plan: Liaison between NATO and would-be entrants should open up new channels, it should promote better understanding of everyone's security concerns, it should transfer some technical expertise, it should be flexible [!], and it should be coordinated with the activities of other European organizations such as the EC, the CSCE, and the WEU. This package of empty calories had its intended effect: The would-be members got the hint "not to press too hard at the NATO door for now."[9]

Ever since 1991 the relationship between NATO and its suitors has been a series of more-or-less nuanced requests followed by "put-offs" of one form or another. The "Partnership for Peace" was largely recognized as such. The German-American campaign for *inclusion* of Visegrad, which began in 1994, however, is no less a "put-off."

The ostensible reasons for the "put-offs" are dismissible easily enough: The Visegrad states should make their military budgets more "transparent." (They are more than eager to do so.) These states should establish civilian control over the armed forces. (Are those who make the objection seriously afraid that some Polish forces may be too pro-Russian? Hardly.) The Visegrad states have equipment that is not interoperable with NATO's. (True, but interoperability could be viewed as a challenge to be met, rather than as a reason to keep out these states.) Indeed, whenever the Visegrad states have asked for a formal list of conditions that they would have to meet in order to become full members of NATO, the answers have been reducible to the Spanish: *mañana*. The inescapable conclusion is that the Partnership's activities—meaningless maneuvers and nebulous joint missions between the Visegrad armies and NATO—are not a preparation for expansion but a substitute for it, and that the reason for this is not any insufficiency on the part of Visegrad. As Poland's foreign minister has noted, the question of Poland's membership is not technical but political:[10] Simply put, none of the NATO governments want to take on added military responsibility.

François Heisbourg writes to this point: "The post-communist states are probably less eager to participate substantially in military burden-sharing than to use membership in NATO as a way of locking themselves into the West."[11] True. But why would European politicians, who are experts at shifting as much of their military burden as possible onto the United States, blame the newly freed states for wanting perhaps to take some more protection than they give? After all, the Visegrad states say to Western Europe precisely what Western Europe says to America: You may be spending more money and supplying more weapons, but we make the inestimable contribution of being your front line of defense. Why don't West Europeans, who have lived by that argument for so long, also accept it?

One answer, of course, is fear. Lots of Western policymakers, not least among them those who most loudly declare the current irrelevance of military matters and the utmost confidence in Russia's peaceableness, in fact, fear war in general and Russia's potential ire in particular. However, theirs is not the sort of prudent fear that leads to prevention. Rather, it is of the sort that leads to what Montaigne called *"le remède du vulgaire,"* the vulgar and imprudent attempt not to think about the object of one's fears.

Circumlocution is the most striking feature of contemporary NATO documents. The Germans are verbally the most evasive. The Federal Ministry of Defense's White Paper 1994–1995 contains no mention of *any* possible threats. The most clear-cut statement in the paper is that "an attack on Germany and its allies" is "most unlikely." Hence, the "mission orientation and size of the Bundeswehr are a crucial prerequisite" for retaining "allies and security partners and, at the same time, exert[ing] influence on NATO,

WEU, CSCE, and UN Policy."[12] In other words, the purpose of the German armed forces is to induce others to do whatever fighting Germany might require for its own interest, and to influence the policies of those who might do the fighting. Yet because the White Paper mentions no threat and outlines no appealing tasks, it is unclear why any German ought to bother paying taxes for the Bundeswehr, much less serve in it. And indeed more and more young Germans choose to opt out of military service as conscientious objectors.

Even more remarkable given the total lack of identification of potential threats is the White Paper's heavy, oft-repeated stress on the maintenance of the "transatlantic link." This stress, to be found in just about every NATO document from every NATO country, is something of a mantra. "Transatlantic link," of course, is NATO-speak for the promise that the United States will wage nuclear war to defend Europe. But against whom? Only one country, only Russia, has the capacity to make war in a way that would require an American nuclear response. Russia is the reason why every West European government, and now even every European socialist party, including former communists, sincerely and wholeheartedly endorse and desire the "transatlantic link" for themselves. And, of course, specific fear of Russia is precisely the reason why the Visegrad states want to be "locked in" under the same American guarantee to make nuclear war on their behalf. Yet if West Europeans believe that NATO's American guarantee is so necessary to defend borders far from Russia, they would not have to be terribly farsighted to want to extend it eastward. Since Russia's invasion of Chechnya, European politicians have become a bit more presbyopic. But they have given no guarantees themselves. Even their approval of an American guarantee of Visegrad is still theoretical at best—and that will not do.

Because American officials do not *want* to extend that guarantee, European officials would have to ask hard and long to get it. What has happened is much less than that. Thus within days of Boris Yel'tsin's revocation of his placet on NATO's inclusion of Visegrad, France's foreign minister, Alain Juppé said, "it was not his thinking right now to admit East European nations,"[13] and German foreign minister Klaus Kinkel declared that NATO should not expand, out of "sensitivity" to Russia's concern, while his predecessor, Hans Dietrich Genscher, advised "the greatest caution with the idea of expanding NATO to the East. . . . We should not do anything that excludes Russia." The reasoning of American officials showed less fear and much muddled hope, but came to the same conclusion. Thus, in proposing the Partnership of Peace, President Clinton said that its purpose was "to do something never before done in the history of the nation state on the European Continent: to unify free and independent nations of their own free will in a Europe that is truly free together rather than have some new and different divisions of Europe." [14] Translated, this means American officials hope that everyone will live happily ever after in Russia and its surroundings, and that to hedge against the possibility that all will not be well would anger Russia.

This deference to the presumed sentiments of Russia obviously runs counter to the original logic of NATO, which was defensive. NATO arose as a response to a threatening Soviet Union. Never, ever, not even under Stalin's worst provocations, did it plan to make war on the Soviet Union. To contend that NATO might harbor aggressive designs on Russia today, or that the Visegrad states want to enter NATO to launch aggression, is akin to believing the wolf in Æsop's fable, who said he felt threatened by the lamb.

Habit better explains this deference than does reason. The stock-in-trade of foreign policy leftists has always been that the very assertion and defense of a collective Western identity and interest, let alone of the identity and interest of any individual Western nation, is somehow improper. Therefore foreign-policy leftists—who long ago became the foreign policy establishment on both sides of the Atlantic—have approached security in two ways that attempt to submerge the very notion of identity and interest. One is collective security—as many nations as possible pledge to join forces against any member that commits aggression. This purposely does not distinguish between potential aggressors and potential victims, between friends and enemies, all of whom are within the fold. This scheme is intentionally agnostic about history and the character of different regimes and, of course, it is value-free. The very concept of collective security negates any notion of an alliance. This is the United Nations, and the Conference on Security and Cooperation in Europe. Another approach was epitomized by America's policy toward the Soviet Union in the early 1970s, labeled "détente," an attempt to ally precisely with the most threatening power. Thus united by the desire to avoid the obvious potential for conflict, the main rivals could presumably settle theirs and their allies' quarrels.

The product of these mental habits is the Partnership for Peace, which comprises NATO's current members, the four Visegrad states, and Russia. It is neither a collective security scheme nor one designed to co-opt a main adversary. Rather, it has the worst features of both. Like a bad co-option scheme, NATO members and especially the Visegrad states entrust their safety to developments within the body politic of the country they fear—developments they have no way of influencing. Like a bad collective security scheme, the Partnership signals a diminution of commitment to enforcing the peace on the part of those in whose interest it is to enforce it. Thus, willy-nilly, the Partnership for Peace must dilute, denature, and decay the remaining moral substance of the NATO alliance.

And indeed it is doing so. Polls in Europe show that while support for membership in NATO is generally higher than it was during the 1980s, support for any military policy other than letting America do whatever might have to be done continues to wane.[15] That is entirely to be expected, given the absence of public discussion of threats and opportunities. All this might be a fiendishly clever plot by European leaders to shelter forever under America's umbrella, if only they were to present to the Americans the kind of case for defense that they do not present to domestic audiences. Yet they make no such case to Americans. Indeed, when they speak to the American people they tend to chide the United States for excessive militarism. This was the case during the last two decades of the Cold War, and it has been the case during the war of Yugoslav dismemberment. Over the years, this message has sunk in: The Europeans are (or think they are) masters at the nonviolent resolution of dispute. This is one more reason the willingness of American public opinion to make war for Europe's safety continues to decline.

During the winter of 1994–95, however, Russia's crushing of Chechnya underlined for some European politicians the twin facts that Russia had already made considerable progress in reassembling the core of the Soviet Union, and that the new Russian Empire was not likely to be benevolent. According to one authoritative account, Germany's entire political spectrum has "dropped the bad habit, adopted in Cold War *Ostpolitik* times, of worrying how hawks in Moscow will react."[16] And indeed European politicians have chastised Mr. Yel'tsin more vigorously over Chechnya than they did any Soviet dictator since the early 1960s. The only concrete action they have taken, however, has been the European Union's postponement of an agreement to liberalize trade with Russia. Yet this surely has less to do with any concern with security than with its ever-deepening protectionism. In sum, even when Europeans do things ostensibly for reasons of security, their wont is actually to serve other purposes. Some of these are more and some less worthy than others, but they really are not about security.

Nothing shows this more clearly than the stump speech that Minister Rühe gave to audiences throughout Europe and North America during the winter of 1994–95.[17] Rühe began by congratulating Germany for having reduced the number of soldiers on its soil from 1.5 million to .5 million during the past three years. He then spoke of how Yel'tsin's intolerable behavior in Chechnya highlights the difference between Russia and the peoples of the Visegrad states who, he emphasized, are just as European as anyone in NATO today. He went on to praise the remarkable integration of French and German forces and the genuine amity that has grown between the two countries. Finally, he proudly mentioned the first joint exercises between Polish and German troops, and wished that eventually Germany would have the same relationship with Poland that it now has with France. All of that is good and worthy for its own sake. But the premise of Rühe's speech is that the purpose of NATO's armies is to get along. Nothing Rühe said bears on whether Germany and the other countries of the EU are willing to fight to prevent Russia from doing in Poland and the other Visegrad countries what it did in Chechnya. The prospect of actually fighting is simply beyond the mentality of Mr. Rühe and many others. Does this mean that NATO's European members are now willing to consider letting the United States give security guarantees to Visegrad, subject of course to European vetoes on how Americans might do it? Probably.

The American position, stated by Mr. Holbrooke in *Foreign Affairs,*[18] starts out forthrightly enough: "If [the great institutions of the West, NATO, the EU, etc.] were to remain closed to new members, they would become progressively . . . less relevant to the problems of the post–Cold War world. . . . The West must expand to central Europe as fast as possible . . . and the United States is ready to lead the way." However, the reader is quickly disabused of reports that the ascendance of Mr. Holbrooke in European affairs represents a reversal of Strobe Talbott's policy of subordinating everything to good relations with Moscow. At most, Holbrooke proposes to talk about "why and how" other states might want to join NATO. And he is terribly clear that the purpose cannot be "anti-Russian" in any way. Presumably, the applicants would be asked to declare that they want in for some reason other than fear of Russia—perhaps to share in the *gemütlichkeit* of Mr. Rühe's maneuvers. The closest Holbrooke gets to the main reason why anyone in *Mitteleuropa* wants to join NATO—fear of Russian imperialism—is that, in the Chechen war, Russia availed itself of Western institutions too little and too late. As for the greatest potential source of conflict on NATO's frontiers— Russia's refusal to accept Ukraine's independence—Holbrooke just expresses satisfaction that Ukraine has pledged to denuclearize itself. Does Ukraine's denuclearization help quench the fires of Russian imperialism or does it whet imperialist appetites? Holbrooke never says. The reason for treating such matters by beating around the bush and whistling past the graveyard is that "each new NATO member . . . extends the U.S. security umbrella." This uninspired treatment can reassure no one in Warsaw or Prague, just as it can no more inspire Americans to make real commitments to new NATO members than to keep commitments to old ones.

Regardless of who realizes it, the underlying reality is that if indeed Russia is civilizing and the world is to live happily ever after, there is no need for NATO, or for any "transatlantic link," no more for France and Germany than for the Visegrad states. However, if there is a chance that something noxious might crawl out of the communist compost pile in the

East to threaten Europe's common identity and interest, then the "trans-atlantic link" would avail Western Europe little unless the European and American publics understood the nature of what might happen and why they should find it intolerable enough to make war against it, as far to the east as possible. The public should know that the Visegrad states are important because they would be the first places where trouble would be likeliest to suck in Western half-commitments. Yet the United States cannot possibly extend that link unless the American public knows that its long-time NATO allies also commit themselves to defend *Mitteleuropa*. In short, because NATO is based on a common understanding of the need for military commitment to protect a common cultural area, it will either live by recognizing the need to expand as the common area has expanded, or it will lose the moral capacity to mobilize itself for any purpose whatever.

CHARACTER

While America's response has been a matter of decisions by one set of policymakers that another set might have made differently, Europe's response has been the reflection of the character of its regimes. No other set of decisions, by any European politicians, would have been acceptable to European bodies politic. Suppose for the sake of argument that de Gaulle and Adenauer came back to life and urged their compatriots to commit to war for the sake of the Poles, Czechs, Slovaks, and Hungarians. These peoples, the old men might say, are no different from ourselves in any important respect. If we succeed in expanding our zone of security and prosperity to them, our strength and our good example will border Russia and Ukraine. We would be able to give them powerful incentives to follow our lead. What a magnet we would be to Belarus' and Ukraine! What a disincentive to reabsorption by Russia would NATO's presence on their borders be! Right now, the old men might say, such a commitment would cost us little. If, nevertheless, we don't make it, we and the whole world will know that we would have neither the foresight nor the courage to take care of ourselves if bigger sacrifices were required of us. Honor and prudent self-interest together compel us to take in our Visegrad kin.

Such an appeal would hardly be understood. Newspapers and politicians might reply: "No different from ourselves?" How dare anyone suggest commitment to war on the basis of cultural discrimination? Yes, showing off strength and prosperity on the borders of the old Soviet Union might bring forth emulation, but it *might* provoke resentment, too. Besides, a military commitment to Visegrad would have to be accompanied by an acceptance of agricultural commodities and other products as well. That would lower a lot of prices in the EU. We would have to let ourselves in for all this trouble for the sake of avoiding dangers that may not come to pass, on behalf of a racist-sounding cultural identity, and in the name of undefinable terms like courage and honor. In fact, right now there is nothing to be gained by making such a commitment, while the potential costs are obvious.

In short, de Gaulle and Adenauer used intellectual currency very different from that used in contemporary Europe. While American politics still contains a modicum of moral sentiment, while it can envisage sacrifice, while it does not entirely exclude appeals to long-run effects, European politics now largely fits Harold Lasswell's definition: It concerns the process for deciding "who gets what, when, and how" and, he might have added, "right now."

It is no coincidence that, after a generation of brokering favors for interest groups, European politicians now suffer from a near-total lack of moral authority. The name varies from place to place from *Parteiverdrossenheit* or "democratic deficit" in Germany to *politica schifosa* in Italy. The phenomenon is the same: The mainstream parties that have been running the welfare-regulatory state have become the object of enormous resentment. Voters are abandoning them in favor of various local alternatives. If any standard politicians were to call for potential sacrifice, it is doubtful anyone would take them seriously.

European electorates have become unforgiving toward politicians who—they believe—are running systems that steal on a grand scale. In France, for example, the party of President François Mitterand garnered only 19 percent of the *vote* in the parliamentary elections of March 1993. The old-line rightist parties won 85 percent of the *seats.* One year later these very parties fell to 19 percent of the vote after they failed to make a difference. The big gainer was a conservative group based in the northwest. In Italy, all the parties that had formed all the governments since World War II ceased to exist in 1994. Their successors risk the same fate because, although they have not been involved in ordinary corruption, they have not lightened the burden of government. In Spain, the political parties are haunted by opinion polls that suggest they will suffer the fate of their Italian counterparts. Representatives of Catalan, Asturian, and Basque regionalism are the gainers. In Great Britain, the ruling Conservatives are polling in the low 20 percent. In Germany, the elections of 1994 produced a Bundesrat firmly in socialist hands, and a Bundestag subject to day-to-day intraparty intrigue.

The chief problem facing Western Europe is the ruin of the welfare state through the working out of its very logic. European governments take and spend about half of their peoples' incomes. Yet they cannot possibly fulfill the promises they have made to provide adequate pensions and medical care. Through various regulations and subsidies, they manage economic, professional, educational, and social life in detail. As the years have passed, the value of connection with government has grown, the size and weight of government has grown, and the proportion of net contributions to net beneficiaries has dropped. The wholesale and retail levels of this mess occupy perhaps four-fifths of the energies of European bodies politic.

Much of the remainder of Europe's political energy is occupied by worries about immigration from the Muslim world and Africa. Unlike immigrants in the new world, Europe's migrants have neither the intention nor the capacity to assimilate. Hence, theirs is more like a gradual occupation. Given Europe's demographic insufficiencies and moral uncertainties, this phenomenon will increasingly poison and cripple Europe in the years to come.

During previous decades it was fashionable to think that any given problem would be ameliorated by Europe's growing integration. Now it is clear that integration, as it has been pursued, is part of the problem. Referenda in Denmark and France, and opinion polls elsewhere, have shown that growing numbers of Europeans see the supranational organs of the European Union as even more alien and autocratic than their own central governments. Moreover, the campaigns for ratification of the Maastricht Treaty of 1993 have brought out rather than suppressed national antagonisms. Thus, in France proponents and opponents of the treaty alike described acceptance (or rejection) of it as the best way of holding in check an otherwise dangerous Germany. In sum, the prospect that European integration, as now practiced, might somehow lift the eyes of European politicians and citizens to their long-term geopolitical interests—never mind noble goals—is nonexistent.

By way of evidence, consider that in 1991-92, as the defense and foreign policy sections of the Maastricht Treaty were being drafted, European governments were making crucial decisions with regard to the war of Yugoslav dismemberment taking place next door. Suffice it to say that in this process the governments of several European states ignored the *procedures* for reaching the common decisions that they were negotiating. If they had, they probably would have reached no decisions at all, because the procedures, while empty of guiding principles, are full of opportunities for obstruction.

As it was, Europe's decisions concerning the Yugoslav conflicts have been of the sort that would get it in trouble while aggravating the local peoples' tribulations. Europe could have left Yugoslavia to work out its own dismemberment. Or it could have chosen sides, effectively supported its favorites, and shaped a congenial outcome. Instead it meddled piecemeal, hesitantly, in a cowardly manner, producing the worst possible outcome. Germany recognized Slovenia and Croatia, dragging its allies into doing the same, but without plans for supporting them against entirely predictable reactions, and without any policy—national or multinational—

toward Serbia and Bosnia. Nevertheless, Western Europeans agreed to an arms embargo that magnified Serbia's relative power. Then when the Bosnian horror began, France and Britain sent troops without a military mission, thereby making hostages of them. There has followed a parody of evenhandedness, by which they imposed economic sanctions on Serbia while pressing Bosnia and Croatia to agree to Serbia's conquests. All of this they did while first soliciting US bombing of Serbian targets and then lobbying the United States against further anti-Serbian action. In sum, incompetence combined with fear of Russia and of terrorism lengthened the slaughter, produced ill will from all sides of the conflict, and showed the European powers to be utterly contemptible.

The United States properly presumed that Europe should take the lead in the Yugoslav crisis; however, the substance of that lead was terrible. In some future crisis involving say, Russia's suppression of Ukraine or demands on Poland regarding Russian territorial access to Kaliningrad, there is every reason to believe that Europe would perform at least as badly. If the United States were to follow Europe's pusillanimous lead, the result might be war with Russia after the most convoluted of half-commitments.

All of this is to say that whatever the shortcomings of America's leadership of NATO, they can only be worsened by deference to West European countries, which seem constitutionally incapable of a coherent foreign policy. The Visegrad countries are not seats of wisdom. But their ruling prejudice is clear, and fundamentally consonant with the interest of NATO. Alas, the US government has chosen to take its lead from the muddles of Bonn, Paris, and London rather than from Warsaw, Budapest, and Prague.

CONSEQUENCES

So what happens when leadership falls through the widening crack between Europe's constitutional impotence and America's supine superpower?

First, the connection between the United States and NATO Europe will shift more and more from common deployments of major armed units and more-or-less realistic plans to the realm of illusion. As the United States effectively pulls back from the Yugoslav disaster, as the controversy over the expansion of NATO stays on the theoretical level, as US troop levels in Europe continue to drop and the US units available cease to match any contingency plans for using them, the US–NATO connection will be reduced to the mythical "transatlantic link." This will serve mainly to dull any residual European instincts about military seriousness.

Second, the impotent European consensus will be blown about by contrary storms, or even by breezes. The regathering Russian Empire is only one (albeit potentially the most serious) of many possible sources of heavy weather. Troubles aplenty will come from the south, where Islamic regimes are rising, dedicated to the proposition that Europe is where the loot is, and that they have a right to it. Any wind at all is dangerous to rudderless ships. Montesquieu wrote of fourth-century Romans: "There was no people so weak that they could not do them harm."

Third, the superpower will remain supine, and any half-baked attempts to rise to meet European problems will be unpleasant enough to convince it to lie down again. The various constituent parts of the US government and of the American public opinion, each for its own reasons, will be happy enough to leave Europe to the Europeans—at least until events unambiguously threaten America's vital interests.

NOTES

1. These states cover the heart of *Mitteleuropa.* They are as Western in culture and as democratic in regime as any of NATO's present members, and have a livelier desire than any of these to defend their freedom.

2. British Broadcasting Corporation, EE/2100, 15 September 1994.

3. SPD press release, "Meeting of the Joint Labor Party working group on Security and Foreign Policy Issues" (Bonn: November 1986). The SED was East Germany's ruling communist party.

4. Ralf Dahrendorf, *Society and Democracy in Germany* (Garden City, NY: Doubleday & Co., 1969), pp. 401, 406, 408.

5. Strobe Talbott, *The Russians and Reagan,* foreword by Cyrus Vance (New York: Random House, Vintage, 1984), p. 75.

6. Michael Mandelbaum and Strobe Talbott, *Reagan and Gorbachev* (New York: Random House, 1987), p. 53 (emphasis in original).

7. Michael Beschloss and Strobe Talbott, *At the Highest Levels: The Inside Story of the End of the Cold War* (Boston: Little, Brown, and Co., 1993).

8. Stephen J. Flanagan, "NATO and Central and Eastern Europe: From Liaison to Security Partnership," *Washington Quarterly,* Spring 1992, p. 144.

9. Ibid., p. 145.

10. British Broadcasting Corporation, EE/2100A, 14 September 1994.

11. François Heisbourg, "The Future of the Atlantic Alliance: Whither NATO, Whether NATO?" *Washington Quarterly,* Spring 1992, p. 127.

12. Federal Ministry of Defense White Paper 1994 (Bonn), p. 85.

13. Jane Perlez, "Bonn Tries to Calm East Europeans on NATO," *The New York Times,* 10 October 1993, p. 6.

14. Henry Kissinger, "It's an Alliance, Not a Relic," *The Washington Post,* 16 August 1994, p. A19.

15. Philippe Manigart and Eric Marlier, "European Public Opinion on the Future of its Security," *Armed Forces and Society* 19:3, Spring 1993, pp. 335-352.

16. Dominique Moisi and Michael Mertes "Europe's Map, Compass, and Horizon" *Foreign Affairs* 74:1, January/February 1995, p. 122.

17. This author heard it at Stanford University on 23 January 1995.

18. Richard Holbrooke, "America, a European Power," *Foreign Affairs* 74:2, March/April 1995, pp. 38-51.

8

Clinton's Russia Policy:
Between Desire and Reality

Paul Quinn-Judge

While the Clinton administration's foreign policy often appears to be an illustration of chaos theory, administration officials, at least prior to Chechnya, were prone to point with pride to a successful and, they would say, embarrassment-free Russia policy. There were some grounds for this claim. Confounding the pessimistic and very plausible predictions of a number of leading Western specialists, the Russian Federation has not disintegrated. Despite armed uprisings, a resurgent rightist movement and profound economic crisis, Boris Yel'tsin is still in power. Economic reforms are erratic and precarious, but are continuing and showing some modest signs of success. The transfer of nuclear warheads from Ukraine, Kazakhstan, and Belarus' back to Russia, a crucial first step in the dismantling of the second largest nuclear arsenal in the world, is well ahead of schedule.

Washington proclaims its belief that Boris Yel'tsin is firmly committed to economic and political reform, and that Russia under his leadership is moving toward the creation of what President Clinton on April 1, 1993 called, with breathtaking optimism, a "nation-state." At the same time Washington declares that it would never countenance the creation of a Russian sphere of influence on the territory of the former USSR.

The policy formulation is elegantly simple, but its foundations are fragile. On closer examination the Clinton administration's Russia policy appears to be one of consistent denial, on at least two planes. It ignores all evidence that Boris Yel'tsin's political stamina or commitment to reform is less than total. And it closes its eyes to Russia's attempts to restore its influence over its neighbors by subversion rather than suasion. In doing so the administration also chooses not to notice the disturbingly prominent role that the Russian military, both regular army and Border Troops, is playing in politics. The two parts of the denial are inextricably related: The admission either of Yel'tsin's weakness or Russia's subversion would mean the unravelling of the US policy. Washington prefers silence.

Washington's policy toward the countries of the Near Abroad is one of diplomatic triage. The administration expresses an unambiguous determination to guarantee the independence and sovereignty of four states: Estonia, Latvia, Lithuania, and Ukraine. It indignantly dismisses suggestions that it is ceding Moscow a sphere of influence over the others. But it is abandoning, certainly discreetly and perhaps regretfully, a number of the other newly independent republics to Russia's tutelage. Senior officials usually cite one of two reasons for doing so: that many of the new republics are not politically viable over the long term; or that the republics are too distant from the United States to allow Washington to exert any serious influence.

Senior analysts and officials in the Clinton administration view large parts of the former Soviet Union as a lost cause. For at least a year now senior intelligence officers have privately cast doubt on the survivability of the two largest and potentially richest states, Ukraine and Kazakhstan. (One should add, though, that since the advent of the Kuchma government, Washington has been evincing greater optimism about Ukraine.)

Warnings by US diplomats of Russian covert interference in Kazakhstan and Ukraine since 1993 have been filed and forgotten. Russian military intervention in Georgia, Azerbaijan, and Moldova has been downplayed or described as the work of rogue military commanders.

The first signs of concern are beginning to emerge, notably in the CIA, where some effort is reportedly being given to studying the chances that a new-style Russian Empire will emerge from the framework of the CIS; however, no such doubts appear to have crept into the minds of the most senior policy-making officials at the State Department or NSC.

This chapter will include a look at the evolution of the Clinton policy toward Russia and its place in the administration's overall foreign policy, noting *inter alia* Russia's diminished importance in the general framework of foreign-policy concerns. Also to be examined is criticism of Russia policy within the administration, and some of the evidence that has been advanced by intramural critics to challenge the prevailing line will be summarized. Because the question of Boris Yel'tsin's health and character is so crucial to both internal reform and the Near Abroad, both issues will be discussed in some detail. Rather than providing an exhaustive chronology of Russian subversion in the south and west, this chapter will try to sketch what the administration really knew at a time when its representatives were pleading ignorance of events, or downplaying Moscow's role in them.

As a journalist, my sources are irritatingly vague. I apologize for the plethora of attributions to "senior officials" and "senior analysts." The information provided is derived largely from conversations in the course of the past two years with high-level officials and policymakers in the area of Russia policy, many of whom I have known in different incarnations for some years. The officials include senior staffers or political appointees at the State Department, NSC, CIA, National Intelligence Council, and Pentagon.

RUSSIA: A RECEDING PRIORITY

Under the Clinton administration, relations with the Kremlin have ceased to be the dominant, defining factor in US foreign and defense policy. Relations with Russia still figure high in any formal listing of foreign-policy issues, of course. But the regular succession of regional crises—starting with Somalia, passing through Bosnia to Haiti, North Korea and the Persian Gulf— have absorbed much of the time and energies of the national security establishment since January 1993.

The diminished priority assigned to Russia has been accompanied by a reduction in media coverage, public interest, and therefore debate about developments in the former Soviet Union. Thus, at a time when Russia policy is arguably more controversial than it has been for years, the intensity of debate has, paradoxically, significantly declined.

When Defense Secretary Les Aspin introduced his long-awaited Bottom Up Review of defense policy on September 1, 1993, he digressed for a moment to marvel at the way the world—and his job—had changed. Throughout his adult life, he said, the overriding preoccupation for people like him had been the Soviet threat. Suddenly that was gone: "history and central casting" had produced a new list of villains, he said, people like Saddam Hussein, Mohamed Farah Aidid, or General Ratko Mladic.

These new villains have pushed Russia off center stage. Under previous administrations, regional crises, be they Vietnam, Afghanistan, or Mozambique, had derived their importance and urgency from their perceived link to the primary threat, the spread of Soviet communism. Under Bill Clinton, conflicts in small countries such as Somalia, Bosnia, or Haiti have become major policy challenges in and of themselves.

This has been a painful and difficult transition. In previous administrations, top national security figures usually have been guaranteed a crash course in Soviet affairs, if they were not already specialists in the field. The Clinton administration's top Russia specialist, Strobe Talbott, has on the other hand been obliged to retool several times as he turned his attention to North Korea, Cuba, or Haiti.

The brutality and volatility of regional conflicts has further diminished President Clinton's already limited enthusiasm for foreign adventures. Candidate Clinton made a point throughout his election campaign of criticizing George Bush for spending too much time on foreign policy (and also, ironically, for being too timid in his pursuit of foreign-policy objectives). President Clinton has done his best to relegate foreign policy to a secondary position, though recent relative successes may cause him to rethink this approach. Time and time again since January 1993, however, Clinton administration officials who handle foreign policy have said the same thing: Their main task is to keep the president's desk clean of foreign-policy questions, thus allowing him to concentrate on domestic reform. However, the daunting nature of regional crises has also deepened the desire for a real foreign-policy success.

These factors—the desire to keep Clinton focused on domestic issues, the general nastiness of regional crises, and the desire for a successful counterpoint to the chaos in the rest of the world—have reinforced the attractions of continuity in US policy toward the former Soviet Union.

During the Clinton transition, these attractions were already self-evident to the people who were to take over Russia policy. Strobe Talbott, Bill Clinton's friend from his Oxford days and a career-long Soviet watcher, had few objections to the Bush administration's handling of relations with the Kremlin, at least in the last phase of the Republican administration.

In their book *At the Highest Levels,* Talbott and his co-author Michael Beschloss fault George Bush for being "so intent on shoring up Gorbachev that he was slow to perceive that by the summer of 1991, the Soviet leader was largely a spent force."[1] The authors then commend Bush for moving quickly after the August 1991 coup to "ditch" his old friend Mikhail Gorbachev gracefully and establish a relationship with Boris Yel'tsin. They also note approvingly that, though he may have stuck with Gorbachev longer than was necessary, Bush nonetheless ensured a peaceful transition to Yel'tsin, a leader "committed to the death of the Communist Party and the dismantlement of the Soviet Union."[2]

Soon after the 1992 presidential elections, Talbott, still at the time a euphoric private citizen, commented that if Clinton were to ask him for one piece of advice—"which he will not," Talbott cautioned rather forcefully—he would urge the president-elect to keep Ed Hewett as the National Security Council's senior point man for the former Soviet Union, special assistant to the president and senior director for Russian, Ukrainian, and Eurasian affairs. After Hewett's tragic and premature death, he was succeeded by his deputy, a career foreign service officer, Nicholas Burns, who has been in the

NSC since the late 1980s. Soon afterwards Talbott himself moved into the administration, as ambassador at large to the newly independent states and special adviser to the secretary of state.

As far as one can ascertain, Talbott has been the prime mover in the administration's Russia policy. At times, indeed perhaps most of the time, he has dealt directly with the president on Russia policy. Whether he has done so with or without the blessing of Warren Christopher is less clear. Nicholas Burns, meanwhile, has proven an able and articulate spokesman for the policy.

The regional crises that have so bedeviled President Clinton have affected Russia policy in at least one other rather surprising way. Quagmire in Bosnia, chaos in Somalia, and a potential nuclear cataclysm coming from North Korea have not just made US-Russia relations look gratifyingly smooth. They have served to distract attention from Russia at times of its greatest crisis in recent years. This in turn has spared the administration the embarrassment of a potentially acrimonious public debate on the merits of its policy.

On March 20, 1993, for example, when Boris Yel'tsin assumed emergency rule, setting off a major political crisis and flurry of speculation about his future, the news had to share space with another crisis: UN and US efforts to establish a no-fly zone over Bosnia, and the possibility that US military power might be committed there. On October 3, shortly after TV viewers here had seen footage of the attack on Ostankino by General Albert Makashov and his supporters, officials in the White House and Pentagon began to receive reports of a pitched battle in Mogadishu between elite US Rangers, Delta Force commandos, and the militia of Mohamed Farah Aidid. Over the next couple of days, attention would be diverted from the events in Moscow to the scenes in Mogadishu of dead US servicemen being dragged through the street, and an interview with a wounded and dazed Special Forces warrant officer who had been taken prisoner by the Somalis. The policy debate and heart-searching that followed centered on Mogadishu, not the charred remains of the Russian White House.

THE THEORY AND EVOLUTION OF RUSSIA POLICY UNDER BILL CLINTON

The Clinton administration lost no time in locking Boris Yel'tsin in a passionate embrace. The hyperbole used to signal this attitude was of the type that one usually associates with a socialist personality cult. Later, following the tumultuous and disturbing events of late 1993, the administration went through a period of self-doubt with regard to its Russia policy. Now, however, it seems to have returned to its basic equation: Boris Yel'tsin = economic reform = democratic change.

On March 23, 1993, Strobe Talbott went before the Senate Foreign Relations Committee for his confirmation hearings. The senators gushed over Talbott. In return, Talbott gushed over Boris Yel'tsin. "President Yel'tsin is the personification of reform in Russia," Talbott told the committee. "He is the leading reformer in Russia today. That is why we support him."

A week later, on April 1, President Clinton went several steps farther in a speech to the American Society of Newspaper Editors.

"President Yel'tsin and his fellow reformers throughout Russia are courageously leading three modern Russian revolutions at once," he declared. "To transform their country from a totalitarian state into a democracy, from a command economy into a market, and from an empire into a modern nation-state that freely let go of countries under its control and now freely respects their integrity."

In the month that followed, prominent Russians and the Russian media provided ample warning to the administration that its basic precepts were simply wrong. Russian politicians who had once been unhesitatingly labelled Western-leaning reformers—Vladimir Lukin, Yevgeni Ambartsumov, or Andrei Kozyrev, to note some of the most obvious examples—started to display nationalist reflexes. Ambartsumov demonstrated this in his reaction to the war in Serbia, Lukin in his support for ethnic Russians living in Ukraine. Other one-time reformers began publicly to rethink their enthusiasm for liberal, Western-style reform.

Had the administration's Russia experts studied the ideological evolution of just one of the most prominent of the post-Soviet generation of politicians, Sergei Stankevich, they would have found ample grounds for doubting their own policy. Even before Bill Clinton was sworn into office, Stankevich— a 40-year-old English-speaking historian who used to be a fixture at US embassy functions—had scornfully rejected the idea of liberal reform for Russia. He later began to speak of the inevitability of the return of the newly independent states to Russia. And in October 1993, using language that seemed to be almost designed to respond to Clinton's Annapolis speech, Stankevich noted that "the dream is fading" in the West "that any minute now a pro-Western government comprising professionals will emerge and— speaking in several European languages—will express views that completely coincide with those held by officials in Washington."[3]

The administration did not heed such remarks, however. Or at the very least they did not allow them to influence their analysis. This might explain in part why they seemed so surprised by the bloodbath of October 1993.

Here a personal illustration of the administration's frame of mind is perhaps in order. In mid-September of that year, intrigued by the menacing talk from Moscow, I asked for a briefing from the key player in US-Russian policy at the time. He in turn referred me to his specialist in internal affairs, the person who, as he self-deprecatingly put it, tells him what to think. Between phone calls—a prominent Ukrainian had just lost his meeting with the president and Talbott was threatening to go directly to Clinton to have the meeting restored—the internal specialist played down the bellicose statements from Moscow. This was the usual *boltovnya,* I was told, "cyclical posturing," the now-traditional maneuverings by parliament and the executive branch before a new session of the legislature.

This happened at best two weeks before Yel'tsin dissolved parliament, and less than a month before the attack on the Russian White House. It is perhaps not inappropriate to note that the destruction of the White House does not figure in the chronology included in a State Department fact sheet issued on September 24, 1994, in preparation for President Yel'tsin's visit to Washington.

The October fighting in Moscow embarrassed the Clinton administration but did not shake its implicit faith in Boris Yel'tsin. Shortly after the October events, a senior State Department official who had reservations about the administration's policy claimed that Talbott continued to "come down rather hard" on officials whose analyses concluded that Yel'tsin "was anything other than a dyed-in-the-wool" democrat. Other officials have subsequently said the same thing.

But the aftermath of the attack—reports of growing alienation by ordinary Russians with the political system, the decline of Yel'tsin's own popularity—coupled with the unnervingly strong showing of Vladimir Zhirinovsky in the December 12 elections did finally seem to sow some questions in the minds of policymakers in Washington. Public statements, at least for several months afterwards, were more cautious.

When Talbott appeared before the House Foreign Affairs Committee on January 25, 1994, for example, he seemed to be hedging his bets somewhat. The mood on Capitol Hill had cooled, both to Talbott and to Russia. The deputy-secretary designate repeated Clinton's assessment that the December elections had been a "wake-up call" for reformers and their international backers. And he laid out the four relatively neutral sounding precepts that guided the administration's policy: (1) Russia is engaged in a "titanic struggle" for its future; (2) the United States has a "huge stake" in the outcome of this struggle; (3) the United States can to some degree influence the outcome; but (4) the process of change is slow, and will require "patience and steadfastness" on the part of the West.

Talbott's discussion of Russia and the chances of reform that day seemed infused with a new sobriety. The administration was still upbeat about reform, but more guardedly so. In the weeks to come, Yel'tsin's name was cited less often, and administration officials did not rush to personify him with reform. Their behavior, in fact, seems in retrospect remarkably similar to the attitude of many Democratic candidates to Bill Clinton during the midterm elections.

The December elections did not, however, lead to a fundamental reassessment of policy, or a discreet distancing of the Clinton administration from Boris Yel'tsin. In fact there are disturbing indications that the administration did its utmost to continue to portray Yel'tsin in the best possible light. Senior US diplomats have privately claimed that the US Embassy in Moscow suppressed cables that alleged electoral irregularities by Yel'tsin supporters.

Parts of the administration did, as we shall see later, start to evince concerns about Yel'tsin himself and his policies toward countries like Georgia, yet these hesitations have not led to a substantial modification of policy. A recent background briefing on Russian policy suggests in fact that the administration has made an almost complete recovery from its doubts about Yel'tsin and his government.

The briefer, a senior White House official with day-to-day responsibility for Russia, described 1993 as "the year of Russia" for the Clinton administration. On three occasions in 1993—in March, when Yel'tsin assumed emergency powers; in September, when he dissolved parliament, triggering the confrontation with the legislature; and in early October, when Russian troops finally stormed the White House—Clinton had to decide whether to support Yel'tsin's decision to take "extra-constitutional measures" to defend himself. Each time Washington did so, stressing that the decision was made as part of a policy of strategic alliance with reform.

Washington's decision to side with Yel'tsin was quickly vindicated, the official continued, by the results of the December 1993 parliamentary elections. The elections, once described by the US administration as a "wake-up call," were in fact a "great triumph" for reform, the official maintained. While the media focused on Vladimir Zhirinovsky, they overlooked the fact that Russia finally had a functioning legislature.

The Russia of 1994, meanwhile, is a country with a greater sense of self-confidence and its own interests, a "difficult partner," the official added. Still, the very fact that it is proving a prickly partner over such issues as Bosnia and Iraq, the argument runs, testifies to the fact that Russia is steadily emerging from its crisis. On Yel'tsin's health, the official remarked that he knew of nothing that prevented Yel'tsin from functioning normally, or running again for the presidency in 1996.

As another senior White House official put it during a background briefing in November 1994, "I wouldn't say that we are any more worried about Russia now than we were two years ago."

DISSENT AND DEBATE WITHIN THE ADMINISTRATION

The official line has been challenged energetically, consistently, but unsuccessfully from within the administration. Some analysts, including senior State Department specialists, question its very foundation. Others, including members of the intelligence community, have slowly come round to the conclusion that Yel'tsin has "potentially serious character flaws"—to use the delicate phrase of one senior intelligence officer. So far, however, the dissenters have failed to shake the administration's confidence.

The fundamental assumption inherent in the official Clinton line is that the Soviet Empire is dead not only physically, but psychologically as well—that Russian expansionism was coterminous with the USSR. Clinton's reference, in his April 1, 1993 Annapolis speech, to an emerging nation-state is particularly telling in this respect. This attitude may come as a surprise to anyone who has read Solovyev, Tyutchev, or even Pushkin in his more splenetic moments. It also presupposes that the security forces and the army are either democratized themselves or completely under the control of the central government. And it assumes that the great intellectual debate between Slavophiles and Westernizers has somehow finally been settled in favor of the Westernizers.

The minority view challenges most of these assumptions. It holds that Russian imperialism is not a purely Soviet phenomenon. It views Boris Yel'tsin as at best a fragile vehicle for democratic change. Proponents of the minority view would probably argue that Yel'tsin bears more resemblance to one of Chaadayev's blank pages than he does to a Westernizing leader. Intramural critics say that Yel'tsin should be viewed as a transitional figure, not the main motive force for change. They stress the urgency for US officials, in the first place the embassy, to reach out to members of the opposition in Moscow to gauge their views and temperaments, but they complain that they are not allowed to do this, on the grounds that Yel'tsin would be offended. Finally, critics say, simple prudence and historical precedents dictate that one should assume that Russia is likely to go through an authoritarian phase before it reaches anything resembling Western democracy.

The dissenters claim that their views have been ignored. While it would be natural for their views to be affected by their own bruised egos, there is considerable evidence to support the case that the administration has been remarkably selective in the reports from Russia which it chooses to read.

DENIAL

Although they no longer call him the personification of reform, administration officials still pin most of their hopes for change in Russia on Boris Yel'tsin. "I don't see anyone else who can pick up the banner [of reform]," a White House official said recently. It therefore follows that the key to success, both in Russian reform and US policy, is the certainty that Boris Yel'tsin is physically and mentally capable of consistently guiding the course of change.

The evidence does not support that assumption. It has not done so for several years. There is no doubt that Yel'tsin is personally brave, and impulsive, and that he possesses a genuine sympathy for ordinary people which distinguishes him sharply from his generation of Soviet apparatchiks.

Neither is there much doubt that Yel'tsin is obsessed with his own inadequacies and lack of qualifications to be head of state, knows little about economics, and prefers the company of his security chief, Aleksandr Korzhakov to, say, Yegor Gaidar. There is no doubt any more that he drinks to the point of incapacitation and is prone to equally debilitating bouts of depression.

At the very least these problems affect his ability to oversee the day-to-day administration of affairs of state. It is more reasonable to assume that Yel'tsin's deepening physical and psychological problems have taken a more serious toll, causing him to leave many key decisions to the closest members of his entourage—or in the case of the Near Abroad, to the armed forces.

The administration continues to claim, however, that Boris Yel'tsin is fine. Such claims are contradicted, of course, by the first volume of Yel'tsin's autobiography. Published in 1990, the autobiography documents a number of disturbing tendencies with striking frankness. The book graphically describes the debilitating headaches that made him "climb the wall," the frequent calls on emergency medical services, the way his head "wouldn't turn off."[4] In the same book he refers to the "apathy" that overwhelms him in times of great pressure: "I didn't want to fight, I didn't want explanations, I didn't want anything other than to forget everything, just to be left in peace."[5] Yel'tsin's tendency to drink himself into paralysis has been known and documented—by journalists as well as by official Russia-watchers—at least since his unscheduled flight to the Latvian resort of Jurmala, immediately after the collapse of the August 1991 coup.

More recently, senior members of the US intelligence community—including some people with a track record of great optimism where Russia is concerned—have begun to voice doubts. One senior analyst, an intelligence officer who is known in the past to have irritated the Bush administration with his positives analyses of Yel'tsin, started to deviate from the "no problem" line sometime after the December 1993 elections. Until then the official had insisted that Yel'tsin was generally healthy and did not suffer to any substantial degree from drinking or other problems. During a background briefing in early January 1994, however, the official stated with almost striking nonchalance that "of course" Yel'tsin had a serious drinking problem and also suffered from what the official described explicitly as "clinical depression."

The available evidence does not indicate that Yel'tsin will abandon office or abandon reform tomorrow, but it is sufficient to raise doubts about his physical ability or psychological stamina to push ahead consistently with reform. His actions over the last four years indicate that his own view of politics is a paradoxical mix of populism and the fist. There are indications that some key elements of policy move ahead largely by automatic pilot. Moreover, Yel'tsin's recent behavior in public—his exuberance in Germany, for example, or his sleepover in Ireland—make it clear that his problems are reaching the point where they no longer can be overlooked. And the administration's continuing embrace of Yel'tsin may make it, too, vulnerable to the charge sometime in the not-too-distant future that it was "so intent on shoring up" a Russian leader that it did not recognize the man was a "spent force."

THE NEAR ABROAD

The pattern of suppressing or ignoring unwelcome information has been repeated in Washington's treatment of Russia's Near Abroad. Here, of course, the administration has flipped its "Yel'tsin is in complete control" argument on its head. When they have been forced to admit Russian military interference in the territories of the former Soviet Union, senior officials have claimed that Yel'tsin was *not* in charge, could not control large bodies of Russian troops, or did not even know they were on the move.

The administration's public line is that it will brook no attempt by Moscow to impose its will on its neighbors by diplomatic, economic, or physical force. In fact it has tried not to notice evidence of top-level Russian involvement in Georgia, and showed similar selectivity in analyzing events in Moldova, Kazakhstan, Ukraine, and Azerbaijan.

The toughest recent articulation of the official US line came on October 28, 1994, when Ambassador Madeleine Albright told the State Department's in-house forum that the United States "does not and will not recognize any extralegal privileges or sphere of influence." It says something for the concern felt by foreign-policy professionals that during a question-and-answer session that followed, one person told Albright that he "applaud[ed] and admire[d]" her statement on the Near Abroad.

Ambassador Albright has, however, often seemed to be a voice in the wilderness on issues of foreign policy. Yet she is also being spoken of as a possible successor, either to Secretary of State Warren Christopher or National Security Adviser Anthony Lake. (Her Open Forum speech seemed to some observers the first salvo in her own campaign for a new job.) If she does move to a more important position, one can confidently expect another titanic struggle in US foreign policy, this one between Dr. Albright and Strobe Talbott.

In the past two years, senior officials in the Clinton administration have received intelligence or diplomatic reports from their own sources documenting Russian efforts to undermine, subvert, or control the governments of Georgia, Azerbaijan, Tajikistan, Kazakhstan, Ukraine, and Moldova.

These operations have been carried out with varying degrees of subtlety. US officials believe, and have reported, that Russian policy on Ukraine aims essentially to keep Kiev so weakened that it is unable to move away from Russia, but not so unstable that it becomes a massive security problem on Russia's western borders. In Georgia, on the other hand, intervention has been cruder, and in Tajikistan more blatant still.

The administration continues officially, however, to claim that Russia is moving—albeit a little more slowly than one might hope—toward a nation-state. The most egregious case of denial by Washington concerns Georgia. US officials have tried to explain away Russian support for Abkhaz separatists in one of several ways. Initially they suggested that any Russian troops in the area were freelancing, hired by local separatists very much in the same way that the warring sides in Nagorno-Karabakh have done. Later they suggested that Russian intervention had been at the behest of the local commander. Finally they agreed that senior officers in the defense ministry might have known about this intervention, but not Yel'tsin.

There are strong indications that Washington and Yel'tsin knew considerably more about the planning and the execution of the Abkhaz operation than either wants to admit. A senior official, citing intelligence reports, asserted in late 1993 that Yel'tsin had discussed Russian military operations in Abkhazia with Defense Minister Pavel Grachev and armed forces Chief of Staff Col.-General Mikhail Kolesnikov. The content of the discussion was not known, the official said, but the meeting corroborated suspicions that Yel'tsin himself was aware of the operation. The same official, whose information has since been confirmed by another well-placed official, also noted that the Russian military's participation in the Abkhaz operation involved coordination between the armed forces, GRU and the SVRR—another factor which undermines the claim that the operation was a rogue initiative.

Moreover a videotaped interview, reportedly made by Georgian intelligence, with a captured Russian who identifies himself as Mikhail Georgevich Demlanov makes further claims about Russian aid to the Abkhaz rebels. One of the claims is that officers provided Abkhaz military leaders with satellite photographs of the Sukhumi area on the eve of their successful attack.

Denial is equally apparent in the administration's discussion of Lt.-General Aleksandr Lebed', who, until recently, was commander of the Fourteenth Army in the Transdniestr region of Moldova. Another chapter in this book discusses the general in greater detail. Suffice it to say that, from the beginning of the Clinton administration and for regular intervals thereafter, senior officials have claimed that—as a White House official put it yet again in early November 1994—"no one really controls Lebed'."[6]

The claim that Lebed' is a loner appears to many quite breathtaking—in its implications, its silliness, and its bizarre willingness to ignore statements that have appeared publicly in the Russian media. The idea that the commander of the Fourteenth Army was able simultaneously to be resupplied by Moscow and flout its writ if true would mean that Yel'tsin was completely powerless. The fact that senior government officials, including Stankevich, visited the general in Moldova undermines the argument that Lebed' is a loner, as do his frequent interviews with the Russian media, both official and independent. And *Rossiiskiye vesti* in 1994 specifically repudiated what it called the "legend" that the general's operations in the Transdniestr area had been carried out in defiance of Moscow.[7] At the beginning of November 1994, just about the time that a White House official suggested Lebed' was out of control, Western wire services reported from Moscow that he was being mentioned as the next defense minister.

US diplomats have warned of growing Russian subversion in Kazakhstan, a republic with immense natural reserves and considerable US investment. They have identified senior members of the Kazakh government who support the Russian moves, either because they are Russian agents of influence, or because they see such a move as furthering their own political careers. Senior CIA analysts have warned of a possible attempt by ethnic Russians in northern Kazakhstan to break away. Their warnings do not seem to have gained much attention in policy-making circles.

Senior State Department officials who are critical of administration policy say that Russia is quietly acquiring equity in Ukraine's strategically vital fuel sector and describe this as an effective way of gaining leverage over Ukrainian political leaders. One official, a particularly well-informed critic, describes Russia's policy toward Ukraine as "very sophisticated, very nuanced and very insidious." The main architect of Moscow's policy toward the Ukraine, officials say, is the one-time liberal Andrei Kozyrev.

In private at least, senior officials will admit that Russia was probably involved in the overthrow of Azerbaijan's president, Abulfaz Elchibey, in June 1993. Meanwhile Tajikistan, they say, is probably beyond hope.

Late in 1993 senior intelligence officers began to refer to some of the largest and potentially most prosperous republics as "pseudo-states." These included Ukraine, at the time mired in economic collapse, and with a depth of corruption that was shocking even by post-Soviet standards—US officials have on a number of occasions said they had plausible evidence that former president Leonid Kravchuk was receiving payoffs. The list also included Kazakhstan, rich in natural resources but with a desperately delicate ethnic balance.[8] The obvious assumption inherent in the term was that these enormous countries were unlikely to survive as independent entities for long. The logical extension of this assumption—occasionally acknowledged by officials—was that restoration of Russian rule in the republics would in the long term be beneficial to regional stability.

CONCLUSION: THE IMPLICATIONS OF RUSSIA'S NEAR ABROAD POLICY

Moscow's intent does not appear at the moment, seen at least from the remoteness of Washington, to be the replication, *mutatis mutandis*, of the empire of the tsars of the Soviets. Moscow's aim seems instead to be two-tiered. Russian leaders would apparently like to restore the Slav core—Russia, Ukraine, Belarus', and at least northern Kazakhstan—as a single entity. They also aspire to control the outer circle of republics by promoting leaders who are compliant, not to say subservient to their will, and overthrowing those who are not. This bears no resemblance to the Clinton administration's picture of development in the lands of the former Soviet Union.

The US policy could change, of course. Madeleine Albright is seen at the moment as the favorite to replace Warren Christopher in Foggy Bottom. Albright's views on the Near Abroad seem, as has been noted, considerably less optimistic than those emanating from other parts of the administration. Regardless of who is secretary of state, one can also expect with a fair degree of confidence a challenge to the current line from inside the administration, perhaps from the intelligence community, perhaps from the Department of Defense. Unless Strobe Talbott's position is weakened or his views change, however, an adjustment in the administration line seems unlikely.

Russia's ambition to a sphere of influence could also prove self-limiting—because of opposition from Russian political opinion, for example, or economic weakness. If it does not, however, the long-term implications seem almost embarrassingly cataclysmic. These start with the need for significantly stronger NATO security guarantees for Poland, Hungary, and the other former Warsaw Pact states. They proceed through the risk of a major strengthening of the German armed forces and the fears that this would revive across Europe. And they extend, of course, to the reorientation of US national security priorities back to some form of containing the threat from the East.

Moreover, the creation of the two circles of Russian control would not guarantee a lasting "Pax Russica" in the region. It could just as likely lead to increased instability, from western Ukraine through to southern Kazakhstan. It is, of course, already present in Tajikistan, where ethnic Tajik guerrillas from Afghanistan are assisting in the struggle against pro-Russian autocrats.

The short-term implications are, however, also deeply disturbing. There is a strong case to be made for the argument that the present Near Abroad policy is military-driven. Either because of his own inclinations, or his political and physical lassitude (both of which the Clinton administration denies, of course), Boris Yel'tsin seems to be allowing the Russian armed forces, notably Defense Minister Grachev and the Border Guards in the person of General Andrei Nikolayev, a large role in determining policy toward the former republics. The Russian security organizations also seem to be actively and enthusiastically involved in these operations.

None of these institutions is famed for its support of democratic ideals. The military's interest in economic reform—other than for the personal gain of some of its senior figures—is slight. The chances of the Clinton administration seeing any of its three revolutions reach fruition are slender indeed if these organizations remain key political players.

Simply and somewhat moralistically put, a nation which plots the subversion of its neighbors—indeed of (nominal) members of its own Federation, as in Chechnya—is not going to be the safe stable democracy that the Clinton administration already feigns to see taking shape and most other observers hope to see in the future. The creation of a civil society goes hand in hand with the recognition of other states' political and territorial integrity. One cannot exist without the other.

NOTES

1. Michael Beschloss and Strobe Talbott, *At the Highest Levels: The Inside Story of the End of the Cold War* (Boston: Little, Brown and Co., 1993), p. xii.

2. Ibid., p. 472.

3. *My/We*, 3 October 1993, as carried by Ethnic News Watch.

4. Boris Yel'tsin, *Ispoved' na zadannuyu temu* (Confessions on an Assigned Theme) (Riga: The Latvian Children's Foundation, 1990), p. 147.

5. Ibid., p. 174.

6. For other examples of this, see Ambassador Thomas Pickering's interview on National Public Radio in October 1993 and the ambassador's briefing to

journalists in Washington in February 1994. During the latter briefing, Pickering also claimed that the Russian armed forces were incapable, because of their weakness, and unwilling, because of a lingering "Afghan syndrome," to engage in any expansionist activities.

7. Gennadi Sovolev, "General Line," *Rossiiskiye vesti* (Moscow), 2 February 1994, p. 2.

8. The CIA 1993-94 Yearbook lists the ethnic breakdown as 40 percent Kazakh, 38 percent Russian, 7 percent other Slavs, 6 percent German, and 9 percent others.

9

Turning the Cold War on Its Head:
The Costs for Russia, Its Neighbors, and the United States

Paul A. Goble

The fall 1994 summit in Washington marked the final inversion of the Cold War, a shift that is certain to have tragic consequences for Russia, its neighbors, and the United States. The meeting's very "normalcy"—something representatives for both sides have insisted upon—defined its real content: the personalization of the relationship between the two states, the assertion and acceptance of parity in the moral as well as the political-military spheres, and the creation of a new international environment in which the interests of the West will be subordinated to the maintenance of what Boris Yel'tsin at the UN called a "strategic partnership." Individually, each of these developments poses a serious challenge to the West; collectively, they threaten to undermine rather than to promote American interests and values.

The personalization of international politics has been expanding at a rapid rate, from George Bush's infatuation with telephone diplomacy to Jimmy Carter's post-presidential excursions into international affairs. The general dangers of such an approach—an overreliance on individual ties rather than on a calculation of national interests and a reinforcement of the natural hubris of national leaders—have aroused much notice. Yet the specific dangers of this personalization for the West's relationship to Russia are even more noteworthy: support for an increasingly authoritarian single leader, in the name of supporting mass democracy, who can exploit the politics of weakness, demanding concessions and any escape from criticism, not because he is in a position of strength at home, but precisely because he is not.

Even more disturbing were Yel'tsin's demand for—and Bill Clinton's apparent acceptance of—the idea that Russia now has achieved a position of moral equivalency with Western democracies. Russian commentators have cleverly exploited American involvement in Haiti to promote a "your backyard, our backyard" image of the world, one that implies that Russian behavior in neighboring countries is exactly equivalent to American behavior. Such a position—which Clinton shows no sign of challenging and every sign of agreeing to—is at odds with the facts: The American Congress was debating how quickly the United States could get out of Haiti while Yel'tsin and his advisors were demanding both permanent bases and a permanent, internationally recognized, right to intervene in what they are pleased to call the Near Abroad.

Another side of this demand and acceptance of parity was the very non-political cast that the Clinton administration gave to the meeting. At the center of the discussions was an effort to promote American private investment in Russia. Whether such investment should be encouraged for a country without a legal system, without defensible contracts, without control over its territory or its nuclear materials, and without a disciplined and reliable military is an open question. By proclaiming that Americans can do business with Russia, the United States is implying that Russia has already made the tough choices and joined the West. Not only is that incorrect, it is also dangerous, for it will only encourage those in Moscow who argue that they need do no more and who want to see a stable but authoritarian Russia rather than a democratic and open one.

Given the natural desire of the American people to focus inward after the exertions of the Cold War, and given both the scope and speed of change in Eurasia, the misreading of Russia and her new neighbors up to now should not have been a surprise to anyone.[1] Yet that does not mean this lack of understanding was without costs or that Americans should not recognize just how wrong their perceptions often were. Numerous shortcomings in Americans' understanding are chronicled elsewhere.[2] Still, there are three misconceptions that must be overcome: the belief that the transitions in Russia and her neighbors will be quick, easy and cheap; the idea that the United States should focus more on Russian domestic affairs than on Moscow's foreign policies; and the notion that the United States and Russia can form a partnership without any costs to traditional allies.

Perhaps the most naïve mistake made was to think that Russia and her neighbors could make a transition to democracy and free markets quickly, easily and at low cost to the United States. Historically, neither Russia nor any other of her new neighbors—with the exception of the Baltic countries—has had either much experience with democracy and a market economy or the broader cultural developments that made possible the emergence of this kind of polity and economy in the West. In addition, no country in the world has ever made this kind of transition without either military occupation or massive outside assistance and without most of the sacrifice and effort being made by the peoples most directly involved. Optimism is one thing; naïveté is quite another.

Americans should be more modest and acknowledge that, while the goals of democracy and a free market are desirable, a detailed road map of how to get there is not available. This is especially important because the United States has not been willing, either as a nation or as the leader of the West, to come up with the kind of funding that would back up its lectures on democratization. A billion dollars is a great deal of money, but spread over a country with 150 million people, such aid works out to approximately 6 dollars per person. Without additional aid, highly inter-ventionist language from the West about domestic changes in Russia and the other countries will inevitably breed a reaction among proud and undefeated peoples.

In US dealings with Russia—and that country has received too much focus relative to its 14 new neighbors—Americans have inverted their tradi-tional approach in foreign relations. Normally, Americans are more con-cerned with how a country acts toward its neighbors or toward the United States than they are with what it does domestically. Even when the focus is on domestic issues—as recently with China –the foreign policy dimension is never ignored. From this inversion flow most of the problems now facing the United States.

First, by focusing almost exclusively on Russian domestic economic difficulties, Americans have been overly invasive without giving much help, and have all too often missed the political and psychological prob-lems that beset Russia and her relations with the 14 other states. The United States unintentionally signaled that it would not oppose the res-toration of the empire, thus undercutting friends in Moscow and aiding those who are most against American principles. For some in Washington, the Russian elections of December 12, 1993 did prove to be a wake-up call, but even then, all too many American analysts reduced the Zhirinovsky vote to economics alone.

Second, by deciding that Boris Yel'tsin alone must be supported, and by insisting that he behave according to an American schema for his domestic reforms, the United States has virtually invited him to use Russian power in the so-called Near Abroad as a means to generate political support via "hurrah patriotism," precisely because of rightist challenges that he is somehow the "West's man in Moscow." Americans have made themselves prisoners to his policies even when those policies change, often praising Russian actions in these new countries that would otherwise be criticized if any other country in the world attempted them.

Third, and most dangerously, Americans all too often have accepted the argument that Russia retains special rights in the new countries and that Moscow should have the same right to defend the 25 million Russian ethnics abroad that other countries have to defend their citizens abroad. Not only does that ignore the 35 million non-Russians living outside their ethnic home territories, and the principle that the Allies fought Germany in World War II to uphold, but it invites Russians to attempt to ethnicize politics throughout the region and destabilize these new countries. Such a notion implies that the United States does not view the other new states in this region as full-fledged sovereign countries.[3] This ignores the fact that even if the United States does not feel threatened by Moscow, its neighbors all too often do—and with justification. This permissive stance gives aid and comfort to the worst people in Moscow rather than the best, leading to greater Russian assertiveness and hence to an expansion rather than contraction of the Russian army and military-industrial complex, thus retarding rather than accelerating the domestic transitions hoped for by the West.

Ultimately it is the third point that is the most distressing. No one wants to make Russia an enemy, but an incautious willingness to allow Russia to veto decisions on NATO membership in Eastern Europe and to demand that oil flow only through Russia undercuts America's traditional allies in Europe, including Turkey. Moreover, the Partnership for Peace, at least as originally advertised, achieves what Moscow has wanted for many years: the diminution of NATO's status and an apparent legitimation of Russian involvement in both the former republics of the Soviet Union and in Eastern Europe. More concretely, the United States' overly celebratory welcoming of Russian involvement in Bosnia will almost certainly come to be seen as a major mistake.

The notion that with communism dead there are no fundamental differences between Russia and the United States in interests, values, or concerns would be laughable if it were not so serious. The idea that the two countries can simply agree on all matters is either deeply insulting to Russia or deeply injurious to the interests and values of the United States. One cannot repeal either history or geography—although, tragically, some have tried.[4] The beginning of wisdom is to recognize both differences and similarities and to acknowledge both interests and limitations. Too often, in the first couple of years of the post-Soviet era, the United States has done neither.

Yel'tsin has already exploited this, demanding American recognition—implicit or otherwise—for Moscow's efforts to dominate and "reintegrate" the former Soviet space, for Moscow's demands that nothing be done in Yugoslavia against Serbian interests, and for American acceptance of Russia as a "strategic" partner. Both because of the usual hype of summitry and because Russia is supposedly the major "success" of Clinton's foreign policy efforts, Washington has been reluctant to say anything against this approach. The absence of criticism has only encouraged Moscow to up the ante rather than to adapt.

Recent reporting from Moscow has focused on two supposedly contradictory tendencies, the collapse of state authority within the Russian Federation and the reassertion of Russian power over her new neighbors. Each of these tendencies has been repeatedly cited as precluding the other: Those who see Moscow restoring the empire have tended to ignore Russian domestic difficulties, and those who believe that Moscow is pursuing a normal course of development with her neighbors have tended to point to these difficulties as a necessary and sufficient explanation for her actions.

This contradiction is more apparent than real. In fact, the reassertion of Russian power over her neighbors precisely reflects an effort by the Moscow authorities to cope with the disintegration of the Russian state. Unfortunately, the cure may be worse than the disease, with its first victims being the countries Russians routinely call the Near Abroad. Moreover, the prospects for the development of democracy and free markets in Russia itself will suffer, and finally, the possibility of a more peaceful and cooperative relationship between Russia and the United States will be undercut.

Here, three main questions arise: What is happening between Russia and the states around her borders? What are the likely consequences of these actions on all the parties involved? What can and should the United States do to promote American interests and values in this region?

Western discussions about Russian intentions toward her neighbors have been remarkably unsophisticated, with the argument focusing on whether Moscow wants to restore the status quo ante or, if after several years of confusion, it merely is pursuing policies normal for a great power surrounded by smaller ones. The simplistic quality of such discussions reflects three aspects of the problem:

1. With regard to Moscow's intentions, there seems to be, in the words of Gertrude Stein, "no there there." No one can be sure at the present time who or what speaks for Russia, and so no one can be certain what is official policy and what is not.
2. There is a "say and do" problem. Whenever Russian officials say something untoward, Americans are routinely enjoined by their supporters to

watch what they do; but whenever Russian officials do something untoward, we are often told that Yel'tsin has assured Washington otherwise.
This is a highly unsatisfactory situation.

3. The debate itself is at an extremely primitive level. On the one hand, there
are those who see any reassertion of Russian influence in the region as
imperialism, ignoring the fact that Russia, just like any other state, has
real and legitimate interests in the countries around its borders. They
forget that the real question concerns the means by which Russia seeks
to advance its interests. On the other hand, there are those who argue
that since Boris Yel'tsin and Andrei Kozyrev—in contrast to someone
like Vladimir Zhirinovsky—have never used the word "empire," and
clearly do not seek to include all the new states within the borders of a
single country, there can be no question that Moscow seeks to dominate
its neighbors in an inappropriate way.

All these problems are exacerbated by the tendency to examine the
issue of Russia's intentions as the sum of bilateral relations between Moscow and each of her neighbors rather than as a general pattern. This perspective allows both sides of this argument to claim victory, with supporters
of the Russians as innocents pointing to the resolution of troop withdrawal
in the Baltic States and with supporters of the idea that the empire is coming
back pointing to the flagrant use of Russian power in Moldova and Georgia.

Is there a way out? Three steps are necessary. First, Americans should stop
fixating on the word "empire" and just look at the specific facts. Secondly, the
United States should seek to define the general patterns of actions, recognizing
that statements alone are often problematic and do not necessarily reflect a
broader policy. And thirdly, the issue should be examined in terms of a series
of policy arenas rather than in terms of specific bilateral relationships. Five
such policy arenas are: economic relations, military involvement, the politics of isolation, "human rights" issues, and linkages among each. The
following paragraphs are meant to suggest the outlines of Moscow's
approach rather than to argue that these outlines explain all of the extremely disorderly Russian approaches to her neighbors.

CURRENT RUSSIAN POLICY

Economic Pressure

No one can contest that the Russian Federation has legitimate economic interests and even equities in the new states, but Moscow officials have pursued a
policy which suggests that these economic assets are a lever for more general
goals. Three examples spring to mind: First, Moscow has not imposed world
prices on raw materials and energy as a general rule but rather has imposed them

selectively and irregularly to destabilize neighboring countries or to increase Russian political influence; secondly, Moscow has insisted that all energy supplies from Central Asia and the Caucasus flow through Russia and has asserted its right to block the export of oil and gas to the West if it would compromise Russian economic goals; and lastly, it has insisted in Belarus', Tajikistan and elsewhere on a very high political price for economic assistance.

Military Pressure

Moscow has deployed troops in Moldova, Tajikistan, and Georgia against the initial interests and wills of the governments involved (that such governments ex post facto were made to agree does not justify earlier uses of force). Russia has dragged its feet on the withdrawal of troops from Estonia and Latvia, and it has provided arms to groups on various sides of civil and international wars in the Caucasus. Curious but seldom noted is the fact that Moscow has used its military force in precisely those countries—Georgia, Azerbaijan, Moldova, and Tajikistan—which had, or appeared likely to have, the greatest doubts about membership in the Russian-dominated Commonwealth of Independent States. Moreover, its military and defense ministry representatives have cast doubt on the genuineness of Moscow's willingness to treat these neighbors as real countries. The West—especially the United States—has also failed to insist on this, all too often seeing the troop issue in the Baltic States as the only one of concern and as an end in itself, and all too often excusing Russian military behavior elsewhere because of CIS agreements and so on.

Political Isolation

Russian politicians from Yel'tsin on down have repeatedly insisted that Russia alone is responsible for what takes place on the territory of the CIS or even of the former Soviet Union. Kozyrev has demanded not only that the West recognize this as legitimate but that it contribute to what he calls "peacekeeping." So far that has not happened, but neither has the West consistently and publicly challenged Moscow on its assertiveness in this respect, leaving many in the new countries to feel that they confront Russian power without any real prospects of assistance. Indeed, Russian discussions about its conditions for joining the PfP are only the latest indication that Russia believes it can play by its own rules, flout those of Europe, and isolate not only the fourteen former Soviet republics, but Eastern Europe as well.

"Human Rights" Issues

Nowhere has Russia been bolder or the West more supine than on the issue of ethnic Russians in the other new countries. The Russian government has a legitimate interest in the fate of its co-ethnics abroad, but this interest must be manifested in ways consistent with the principles of international law and the higher standing of citizenship. Of the often-mentioned 25.4 million ethnic Russians living outside the Russian Federation, only 150,000 are citizens of the Russian Federation. All but 800,000 of the remainder are citizens of the other countries. Unfortunately, not only has the West allowed Moscow to make claims about the need to protect these persons—a claim that would be objectionable if it were made by any other nation (as, for example, Germany)—but the United States has forgotten to worry about or direct the CSCE High Commissioner on National Minorities to concern himself with the fate of the 35 million other people in this region who either live outside their own country or are not members of a titular nationality. This failure has led to assumptions in Moscow and in other capitals that some countries are "normal" and others are simply "inconvenient," thereby reinforcing the isolation of these countries and the tendency of the West to view them only through Russian eyes.

Linkage Issues

In each of the cases listed above, there are some legitimate reasons for Russian statements and actions. Unfortunately, in every case, the Moscow authorities have used their leverage to seek to reintegrate these countries under Russian domination even when the initial Russian action may be welcome. Russian involvement in the Karabakh conflict is a case in point: Russian diplomatic actions sometimes have been useful, particularly given the failure of other states to be more active, but these welcome Russian actions have always been accompanied by other less welcome signs that Moscow's intentions are less benign than advertised.

Can it be said that Moscow is seeking to reimpose a single imperial state? So far, the evidence for that is lacking. Evidence does exist, however, to back up the claim that Moscow wishes to dominate these countries in ways that are inappropriate and inconsistent with international law. The conversion of some, or eventually most, of these countries into simple satellites is proceeding so rapidly that the question of empire may, in fact, become a genuine one, especially since so many Russians regret the end of the Soviet Union, and since so many politicians see the restoration of Russian suzerainty over these states as a solution to—or at least a distraction from—Russia's own enormous domestic problems.

DANGEROUS CONSEQUENCES FOR EVERYONE

There will be three victims of the reassertion of Russian power if it continues in the forms it is now assuming and if the United States simply concedes the game. The first and mos't obvious victims will be the new countries themselves, some of which will retreat into ever more extreme forms of nationalism and seek to resist their far larger neighbor with all the negative and self-defeating consequences of such reactions. Others will simply give way to Russian demands, thus leading to additional demands and the sacrifice of the freedom they had obtained.

However, the two other victims—and they will flow inevitably from the first—should disturb the United States even more. The first of these is Russia itself. If Moscow seeks to become a new imperial state, it will not be liberal, either politically or economically. Indeed, it will give up all chance of that as a result of an ever-larger military and military-industrial complex and, thus, quickly find itself in the same trap as the Soviet Union did. A liberal Russia may be possible, but a liberal empire is a contradiction in terms. Even more, the Russian attempt to resubordinate its neighbors—whether it goes as far as a drive to include them all in a single state or not—will ultimately fail and again for the same reasons, with many victims on both sides. (As Chechnya demonstrates, even regions nominally part of the Russian Federation are not exempt from these perils.)

Unfortunately, however, the largest victim may be the West. A resurgent, non-liberal Russia will ultimately have to posit an enemy larger than the Estonians—that *Feindbild* will work only so long. Many Russians believe that they can count on an alliance with the West against China or against Islam, but they are almost certain to be wrong, because neither of those powers is as immediately threatening as many Russians and Americans believe, and because it will be difficult for the United States and the West to ally themselves with an authoritarian Russia. As a result—and this is already visible—a Russia unrestrained in its drive for regional hegemony is likely to turn on the West, blaming the West for its problems and issuing challenges in more and more places. It will not be able to do that as effectively in the past, but even its limited efforts will preclude many of the changes hoped for in the post–Cold War environment.

WHAT IS TO BE DONE?

Only a few years have elapsed since the end of the Soviet Union. Unfortunately, neither the West nor the Russians has made especially good use of the time. The United States largely has passed on the opportunity former Secretary of State James Baker outlined to restructure the world in ways that would guarantee a generation of peace, but it is not too late to get involved and to limit the damage that has already taken place.

Three measures can and should be taken:

1. The United States should treat *all* the countries of the region as sovereign states. That means more than opening an embassy there. It

means insisting that other countries respect these states and play by the international rules of the game; it means that no countries and ethnic groups will receive extra privileges; and it means that aggression will not be allowed to be profitable, lest it is encouraged.

2. The West should end its inverted approach to Russia. Unlike America's dealings with other countries, Washington has been obsessed with what Russia does domestically—while providing relatively little aid to go along with its improving speeches—and largely has ignored what Russia is doing to her neighbors. The United States should both provide more aid to Russia, while keeping expectations on Russian domestic change modest, and be more insistent that Moscow play according to the normal rules of the game vis-à-vis its neighbors.

3. The West should stop allowing Moscow to assume that the "ordinary yardstick" of international relations does not apply to Russia, that Russia will be allowed to make up the rules or exempt itself from them as it goes along.

In each case, America may not always be able to enforce its principles, but should not forget them or fail to articulate them to others. That is not only the source of American influence in the world but also—and even more important—the basis for the peaceful and democratic world that everyone would like to see in the future. The United States should pursue cooperation with Russia on the sure basis of its own interests and values rather than on the much shakier foundation of cooperation in the name of cooperation. Trying to pretend that there will be no disagreements simply passes the whip hand of policy to a Russia not yet fully integrated into the West, and guarantees an eventual fragmentation of the relationship when the degree of the two countries' real differences becomes apparent.

NOTES

1. That democracies usually react this way to victories and periods of rapid change is captured in Winston Churchill's *The Aftermath* (New York: C. Scribner's Sons, 1929), his insightful study on Western reaction to the end of World War I. He writes:

> To the faithful, toil-burdened masses the victory was so complete that no further effort seemed required. Germany had fallen, and with her the world combination that had crushed her. Authority was dispersed; the world unshackled; the weak became the strong; the sheltered became the aggressive; the contrast between victors and vanquished tended continually to diminish. A vast fatigue dominated collective action. Though every subversive element endeavored to assert itself, revolutionary rage like every other form of psychic energy burnt low. Through

all its five acts the drama has run its course; the light of history is switched off, the world stage dims, the actors shrivel, the chorus sinks. The war of the giants has ended; the quarrels of the pygmies have begun.

These words were published just four years before Hitler came to power and just a decade before the world was engulfed in a general war.

2. See Paul Goble, "Ten Issues in Search of a Policy: America's Failed Approach to the Post-Soviet States," *Current History,* October 1993, pp. 305–308.

3. On this difficult problem, see Paul Goble, "Russia and Its Neighbors," *Foreign Policy,* Spring 1993, pp. 79-88; "Can We Help Russia Become a Good Neighbor?" *Demokratizatsiya* (Washington, D.C.), Winter 1993-94, pp. 3-8; and "Russia as a Eurasian Power: Moscow and the Post-Soviet Successor States," in Stephen Sestanovich, ed., *Rethinking Russia's National Interests* (Washington, DC: 1994), pp. 42-51. Administration officials often point out how much the United States supports the statehood of the three Baltic States without acknowledging that this policy also can have unintended and counterproductive consequences. On that issue, see Paul Goble, "The Rebirth of Baltic Exceptionalism," *The Baltic Independent,* 8-14 October 1993.

4. See Paul Goble, "Let's not be revisionists on Soviet history," *The Philadelphia Inquirer,* 1 December 1993, p. A17, for a discussion of the implications of this approach. On the more general problem of ignoring geographically based conflicts, see David Hooson, "The Return of Geography," in Ian Bremmer and Norman Naimark, eds., *Soviet Nationalities Problems* (Stanford, 1990), pp. 61-68.

About the Contributors

Harry H. Almond, Jr. currently serves as Adjunct Professor of Strategic Studies in the National Security Studies Program at Georgetown University, where he focuses on matters involving law and national security. Previously he served as Senior Attorney Advisor for International Affairs at the Department of Defense, Office of General Counsel, and Professor of Strategy and International Law at the National War College. He has written articles on international law, the law of war, arms control and disarmament, economic warfare, terrorism, the law of the sea, the law of outer space, and numerous other fields for professional journals. Prof. Almond has been a member of US delegations to United Nations conferences on outer space, arms control, and the law of war. He was educated at Yale University, Cornell University, Harvard University, the London School of Economics, and the National War College.

Angelo M. Codevilla is Senior Research Fellow at Stanford University's Hoover Institution. He was educated at Rutgers University, University of Notre Dame, and Claremont Graduate School. After receiving his Ph.D. in 1973, Dr. Codevilla taught political science. In 1977 he became a US Foreign Service Officer. He then joined the staff of the US Senate Select Committee on Intelligence. At the same time he served as legislative assistant to Sen. Malcolm Wallop (R-WY), and helped to conceive the technology programs that, in 1983, were relabeled SDI. In 1980 he was appointed to the teams preparing the presidential transition for the Department of State and the Central Intelligence Agency. Throughout his time in government, Codevilla published articles on intelligence and national security. He has taught at Georgetown University, Boston University, and the US Naval Postgraduate School. Codevilla's books and articles range from French, Italian, and Chilean politics, to the thoughts of Machiavelli and Montesquieu, to the role of intelligence in statecraft, war, the technology of ballistic missile defenses, arms control, and a broad range of international topics. He has been published by *Commentary, Foreign Affairs, National Review, The New Republic, The National Interest, The New York Times, The Wall Street Journal,* and *The Washington Post.*

Ariel Cohen is the Salvatori Fellow in Russian and Eurasian Studies at The Heritage Foundation. Educated at the Fletcher School of Law and Diplomacy, Tufts University, and Bar Ilan University School of Law, he is well-versed in international law and international relations. Dr. Cohen has served as a parliamentary advisor to the Knesset, a researcher for Radio Liberty Media & Opinion Research, an adjunct faculty member of several universities, and an attorney in private practice. Dr. Cohen has been published by *La Pensée Russe, Radio Free Europe/Radio Liberty* (Paris), and *Yediot Aharonot.*

Paul A. Goble is Senior Associate at the Carnegie Endowment for International Peace, working on the Problems of the Post-Soviet Successor States. Prior to joining the Endowment in January 1992, he served as Special Advisor on Soviet Nationality Problems to the Assistant Secretary for European Affairs and Desk Officer for Estonia, Latvia, and Lithuania at the US Department of State. Earlier he worked as Director of Research at Radio Liberty, Special Assistant for Soviet Nationalities in the US State Department's Bureau of Intelligence and Research, and a Soviet Affairs Analyst at the Central Intelligence Agency (CIA) and Foreign Broadcast Information Service (FBIS). Trained at Miami University and the University of Chicago, he has written numerous articles on Soviet nationality problems.

Sergei Grigoriev is Visiting Professor of Political Science and Journalism at Northeastern University. He is also involved with the Strengthening Democratic Institutions Project at Harvard University. Educated at Moscow State University, Harvard University, and Tufts University, he was Deputy Spokesman and Press Officer for the Office of the President of the USSR from 1990 to 1991. Previously he acted as an Interpreter for the International Department of the Central Committee of the CPSU. After leaving Moscow for the United States in 1991, he served as a consultant for ABC News and as a Fellow at Harvard's John F. Kennedy School of Government and, earlier, at the Woodrow Wilson School of Public and International Affairs at Princeton. His articles have appeared in a number of international and US publications, including *Newsweek International.*

Adrian Karatnycky is President of Freedom House, a non-partisan, non-profit organization that promotes democracy, the civil society and the rule of law and monitors human rights, political rights and civil liberties around the world. Previously he served in many capacities for the AFL-CIO, including Assistant to the President, Director of Research for the Department of International Affairs, Editor of the Interco Press Service (the AFL-CIO's international editorial features service), and Research Director for the Free Trade Union Institute. From 1980 to 1984, he was Research Director of the A. Philip Randolph Institute, a civil rights group. In 1979, he served as Assistant Director of the International Sakharov Hearings. A graduate of Columbia University, Dr. Karatnycky has written scores of articles on East European and post-Soviet issues for publications such as *Foreign Affairs, Orbis, The New Republic, Commentary, Freedom Review, The Wall Street Journal, National Review, New Leader, Los Angeles Times, The Washington Post,* and *American Spectator.* His books include *Workers' Rights, East and West* (co-authored with Adolph Sturmthal and published by Transaction Books), *The Hidden Nations: The People Challenge the Soviet Union* (co-authored with Nadia Diuk and published by William Morrow and Company, 1990), and *New Nations Rising: The Fall of the Soviets and the Challenge of Independence* (John Wiley and Sons, 1993).

Mark Kramer is Deputy Director of the European Security Project at Brown University's Center for Foreign Policy Development. He is also a Fellow of Harvard University's Russian Research Center and an Adjunct Research Fellow at Harvard's Center for Science and International Affairs. Prof. Kramer taught for three years in the Government Department at Harvard and currently teaches in the International Relations Department at Brown. His book on *Crisis in Czechoslovakia, 1968: The Prague Spring and the Soviet Invasion* will be published in 1996 by The New Press of W.W. Norton. He has nearly completed another book on a reassessment of Soviet–East European relations from 1945 to 1991 and has also been co-editing a book on the role of blue-collar workers in the post-communist transitions in Eastern Europe and the former Soviet Union.

Kate Martin is Assistant Director of the Institute for the Study of Conflict, Ideology and Policy at Boston University. A former journalist, she is the editor of the journal *Perspective* and co-editor (with Uri Ra'anan and Keith Armes) of the books *Russian Pluralism—Now Irreversible?* (St. Martin's Press, 1992) and *State and Nation in Multi-Ethnic Societies: The Breakup of Multinational States* (Manchester University Press, 1991). She was educated at Northeastern University and Boston University.

Paul Quinn-Judge is a Washington-based Diplomatic Correspondent for *The Boston Globe.* His previous positions include Moscow Bureau Chief for *The Boston Globe* and for the *Christian Science Monitor,* Southeast Asia Correspondent for the *Christian Science Monitor,* and Indochina Correspondent for *Far Eastern Economic Review.* He was educated at Cambridge University.

Uri Ra'anan is University Professor in the University Professors Program, and Director of the Institute for the Study of Conflict, Ideology, and Policy, at Boston University. He is a Fellow of the Russian Research Center at Harvard University. Author, co-author, editor, or co-editor of 23 books, and contributor to 19 others, as well as 21 monographs and Congressional Publications, his latest publications include *Russian Pluralism—Now Irreversible?* (St. Martin's Press, 1992); *State and Nation in Multi-Ethnic Societies: The Breakup of Multinational States* (Manchester University Press, 1991); *Inside The Apparat* (D.C. Heath, 1990); *Gorbachev's USSR: A System in Crisis* (Macmillan, 1990); and *The Soviet Empire: The Challenge of National and Democratic Movements* (D.C. Heath, 1990). His current research work focuses on neo-imperial trends in Russia's foreign policy. Prior to his current appointments, he was Professor of International Politics and Director of the International Security Studies Program at the Fletcher School of Law and Diplomacy, where he taught for two decades. Before joining the Fletcher School, he taught (briefly) at the Massachusetts Institute of Technology, and, previous to that, at Columbia University and the City University of New York. He obtained his undergraduate and graduate education and degrees at Oxford University (Wadham College, 1945–1950).

Index